Research within the Disciplines

Foundations for Reference and Library Instruction

Peggy Keeran, Suzanne L. Moulton-Gertig,
Michael Levine-Clark, Nonny Schlotzhauer,
Esther Gil, Christopher C. Brown, Joseph R. Kraus,
Carrie Forbes, and Jennifer Bowers

The Scarecrow Press, Inc.
Lanham, Maryland • Toronto • Plymouth, UK
2007

Scarecrow Press, Inc.

Published in the United States of America
by Scarecrow Press, Inc.
A wholly owned subsidary of The Rowman & Littlefield Publishing Group, Inc.
4501 Forbes Boulevard, Suite 200, Lanham, Maryland 20706
www.scarecrowpress.com

Estover
Plymouth PL6 7PY
United Kingdom

British Library Cataloguing in Publication Information Available

Library of Congress Cataloging-in-Publication Data

Research within the disciplines : foundations for reference and library
instruction / Peggy Keeran ... [et al.].
     p. cm.
 Includes bibliographical references and index.
 ISBN-13: 978-0-8108-5688-2 (pbk. : alk. paper)
 ISBN-10: 0-8108-5688-3 (pbk. : alk. paper)
 1. Library research. 2. Reference services (Libraries) 3. Research—
Methodology. 4. Library orientation. I. Keeran, Peggy, 1959–
 Z710.R47 2007
 020.72—dc22

                                                2006032340

∞™ The paper used in this publication meets the minimum requirements of
American National Standard for Information Sciences—Permanence of Paper
for Printed Library Materials, ANSI/NISO Z39.48-1992.
Manufactured in the United States of America.

Contents

Preface

This book, a collaborative project of the reference librarians at the University of Denver and Nonny Schlotzhauer (a former University of Denver reference librarian who is now at Pennsylvania State University), grew out of our team discussions about teaching research and writing within the disciplines, which were in response to new initiatives at our institution. As the university moved to integrate writing and research into the whole of the undergraduate curriculum, we used our collective experiences as a basis to describe our roles in this new plan. Because of our interests, and because of the lack of such a volume, we decided to write a book that would serve as a foundation for research within the disciplines, one that we hope will be of value to others.

We all participated in the development of this book; not only has each person written a chapter in his or her specific subject area, but we have actively made editorial decisions through discussions and by consensus. This collaboration included several conference calls involving all the authors, as well as different threads of conversation among two or more authors, to determine how to achieve the goal of the book as described in the introduction. All authors were involved in the editorial processes of reading each of the chapters, offering feedback for improvement, rereading revised chapters, reflecting on and debating the path the book was taking, and revisiting and revising our original goals.

We want to thank Lois Jones, Barbara Berliner, Ann Dobyns, and Tracie Kruse who provided valuable feedback toward refining the text. We also want to thank Martin Dillon, our consulting editor at Scarecrow Press, who was very supportive throughout the process. Lastly, we want to thank Niki Guinan, our Scarecrow production editor, and Matt Evans, our Scarecrow copy editor.

We hope that readers of our book will find the information relevant and useful as they proceed to conduct reference interviews, engage in library instruction, or begin to do research in their fields of study.

Introduction

Research lies at the heart of all academic disciplines. This book is an expansion of that concept. While it acknowledges that there exist some common threads and elements that run through what we identify as "research," the book's main objective is to provide a degree of orientation toward conducting research within specific disciplines and across others. What emerges is a window for readers into the full intellectual investigative tools that exist among many disparate fields of study and at all levels.

The aim of this book is to give a flavor of the many facets of the research process, with an emphasis on how to make the most of the experience through the utilization of library resources. By design, this book is broad in scope and is meant to serve a diverse audience, though principally it is addressed to entry-level librarians working with a wide variety of disciplines, as well as to graduate students in library and information science. A secondary audience, we hope, will be found among undergraduates, graduate students, faculty, and practitioners in specific fields of study.

This book contains discussions of a wide range of subjects that have been selected to be of the most direct value to readers. Obviously, it is not possible to include everything of relevance within a book of this length; in fairness to the authors, that is not our intent. It is meant to supplement the existing body of work within the field of library science, fill any gaps that may be present, and introduce a pertinent element to the research literature in a wide array of disciplines, from the arts, business, humanities, sciences, and social sciences.

This book is organized in a logical manner that reflects a connection among the sections. Thus, the chapter discussing the humanities is followed by chapters on music and history that appropriately highlight the research practices among individual disciplines from the broader field of study. Subsequently, chapters on business and government documents follow the chapter treating the broad scope of the social sciences. These are followed by a chapter covering the sciences and then one with a focus on engineering. The penultimate chapter discusses the role of library instruction and information literacy in teaching and assessing discipline-based research skills. The book concludes by summarizing the foundations of disciplinary research and providing an overview of interdisciplinary research. General research strategies, applicable to any discipline, are interspersed with specialized searching techniques.

The book will provide library school students and general reference librarians with a foundation about research within the disciplines that they can apply to their profession. Undergraduates can use the book to increase their knowledge about research within specific majors. Faculty can recommend the appropriate chapters to graduate and undergraduate students they teach, and faculty and graduate students can utilize information about other disciplines to further their own research knowledgeably.

In addition to the broad perspective, the individual chapters also stand independently, should a reader wish to focus on a specific discipline. Once you are familiar with the contents, the book then serves as a reference book. We hope that you will find it useful to use different chapters when appropriate, since individual chapters of the book may offer greater relevance to some readers, and since certain sections can be consulted at different stages of the research process.

The main theme that runs throughout the ten chapters is the rich nature of the research process. It is a process that demands the full understanding of the possibilities and limitations of research. Indeed, to be a savvy researcher nowadays, and in turn a proficient librarian, you must, according to Michael Mann, be acutely "aware of the trade-offs between virtual and real libraries."[1] Even in today's increasingly technological world, where we are privileged to live in the information age, it can nonetheless be hard to find the resources you want, given some inescapable restrictions such as cost and access.[2]

For librarians whose principal role involves facilitating the use of the library and its abundance of resources, conveying the *nuts* and *bolts* of research to students and other users necessitates a full understanding of the role of information. Carrie Forbes, in chapter 9, presents a sound case for the significance of information literacy within the research process. She provides a historical overview of how library instruction has grown over the years to occupy a principal place in academia, with its role in formulating the concepts of critical-thinking skills and lifelong learning as central tenets within the library. Finally, she shows how information literacy across the curriculum, coupled with a subject-specific emphasis, offers the necessary skills to all students, many of whom will become our researchers of the future.

Michael Levine-Clark's chapter 3 on historical research provides an introduction to the methods and resources within a field of study that crosses disciplinary boundaries. He explains in depth the central role that primary and secondary sources play in historical research, and he shows the different tasks and demands that delving into the past entails. Chapter 6, by Christopher C. Brown, highlights the interdisciplinary nature of research by providing a general road map for using government documents for researchers in all fields. Despite their complexity in scope and format, the chapter offers a clear explanation of their organization, distribution, and necessity for researchers in any discipline. In chapter 8 on research in engineering, Joseph R. Kraus discusses the unique nature of research among engineers. Their library use, while not analogous to other disciplines, nonetheless necessitates a clear understanding about their information needs on the part of the librarian serving the discipline.

Chapter 2 is a little more specialized. It provides a guide to research in the discipline of music. Suzanne L. Moulton-Gertig covers the research process by looking at the abundance of resources available to researchers at all levels. Though music research, not unlike other fields of inquiry, follows a systemic procedure, it draws on a significant amount of knowledge from other disciplines. She offers some guidance for using nonmusical work and covers the unique types of sources used in the field.

In business, as Esther Gil points out in chapter 5, research strategies depend on the type of information one needs within a wide range of subjects—accounting, economics, marketing, and the like—and often involve time constraints. Within the academic environment, much research is project driven as students work to complete class assignments, which often necessitates working closely with librarians to assist in navigating both primary and secondary resources. Business research can entail looking at individual company performance, market analysis, surveys of industry, or statistics, each requiring its own set of resources and approaches. She shows how this complexity, though challenging, can be addressed with well-rounded reference and instruction.

The remaining chapters cover research across the vast array of subjects in the humanities, the sciences, and the social sciences. These chapters show that while standard research practices are common to their respective disciplines, all fields have unique requirements that demand certain methods and resources. Peggy Keeran, in chapter 1, shows how the needs of practicing artists differ from the scholar, and how these different needs shape librarians' roles. Similarly, chapter 4, by Nonny Schlotzhauer, demonstrates how research that is conducted for practical purposes—that is, to enact policy—often utilizes different approaches than assignments by students or research papers by scholars. In addition, he also provides an overview of some common research methods and techniques within the social sciences to illustrate how certain fields utilize resources. Finally, Joseph R. Kraus, in chapter 7, describes the various science fields and guides the reader through the key resources associated with each.

The boundaries provided by the chapters are somewhat artificial and certainly malleable. This, in fact, is addressed in a coherent way by Jennifer Bowers in her concluding chapter 10 on interdisciplinary research. She writes about how disciplines are constantly changing, adding to a renewed vitality among scholars and within several fields, and about how disciplinary and interdisciplinary research share a dynamic and interdependent relationship that can inspire new ways of looking at the world.

However we slice it, the underlying concern of this book—true across all disciplines—is the continued necessity of understanding the foundations of research, whether within a bricks-and-mortar structure or via the electronic environment. Together with the tremendous opportunities it has opened up, the growth of information technology has presented some real challenges, particularly with the exponential growth of the Internet over the past decade. Expectations among students and researchers have grown along with the technological advancements, as the "Googlization" of society has dramatically increased access to information and enhanced scholarly communication.

The new research atmosphere has affected what people learn and how they learn, and some traditional arrangements are being unsettled. The spiraling costs of journals have led to the "open access" movement, wherein scholarly articles, solely the domain of subscription-based publications, are now appearing on the Internet as free, publicly distributed works for all to read. Though yet to catch on as a serious threat to the high-cost periodicals that form the backbone of scholarship, this adds to an ever-increasing array of choices confronting students and others looking for research material.[3]

For librarians, the challenge exists to make order of the volatile world of information and provide a way to turn information into knowledge. The library remains central to research, and librarians can bring clarity to the process. All of the contributors to this book are practicing academic librarians, and all know the value of information and how to use it. They all recognize that in this dynamic environment, distinctions among forms of information are becoming less clear, and the process at times appears less certain. Whatever its nature, when it comes to research, the librarian maintains the expertise that students and scholars need to engage the information, and can provide the foundations for research across the disciplines.

NOTES

1. Michael Mann, *The Oxford Guide to Library Research*, 3rd ed. (New York: Oxford University Press, 2005).

2. William B. Bradke, *Research Strategies: Finding Your Way through the Information Fog*, 2nd ed. (New York: IUniverse Inc., 2004).

3. Though it holds wide appeal, open access presents several challenges for librarians. One is the very fact that it is free. For many years, librarians have differentiated between resources that were paid for by the library and contained on its network and those that were available "free" on the Internet. There was a value to a resource with a cost, whereas something free was of dubious worth. Such distinctions have now gotten a bit murkier, and librarians again need to step in, harness the technology, and develop delivery platforms for the new scholarship on the Web.

1

Research in the Humanities

Peggy Keeran

The humanities grew out of the study of ancient Greek and Latin classics from the Middle Ages through the Renaissance. Today the term encompasses the academic disciplines that allow us to explore ourselves through human culture, including art, architecture, archaeology, classics, dance, film, history, literature, music, philosophy, religion, and theater. Humanities research is primarily qualitative rather than quantitative, acknowledging multiple perspectives and paradigms about our cultures that reflect the diversity of the human condition. The evidence to support an argument is cumulative, allowing researchers to legitimately draw from both past and present. As a result, the investigative methods used by humanists differ from those of social scientists and scientists. In this chapter, I provide an overview of research within the humanities to serve as a foundation for understanding the various processes. Music and history are discussed in depth in separate chapters, but the basics here are applicable to both of those disciplines as well.

Humanities research topics can be investigations into or creations of a "text," for example, a poem, a dance, a piece of music, a painting, or a film. The text may be prehistoric or recently produced. The humanities researcher formulates a question that reflects a personal interest in the topic. Two people analyzing the same piece may come to very different conclusions based on the interpretation of the text, the supporting evidence used, the theoretical approach applied, the political or philosophical beliefs of the individual, or the goals of the research. In terms of goals, an artist seeking images of horses to use as models for a painting has very different intentions from a scholar analyzing the depiction of horses in public sculpture. Whatever the goals of the question being explored, whether researching an academic topic or making a work of art, the individual is participating as part of a larger community. The practitioner, in creating a work of art, is part of a tradition that can include the themes, tools, and techniques used during the creative process. A scholar, in exploring an issue about an aspect of human culture, enters an ongoing conversation that could be hundreds of years old. The resources required by the humanities community are not limited by time or format: the question being asked and explored determines the needs of the individual.

The following list highlights a few of the many different types of issues explored by researchers within the humanities discipline:

- The costume designer for a play needs books with images of historical clothing.
- An actor wants recordings of regional accents.
- A playwright requires slang dictionaries to browse for authentic historic vocabulary.
- A set designer researching staging needs access to Shakespearean video recordings of various performances.
- A graduate student must find funding to travel and examine the archival papers and prompt books of a theatrical director.
- A student needs to borrow from another institution microfilm of a nineteenth-century publisher's records.
- A student is required to discover an authoritative website with images of medieval manuscripts.
- A scholar needs to identify play reviews in newspapers and popular periodicals, ranging from the nineteenth through the twenty-first centuries.
- A choreographer needs videotapes of various dances from around the world.
- A poet needs a thesaurus or rhyming dictionary.
- An artist wants technical specifications on different types of ceramic glazes.
- A student has an assignment that requires criticism about the theme of marriage in Jane Austen novels.

- An undergraduate needs comparisons of the writings of Socrates and Plato.
- A scholar needs to investigate the role of public art at the end of the twentieth century.

These projects reflect the diversity of topics explored within humanities, the wide range of formats used, the vast period of times studied, and the many types of primary and secondary sources required.

THE TRADITIONAL HUMANITIES RESEARCHER AND TECHNOLOGY

Since Rebecca Watson-Boone's 1994 article summarizing sixteen studies published between 1983 and 1992 in which the information-seeking habits of humanities scholars were examined, technology has become an important element in research.[1] As a result of her analysis of the literature, Watson-Boone created a portrait of the traditional humanities scholar as one who works alone, builds a personal library to form the foundation for research, "grazes"[2] library collections for inspiration or relevant materials, and, through the process, accumulates, selects, and interprets the information gathered to transform it into knowledge. Though humanities scholars do not use what they do not need, they do need to interact with the material to determine if it is useful. They look within the literature itself, through the bibliographies and notes of sources they use, to find additional sources. They consult colleagues and other experts who can give sound advice and direction. Computer technology doesn't make any of these characteristics obsolete, nor has it changed the basic characteristics of the humanities researcher; instead, the humanists have adapted and integrated technology to meet their communication and research needs.

Humanists don't have a single method for discovering primary and secondary sources. Humanities research is cumulative, and humanists accumulate the strategies and technologies that enrich their research and writing. Carole L. Palmer and Laura J. Neumann's thoughtful essay about the work of interdisciplinary humanities scholars, and the use of personal contacts and technology as part of the research process, reveals the adaptive nature of humanities researchers.[3] Human contacts continue to be important, for "colleagues are the most valued and effective authoritative sources."[4] Technologies are tools that are used when "they fit into the established patterns of research."[5]

> Information and its technologies aggregate instead of dissipating through obsolescence; books and textbases, indexes and databases, microfilm readers and scanners are all at play. The increased mobility of networked information appears to have accelerated the accumulation process for some, as predicted by Latour, but it has also increased the possible sources of evidence. For example, in developing a paper for an audience in religious studies, one literary scholar easily added episode transcripts from a Star Trek fan Web site to his already diverse and scattered mix of source material.[6]

In their study of English literature scholars, both in the United Kingdom and abroad, David Ellis and Hanna Oldman discovered that as long as technology served a need, such as e-mail and distribution lists to communicate and collaborate with colleagues, or online catalogs and databases to conduct research, the researchers would use it.[7] But, in keeping with the traditional humanist habit of using only what is needed, the "general standard of the [newsgroup] discussions is considered low and non-academic and as a result not many academics take up the opportunity to participate or to consider this medium seriously."[8] Although digital tools can help humanists conduct cumulative research, academics in the Ellis and Oldman study view the idea of the total digital library with skepticism and dislike, for it doesn't take into account the "necessity to feel the real object," and therefore digital access to materials shouldn't completely replace the object.[9]

Bibliographic citation tracing to find additional resources remains relevant. George Buchanan, Sally Jo Cunningham, and their colleagues examined the use of digital libraries by humanities academics and scholars and found that those with better search skills had higher success using digital libraries, but that "chaining," or discovering additional resources by searching through bibliographies and notes to discover relevant materials, remains very important, and that those with weaker search skills had very strong academic networks that negated the need to do independent information seeking.[10] The avenue of research didn't change, but technology that allows bibliographic citations to be traced was added to the repertoire.

The authors, studying the information-seeking habits of humanists and noting how technology enhances the humanities research process, recommend developing tools that will meet the needs of this community. For example, because chaining is one of the standard methods for researching within the humanities, "better citation chaining tools should considerably improve their experience of DL [digital library] systems."[11] Humanities scholars build extensive personal collections "to support rereading." They don't read a text once, but read and reread it as they ponder its meaning. This essential part of the process needs to be supported by allowing scholars to develop personal digital libraries, including texts and images.[12] Because humanists browse for creativity and to enhance research, access to materials placed in storage or available in digital form must allow this mode of discovery. Developing databases that allow the identification of nontext resources, such as images, audio clips, and music, and that pull together resources by theme, technique, or material type, would respond to the ways that parts of the academic community have traditionally mined library collections. Humanists depend on libraries and archives in their research; librarians could take advantage of discussion technology by offering "electronic discussion forums with archivists and other experienced users of a collection."[13] As Palmer and Neumann conclude, "Some of the most interesting and challenging information problems exist within the humanities, where texts, images, and artifacts are commonplace sources of data. . . . At minimum, the humanities offer an optimal test bed from which to learn how to develop and exploit heterogeneous information for the purposes of innovative inquiry."[14]

BECOMING A HUMANITIES RESEARCHER

As is true in any field of study, humanists go through a process, via their education and professional development, to acquire the skills and confidence to become effective researchers. This transition may be most evident during the career of graduate students. As Gloria J. Leckie notes, "Obtaining a PhD is a subtle process of both technical and social acculturation into a discipline or area of study."[15] She identifies a gap between the faculty, who have developed their understanding over time, and undergraduates, who adopt "coping" strategies because they don't know or understand the strategies used by their professors. In their 1982 article illustrating undergraduate anxiety, for example, Schwegler and Shamoon found that "students viewed the research paper as a closed-ended, informative, skills-oriented exercise written for an expert audience by novices pretending to be experts," while their professors "view the research paper as open-ended and interpretive, written for an audience of fellow inquirers."[16] The literature discussing the undergraduate researcher reveals that faculty may not remember how they learned to become scholars and may not understand the anxiety students feel because of deadlines and because of the need to sound authoritative on a topic in a short span of time. Undergraduates don't envision their research continuing past the completion of the assignment.[17] This tension needs to be addressed by the academic community, and the integration of writing and research into the curriculum may be the opportunity to do so in a meaningful way.

Graduate students have more time in their academic career to develop from the anxious undergraduate to the confident professional. Perhaps an examination of that development could provide faculty and librarians with ideas about raising the comfort level of undergraduates. Two articles illustrate this process. Robert Delgadillo and Beverly P. Lynch interviewed fifteen graduate history students at the University of California, Los Angeles, and found a distinct difference in the research abilities of the students as they progressed through their programs. Initially, the students depended heavily on secondary sources, but as they progressed and began to define their own research interests, they began to exhibit the traditional characteristics of the humanities researcher, including incorporating the "invisible college" into the process: talking to the instructor or adviser, attending conferences, reading secondary-source material and tracing bibliographies, and consulting with subject bibliographers in the library.[18] In his article summarizing a study on the information-seeking habits of humanities graduate students, Andy Barrett contrasts the undergraduate, who is often trying just to get the assignment done, with the experienced scholar, who often concludes the process only because of time constraints, but accepts that limitation.[19] The graduate student's development—from the deadline-driven behavior of an undergraduate to the complex information-seeking behavior of a professional—illustrates the stages of development from novice to expert. Barrett found that graduate students exhibit behavior found in both the undergraduate (i.e., use of information technology and generic Internet search engines to find general information, relying heavily on advisers and instructors for assignments, and lacking personal collections and subject expertise) and faculty (i.e., relying on subject experts and colleagues; interest in primary source materials; comfort with the "detective" approach to research, including browsing, citation chasing, and reading widely; and not anxious about deadlines). During the transition from one stage to another, graduate students do reveal their own distinct research nature (i.e., relying heavily on research supervisors or mentors during the initial phases of their project and learning to deal with the various deadline pressures to complete their graduate study), which characterizes this group; graduate students exhibit a different type of anxiety and comfort level of their own with the research process.[20] Those who work with the different populations in terms of research and writing need to understand these vital stages, from the novice to the transitional graduate student to the expert, to help alleviate anxiety and to educate and validate the various approaches to research.

AVENUES OF INQUIRY

Both scholars and practitioners within the humanities are the main focus of this chapter; although they both do research to solve problems, for the purposes of distinguishing processes in this chapter, *scholars* explain and analyze cultural objects/pieces, while *practitioners* create them. Both may be in search of financial backing for the project itself. Scholars may be more visible as researchers because they require secondary research sources to develop their arguments, and therefore they are more likely to ask for assistance finding relevant information. The practitioner may be invisible as a user but may still be a member of the community who uses the collections to research the creation of a piece, to explore new techniques within an art form, and to discover business practices necessary for establishing and maintaining a career. Neither of these groups is mutually exclusive—artists write critical works, and scholars can be practitioners.

As described above, scholars identify a question to be explored and answered about some aspect of human culture. The question may be prompted, for example, by personal interest or a response to a cultural experience, or may result from conversations with scholars and practitioners. The discovery and selection of primary sources to be analyzed may be through previous knowledge of the field; in-depth reading; recommendations from colleagues, faculty, or advisers; browsing book collections, museums, or archives; attending live performances; or serendipitous discoveries. Research for secondary sources and supporting evidence may include personal libraries; bibliographies found in books or articles; recommendations of colleagues, faculty, or advisers; browsing through libraries, book/film/image collections, museums, galleries, or published catalogs; and the use of library catalogs, indexes, subject bibliographies, encyclopedias, dictionaries, companions, and directories.

The practitioner, in the creative process, may be inspired by almost anything, from the immediate environment to a cultural or newsworthy event to materials found in the library collection. On a pragmatic level, an artist may need to create a piece in response to the theme of a challenge/competition opportunity or a piece commissioned by a patron. The secondary research required to accomplish the practitioner's goals may include the same types of resources as the scholar: personal collections (e.g., books, music, art, images); bibliographies; and browsing through book/film/image collections, museums, libraries, galleries, and published catalogs. To discover the voices behind other creations, the practitioner may need to access interviews, attend lectures, read biographies and artist statements, and view documentaries. Research may include exploring the types of tools required to accomplish completion of the piece, such as computer programs, color wheels, ceramic glazes, or specialized dictionaries for slang or dialect. To further their careers, artists may require guides to their professions offering advice on business practices, marketing, and promotion. Reference sources, including dictionaries, handbooks, and manuals, are important tools for enhancing and expanding technical skills: for example, grammar manuals, rhyming dictionaries, thesauri, color theory principles, lighting (theater or photography) or acoustics guides, graphic design handbooks, or textile encyclopedias. Artists may need tools for discovering sources of funding or career opportunities such as grants, internships, scholarships, fellowships, locations of writer/artist colonies, and listings of competitions, auditions, and casting calls.

RESEARCH TOOLS WITHIN THE HUMANITIES

The breadth of possibilities for inquiry within the humanities means the librarian must accumulate the collections, research tools, and technologies to promote the success of this community. Humanities researchers require access to a wide variety of sources, from the very scholarly to the very popular, from the most canonical texts to ephemera. Their needs are not bound by time or format. Books and periodicals play a vital role in all humanities research, while microforms, digital audio files, texts and images, films, documentaries, and audiotapes all have their place as well. The ideas, creations, and interpretations generated over time, not just the most current publications, are central to the conversations within the disciplines. Books are still the primary format for communicating within the humanities. But as is generally true in publishing overall, the latest theories and discussions of emerging movements and artists enter through the periodical literature.[21] Scholarly periodicals within the humanities range from broad coverage (e.g., *PMLA*, *Art History*, *Dance Research*, *Theatre Research International*, *Film Quarterly*), to the specialized (*Keats-Shelley*, *AfterImage*, *Restoration and 18th Century Theatre Research*), to trade publications (*Dance Magazine*, *Variety*, *Ceramics Monthly*). Many periodicals also serve to communicate professional opportunities, including job announcements, competitions and contests, casting calls, auditions, conferences, juried exhibitions, grants, fellowships, scholarships, internships, residencies, and workshops.

Traditionally, scholarly researchers within the humanities depended on bibliographies in the books and articles found on the topic to identify secondary resources, even though library catalogs, bibliographies, and indexes have long existed to provide access into the literature. With the advent of computer-based tools, our rich cultural history has been opened up in new ways. Web-based digital collections, library catalogs, bibliographies, and indexes allow researchers to find relevant materials from across decades and even centuries, searching by keywords. Streaming media, image databases, and electronic access to audio files and music are beginning to make our nonprint culture more accessible for exploration. Electronic access to information is an important addition to the research process as a whole within the humanities, expanding access to collections available in a variety of formats. Both standard library research tools and innovative ways to use the Web to communicate and share resources have brought new depth and breadth to the disciplines.

Research Guides within the Disciplines

Annotated research guides within the disciplines are invaluable for discovering tools to aid in the research process. *The Humanities: A Selective Guide to Information Sources* by Ron Blazek and Elizabeth Aversa provides working definitions of the humanities and the selected disciplines (philosophy, religion, mythology, folklore, visual arts, performing arts, and languages and literatures). Each chapter includes an overview of the discipline covered; major divisions within the field; users and uses of information; information-seeking behaviors; major classification schemes; important subject headings; major societies; annotated lists of standard research tools (e.g., bibliographies, periodicals, indexes, biographical sources, directories, dictionaries, handbooks, manuals); and specialized sources within the individual disciplines, such as versions and editions of the Bible, concordances and quotations, sales and exhibition catalogs, ethnic and regional dance sources, writers' guides and directories, and directories of plays, films, and videos, to name a few. Researchers can also consult specialized annotated guides within the discipline, which will provide much more comprehensive coverage, such as Hans E. Bynagle's *Philosophy: A Guide to the Reference Literature* and Martin Dillon and Shannon Graff Hysell's *ARBA In-Depth: Philosophy and Religion*.

Because of the impact of the Web on research, some discipline-based reference guides focus on using the Internet in the research process and direct researchers toward quality sites. Since the Web is not stable, these books are sometimes out of date by the time they are published, but the annotations for even defunct sites will provide researchers with evaluative criteria for determining the authority of other websites discovered. Louis E. Catron describes important websites for both scholars and practitioners in *Theatre Sources Dot Com: A Complete Guide to Online Theatre Sources and Dance Sources*, and, although dated, Lois Swan Jones's *Art Information and the Internet: How to Find It, How to Use It* gives valuable advice for using the Web in the research process. Directories to important sites within the disciplines can be found on the Web itself; researchers should focus on those directories established by societies, associations, or educational institutions to ensure that some level of authority is attached to the site used. For example, *Voice of the Shuttle*, a reputable portal directory to humanities websites, was created and is maintained by Professor Alan Liu, English Department, with the assistance of graduate students and others at the University of California, Santa Barbara.

Library Catalogs

At present, the library catalog remains a core research tool in the humanities, bringing together records of the print, electronic, digital, visual, recorded, and Web-based materials the library owns or to which it provides access. Keyword searching in the Web-based library catalog allows the researcher to focus the search on particular aspects of a topic and opens up the topic to cross-disciplinary discoveries and voices. Books, whether print or electronic, remain an important publication format within the humanities, whereas in the social sciences and sciences, as discussed in other chapters in this volume, the periodical literature serves as the main avenue of scholarly communication. In the humanities, books provide both primary and secondary materials: scholars write criticism; literary writers compose fiction, poetry, memoirs, or short stories; and images of art are organized by artist, movement, or theme. Library users can search for resources available in a variety of formats: video recordings of dance, operatic, or theatrical performances; microforms of historical newspapers and periodicals; dramatic readings by authors; documentaries illustrating the practices of artists or revealing the excavation of an ancient ruin; or feature films by genre (e.g., film noir, science fiction, westerns, war). Commercial and free digital collections of books, journals, and images allow online access to resources, some centuries old but newly discovered through technology. Additionally, the Web-based catalog allows virtual browsing of the collection. The researcher can search online by call number and discover all the materials the library owns within a certain classification number, whether the items are located in the book stacks, in storage, in a special collection, or in digital format.

The library catalog continues to be a core research tool within the humanities, but it can be improved. It isn't an effective tool to discover parts of monographs, such as short critical analyses of poems and short stories or images. As noted by Suzanne L. Moulton-Gertig in chapter 2, the library catalog has its shortcomings in music research for various reasons. The strength of the library catalog is the access it provides to the larger collections, but it must be supplemented by other sources, for example indexes, bibliographies, other reference tools, and even the Web. Librarians are expanding the value of this standard resource by understanding the humanist and by including item- and collection-level records for Web-based digital and microform collections, tables of contents of monographs, and access to audio and visual collections. Through technology, librarians can make the library catalog a vital portal into the world of traditional and electronic resources.

Local union catalogs, subscription databases such as *WorldCat* and initiatives such as *Google Scholar* allow researchers to reach far beyond the materials physically located in their home libraries. For the humanist, these types of resources offer the opportunity to discover additional potentially valuable materials, particularly because union catalogs bring together records from a variety of institutions. In cross-disciplinary work, an art historian conducting research on the history of medical anatomy lessons may find valuable resources in the more specialized medical and law collections. Public libraries may purchase how-to books valuable to an artist, or popular culture materials such as video recordings of television shows. A scholar researching the periodical literature of the late eighteenth century can identify titles available on microfilm to borrow through the Interlibrary Loan Department. Some libraries may include tables of contents for materials, which allow researchers to retrieve materials published in anthologies, such as essays, speeches, poems, and plays. A local library with a strong program in American studies may catalog titles found in free Web-based collections such as the nineteenth-century books and periodicals available digitally in the *Making of America* project, or include a record pointing to the collection of images of African Americans during the nineteenth century from the New York Public Library *Digital Schomburg* collection. In union catalogs, the combined cataloging practices of a variety of libraries, with different missions and communities served, will have an impact on the research process and bring to light a rich assortment of primary and secondary sources.

Bibliographies and Indexes

Bibliographies and indexes continue to serve as the best access to the literature within the various disciplines in the humanities, including periodical and newspaper literature both past and present. Standard academic subject indexes, once available only in print, are becoming more widely used through Web-based subscriptions. Decades of secondary research can be searched: the Modern Language Association's *MLA International Bibliography* (1920s–present) and the *Annual Bibliography of English Language and Literature (ABELL)* (1920–present) for literature, the *Philosophers Index* (1940–present) for philosophy, the American Theological Library Association's *ATLA Religion Database* (with citations back to the nineteenth century) for religion, *Art Abstracts* (1983–present) and the *Bibliography of the History of Art* (1970–present) for art and art history, and the *International Bibliography of Theatre and Dance* (1960s–present) for the performing arts. Some standard sources, however, are available only in print, such as the New York Public Library's dance catalog published as the *Bibliographic Guide to Dance*. Interdisciplinary databases, such as the *Chicano Database*, *HAPI (Hispanic American Periodicals Index) Online*, the *Handbook of Latin American Studies*, and *Fuente Academica* provide access to a variety of sources for Spanish language and cultural topics from various geographic regions, while *L'Année Philologique* provides interdisciplinary access to scholarly literature of Greek and Roman archaeology, history, mythology, religion, epigraphy, numismatics, and paleography. Sometimes identifying relevant indexes can be difficult because the publications are scattered and the knowledge to create adequate directories falls upon a group of experts within the field. In such cases, websites maintained by librarians associated with the field of study can be fruitful for discovery, such as the Web-based site *Indexes and Guides to Western European Periodicals in the Humanities and Social Sciences*, which lists research tools arranged by language and by century, and which is maintained by the Western European Studies Section of the Association of College and Research Libraries.

Online bibliographic databases also provide access to the periodical literature of previous centuries. *Periodicals Archives Online*, *C19: The Nineteenth Century Index* (which includes *Poole's Index to Periodical Literature*, *Periodicals Index Online*, and the *Wellesley Index to Victorian Periodicals,*

1824–1900), the *Making of America Digital Journal Collection* (a digital collection of over thirty journals from the antebellum period through reconstruction), the *Times Digital Archives* (1785–1985), and ProQuest's *Historical Newspapers*, including the *New York Times* (1851–2003), the *Wall Street Journal* (1889–1989), the *Washington Post* (1877–1990), the *Los Angeles Times* (1881–1985), the *Chicago Tribune* (1849–1985), and the *Boston Globe* (1872–1923), are all examples. These types of digital projects continue to be developed, providing access to materials that might otherwise not be available for purchase or loan.

Bibliographies and indexes that focus on a single type of publication, topic, or artist are excellent resources. The multivolume sets by William S. Ward, *Literary Reviews in British Periodicals* (1798–1826), Angela Forster's volumes titled *Index to Book Reviews in England* (1749–1800), the *Index to 19th-Century American Art Periodicals*, and *American Literary and Drama Reviews: An Index to Late 19th Century Periodicals* are invaluable for providing high-quality access to pockets of periodical literature that were only sketchily covered, if covered at all, by larger indexing projects such as *Poole's Index to Periodical Literature*. Compilations of reprints analyzing the writings of individuals, such as *Nietzsche: Critical Assessments* and *Karl Popper: Critical Assessments of Leading Philosophers*, or bibliographies to cultural thoughts and beliefs, such as *Judaism and Human Rights in Contemporary Thought: A Bibliographic Survey*, *South Asian Religions in the Americas: An Annotated Bibliography of Immigrant Religious Traditions*, and *Death and Dying: A Bibliographic Survey*—all part of the *Bibliographies and Indexes in Religious Studies* series—provide valuable access to historical and contemporary literature reviews. Before digital collections came into being, facsimile reproductions on a particular topic were gathered and bound together. In the *Romantics Reviewed*, contemporary reviews for the works of the canonical Romantic poets and selected literary figures were reproduced. The *New York Theatre Critics' Reviews* reproduced reviews from the New York City press of plays produced in New York from 1940 to 1996. The *New York Times Film Reviews* contains reprints from the newspaper from 1913 to 1996. Projects similar to these latter works have begun to disappear with the advent of digital collections, but the change is due to developments in technology, not changes in the research habits of the humanist.

Despite these various types of periodical and newspaper indexes, available both in print and online, coverage is selective for periodical literature, especially for newspaper literature prior to the end of the twentieth century. Because there is no comprehensive coverage, researchers may have to go through periodicals page by page in search of the material they need. This form of browsing may never disappear.

The titles above represent a small portion of sources available electronically and in print providing access to our periodical heritage, but though they share a common purpose, they have their own strengths and weaknesses that affect research. Understanding the scope of a resource is critical for the researcher. Three indexes that cover nineteenth-century periodicals illustrate this point: *Periodical Index Online (PIO)*, *Poole's Index to Periodical Literature*, and the *Wellesley Index to Victorian Literature*. *Poole's* is the oldest of these three indexes, published in the second half of the nineteenth century, to provide access to the literature of that time back to 1802. *Wellesley* lists the tables of contents for forty-two British Victorian periodicals from 1824 to 1900. *PIO* is an online periodical index, developed in the late twentieth century, providing keyword access to the contents of journals back to the eighteenth century. All three of these index the *Quarterly Review*, the journal in which Sir Walter Scott reviewed Jane Austen's novel *Emma*, but if the researcher doesn't understand the scope of each of these resources, the search results can be frustrating. For example, *PIO* doesn't analyze the contents of a journal, but instead simply transcribes what was printed on the page at the time. Austen published *Emma* anonymously. Therefore, to find reviews of *Emma*, the researcher would need to search by keyword "emma" and limit to a range of years during which the book was published, because reviews can't be found by a search on Austen's name. In contrast, *Poole's*, the oldest of the three indexes, was created in the latter half of the nineteenth century, when Jane Austen's identity was known; she was included as a subject in the index, and therefore articles about her and her books can be found. In the creation of the *Wellesley Index to Victorian Literature*, many of the anonymous authors of Victorian periodical articles were identified, making that index a key resource for scholars working with Victorian periodicals. Title entries were enhanced to clarify article titles. But the tables of contents for the *Quarterly Review* begin with volume thirty in 1824, eight years after *Emma* was reviewed. These three indexes are vital to periodical research done in nineteenth-century periodicals, but they are neither comprehensive nor infallible. Actually, ironically, the scholar seeking reviews of *Emma* will have the most success using Ward's printed volumes, *Literary Reviews in British Periodicals*, or using a bibliography devoted to the critical assessment of Austen, not any online article database.

Other sources, beyond books and discipline-based periodicals, have their place in the humanities research process. Contemporary reviews found in the popular press may be the only secondary sources available for early discussions of emerging arts and artists. The first in-depth scholarly analyses of contemporary authors, musicians, dancers, and other artists are often found in dissertations. Some scholarly websites devoted to individual artists or movements may contain more complete, up-to-date bibliographies on individuals or movements than the standard bibliographic databases. Blogs and electronic distribution lists have roles to play in communication within disciplines, from discussions about new research and techniques, to information about conferences, to soliciting advice from fellow scholars and practitioners. Research within the humanities requires broad access to a variety of formats and technologies, as well as the willingness to learn to use what is necessary to retrieve the required information.

Unique, Yet Representative, Types of Research Tools

As with any branch of knowledge, each discipline within the humanities has its own dictionaries, encyclopedias, handbooks, companions, guides, directories, and chronologies. Language dictionaries or dictionaries defining critical or theoretical approaches are examples of reference tools that serve specific roles within the research process; the former aid in translations of text, and the latter aid in providing specialized interpretations of vocabulary within a field. Traditional descriptive bibliographies detail the publication history of authors, including such information as the size and length of novels and the number of editions. Concordances—alphabetical indexes to all of the words, in context, occurring in a text or body of works—provide entry to a text or group of texts, such as the works of Chaucer or Shakespeare, or religious texts such as the Bible or the Koran. Concordances may eventually become obsolete in print as online search technology becomes more sophisticated, but at this point the print remains relevant.

Commercial and academic cooperative initiatives are taking advantage of the Web, which is flexible and easily updated, and which encourages linking within the site as well as out to relevant materials. For example, *Grove Art Online*, published commercially, is a core scholarly encyclopedia for art and art history. In the past, a print reference tool of this quality would be valued, but it would grow slowly dated as time wore on. The online version not only takes advantage of the Web by linking within the text to other relevant entries and linking out to images at museum sites, but entries are updated regularly with new developments and bibliographies, and new scholarly essays on traditional and contemporary arts are added. The *Perseus Digital Library*, a free Web-based resource, provides access to primary and secondary texts, as well as images, from Ancient Rome and Greece. The *Stanford Encyclopedia of Philosophy* is another cooperative initiative in which a "free" Web-based scholarly resource is updated dynamically as new scholarship emerges; the success of this type of project, however, depends on the willingness of users to help fund it through donations, and on the dependability of contributors to provide the content. Outside of academia, *Wikipedia* and the *Internet Movie Database* are two nonscholarly websites that use their communities both to provide content and monitor quality; both represent how the Web can be used to create reference tools by cooperatively archiving the collective knowledge of our society.

Print and electronic resources from a variety of origins can enhance research within a discipline in a variety of ways. The creators of *ARTstor* are building an image database containing images from all aspects of human visual culture, not only art objects. Print or online art sales catalogs provide prices for specific works of art for someone who may want the latest sales figures, or to trace sales trends over time. An art historian interested in identifying the origins of cemetery sculpture at the end of the nineteenth century might find mail-order catalogs important sources for images, while a theater designer wishing to find images of everyday tools and clothing might find those same mail-order catalogs sources of inspiration. The art historian working on nineteenth-century cemetery sculpture, who might use city directories to identify individuals by occupation, would welcome the Tufts Digital Library initiative *Boston Streets: Mapping Directory Data* at dca.tufts.edu/features/bostonstreets. This website is an innovative approach to providing researchers with the data needed for such a project:

> *Boston Streets* combines three heavily used resources in historical research libraries[—]photographs, maps, and city directories[—]in a way that transcends their use in the physical world. Underlying the entire project is the idea that [it] is possible to organize data by spatial location and then link this data to many other sources of information that share the same location without having to extensively catalog them by subject, name, or other subjective terminology. At the same time, any subjective terms that are added become discoverable though their relationship to the location.

The art historian not only can identify the individuals within an occupation but can find digital maps and images to enrich the information discovered. Such an initiative responds to how particular historical documents are used and digitizes them to allow both browsing and keyword/subject searching of the data.

Archives and special collections, whether kept within a physical location or distributed digitally or via microforms, are rich sources of primary materials valued by humanists. Michael Levine-Clark discusses archival research in chapter 3. Print and Web-based directories list information about the location of manuscripts and other archival materials. In the United States the *National Union Catalog of Manuscript Collections* and in the United Kingdom *Archon* provide bibliographic records to archival and manuscript repositories, including business, government, literary, and cultural documents. The *Archives of American Art*, which began as a microfilm repository and is being replaced by a digital collection, makes available "roughly 16 million letters, photographs, diaries, sketches, scrapbooks, business records and other documentation concerning the visual arts" in the United States; the catalog and digital archive are available through the Smithsonian website, and the microfilm can be borrowed via Interlibrary Loan.

The cumulative nature of the humanities disciplines can have an effect on the ongoing reinvention of resources that are of value to humanists. For example, two large-scale bibliographic projects were the foundation for the digital collection titled *Early English Books Online*: Alfred W. Pollard and G. R. Redgrave's *A Short-Title Catalogue of Books Printed in En-*

gland, Scotland, and Ireland and English Books Printed Abroad, 1475–1640, and Donald Wing's *Short-Title Catalogue of Books Printed in England, Scotland, Ireland, Wales, and British America, and of English Books Printed in Other Countries, 1641–1700*. The compilers of the bibliographies sought to identify everything published in the English language in Britain and all its colonies. With the advent of microform technology, these bibliographies were used to create microfilm collections that were then purchased by libraries from around the world, thus allowing scholars remote access to rare materials. With advances in digital technology, the microfilm was reformatted into a Web-based digital collection. The need for the content didn't change; the format and access were just adapted to new technologies.

With the introduction of digital microform scanners, microforms, often greeted with moans of dismay by researchers, are also getting a new life. In the past, researchers had to print what was readable on the screen, which sometimes necessitated taping together pieces of paper, especially when trying to capture a whole page of a newspaper. With the digital scanner, the whole page of a newspaper can be captured as one image, and then software is used to enlarge the page to read it. The quality of the images created is excellent, although the better the quality of the microform itself, the higher the quality of the resulting image. Scholars can use this technology to create their own databases of primary source materials.

As stated above, the humanities scholar enters an ongoing conversation when he or she begins to research and write. This conversation is with the text itself and with the published materials found to support an academic argument, but the conversation also includes colleagues and experts within the field of study—individuals who can be met at conferences or in performance/gallery spaces. The Web also provides opportunities for communication: for example, studio artists can find websites devoted to stock imagery, and blogs and electronic distribution lists devoted to every media. They can use the Web to find images for inspiration, and to find fellow practitioners from whom advice can be sought. For individuals in the humanities, who are often working in isolation, these sources for communicating with like-minded individuals allow virtual communities to be built.

BROWSING AS A RESEARCH STRATEGY

Not every discussion within the humanities will be found using standard research tools such as library catalogs, bibliographies, and indexes. For example, students may not be able to use the library catalog, or even a standard subject-based index, to find scholarly criticism on a specific novel,
short story, poem, painting, or film. Some of the individual plays of Shakespeare and Ibsen, and the individual novels of Jane Austen and Herman
Melville, have had whole books of critical analysis devoted to single works,
but this is not always the case. Students may want to use the library catalog
to find criticism, but they may really need to use a subject-based index such
as the *MLA International Bibliography*, *Art Abstracts*, or the *Film & Television Literature Index* to find research on specific works. Even that may not
be sufficient because those resources don't analyze the parts of works the
way an even more specialized research tool would. *Short Story Explication*,
for example, is a print index that identifies discussions of short stories
within chapters in books, even if the discussion is less than a page long. *Illustration Index* is another source that indexes a specific element of a larger
work: illustrations in magazines. Both *Short Story Explication* and *Illustration Index* are intended to help researchers find relevant materials using a
standard research resource—an index—to discover information that otherwise can only be found by browsing. These tools are not comprehensive,
however, and therefore browsing may still be necessary. If no analysis of a
particular short story, poem, or play can be found using the print and electronic reference tools available, humanities librarians need to encourage the
researcher to go to the shelves containing the works of and about a particular author and look through the tables of contents and indexes of volumes
found in that section. Browsing within the volumes themselves can sometimes be more rewarding than using print or electronic reference sources. A
costume designer in need of images for a Greek tragedy can look through
art books, history books, and costume books for inspiration, and browsing
call numbers in the areas of costumes or ancient Greek art or daily life in
ancient Greece may all provide illustrations for the designer to examine.
Creativity and flexibility are core to successful humanities research, and it
is important for the librarian to stress the need to develop these skills as part
of the process. Even browsing within the issues of a periodical can bring
about serendipitous discoveries that can't always be found through tradi-

tional research tools. For example, an essay written about women in a magazine during World War II, when juxtaposed with the advertisements within the magazine, may reveal the messages, sometimes conflicting, that women received about their domestic and public roles. At times, only by browsing through the periodical literature of the era will a researcher be able to gather together the primary source evidence.

Browsing the bibliographies of the secondary sources used in a research project allows the researcher not only to identify additional readings, but also to discover who is being cited. Thus the researcher begins to develop a sense of the various voices in the conversation that he or she is to join, and learns to evaluate the authority and critical approaches of the different scholars. As a research project becomes more focused, the researcher may detect a pattern to the scholars cited and start to recognize the names of established authorities within the topic being researched. By beginning to recognize who the scholars are who have worked or are working within a discipline, the student is learning to think independently of his or her professor and is establishing a framework for his or her own work.

Browsing is an important skill in humanities research and is practiced in a variety of ways. Faculty, graduate students, and practitioners do it as a matter of course and learn to build it into their research process. Undergraduates browse too, but they often do not understand its value or relevance, for they believe that the discovery of materials found in such a manner is accidental or even a form of cheating. They have to understand that the books in a library are deliberately grouped by subject and are arranged by a classification system such as the Library of Congress or Dewey Decimal system to allow browsing. Librarians and faculty need to address this gap in undergraduate abilities. Because browsing can be very time consuming, the nature of the research project, and an understanding of the strengths and weaknesses of the research tools available, can help determine if browsing is warranted and necessary.

THE ROLE OF THE LIBRARY AND LIBRARIANS IN THE RESEARCH PROCESS

It is difficult to generalize about which research standards are necessary and common across the many branches of the humanities. Scholars and practitioners have different goals, and therefore the basic skills they need for lifelong learning and research literacy vary. Within the practice of an art, some forms such as film, theater, and dance may be much more collaborative than others, such as writing poetry or painting, but both creative endeavors require research, whether locating images of Roman dress for a staging of *Julius Caesar* or exploring how one's own work fits into the tradition of ekphrasis in poetry. Sound searching skills, knowledgeable use of collections, critical thinking, and willingness to ask for help are all core to the successful research project.

Librarians must assess the level of need for the individual seeking help in the humanities: freshman papers do not require the same rigorous research as is necessary in upper-level undergraduate or graduate student projects. Sometimes an interdisciplinary article database, such as *Academic Search Premier* or *Expanded Academic ASAP*, will provide enough critical content to get a novice researcher started. Research literacy within the discipline, however, does require scholars and practitioners to build essential skills to allow them to navigate successfully through the material relevant to their individual projects.

Even though humanists do create their own personal libraries, they can't own everything, so by using the library they are extending their collections. For example, a fiber arts artist may have a collection at home that includes manuals about different types of textiles and books illustrating the works of artists within the medium. The library, through its collections of books and periodicals, provides access to more images from across the centuries and around the world, articles evaluating works in exhibitions, interviews with artists explaining their work, handbooks about care and maintenance of textiles, and periodicals listing workshops, contests, grants, and residency programs. Academic and public libraries have different missions, so a public library may offer a greater variety of how-to books, many aimed at the amateur artist but still of practical worth, or a wider variety of coffee-table picture books for visual inspiration. Because of the specialization of the community served, the librarian at an arts college may have more in-depth knowledge about sources. The librarian working with such a student or group of students can show how the library or libraries in the area can serve as an extension of his or her own libraries, the classroom, and the studio.

By explaining the standard research practices, the librarian can engage in a conversation about the larger goals of research within the discipline and can illustrate how the various sources available can be used to push the boundaries of a topic. Because the personal interaction between the researcher and the text is core to the process, humanities research often requires collaboration between the researcher and the librarian to find relevant materials. For a class on the representations of women during World War II, students may need access to films, novels, short stories, memoirs, advertisements, documentaries, newspapers, and periodicals from the time, lists of films and books by topic, and current scholarly historical, film, literary, and cultural studies research. Newspapers from the period may be available on microfilm or digitally. Students may need to browse through periodicals to find advertisements about women, or they may find websites with images published as posters. There is no one avenue for the class to take into the primary and secondary material because the paths taken depend on the questions being asked by the researchers; each student in a class of this sort could have a unique approach or interest in the topic. One student might compare two novels, another might need to analyze the representation of women in war films presented across several decades and need help identifying which films to use, and another might wish to analyze the domestic and public realms that women inhabited by looking at diaries and letters they wrote during the war. With such diversity within a class, the librarian can provide a broad overview of sources relevant to the theme, but this can be overwhelming; the librarian may also need to provide individual follow-up sessions to ensure that students are successfully locating relevant materials.

Research Skills within the Humanities

The following list of evidence of research literacy is more ideal than realistic for the individual humanities researcher, but these are the skills the humanities librarian must have. The basics of research literacy covered by Carrie Forbes in chapter 9 are vital. Beyond those, students within the discipline may develop some of the following that are most relevant to their continued research needs. Humanities researchers should at least be introduced to the overview of humanities research literacy and know that they can work with reference librarians to get assistance when the research is beyond their skills. As the materials required in humanities projects may include anything from archival documents to microforms to books to digital collections, the researcher must be fairly proficient at using technology.

I. Understand the structure of information available and avenues of communication within the discipline.

II. Identify and differentiate between various types of sources:
   - Identify sources as either primary or secondary, depending on the topic.
   - Differentiate between different editions, both online and in print, to determine which are authoritative.
   - Differentiate between scholarly criticism and popular reviews.
   - Know how to find the "texts" within the discipline, that is, visual resources, authoritative editions, productions, reviews, facsimiles, prompt books, letters, diaries, and so on.
   - Begin to understand the role of critical theory in scholarship within the disciplines and to recognize the use of critical theory in the literature.

III. Identify and use key research tools to locate relevant information:
   - Know the relevant interdisciplinary sources to find nondiscipline discussions as well as popular responses and reviews to cultural events (general magazines, newspapers, reviews, interviews, transcripts, and the like).

IV. Plan effective search strategies and modify search strategies as needed:
   - Know the terminology/vocabulary of the discipline to describe eras, theories, movements, genres, and so on.
   - Know how to discover the controlled vocabulary within the specific research tool for searching (standardized spellings for transliterated words and names), as well as the alternative spellings that may be used.
   - Know how to find locations of primary sources in archives, museums, special collections, and other repositories.
   - Be able to use a variety of technologies necessary to use materials, including various search engines, digital collections, digital microform scanners, and traditional microform readers.
   - Understand archival research practices.

CONCLUSION

The research practices and needs within the humanities offer the librarian both challenges and opportunities. The librarian must be able to prove to the researcher that it is worth his or her while to develop strong research skills and learn to use the library creatively. Because relevant materials are not bound by time, those working within the humanities must be more flexible than in other disciplines about using a wide variety of formats, and must be willing to broaden the search parameters of the topic being explored. Using bibliographies within books and articles, for example, is one method for discovering the conversations within a discipline, but subject and keyword searches within library catalogs and subject indexes are vital to the community as well. Electronic access to library catalogs and indexes allows whole collections and multiple years of research to be searched at once. Voices that may have been lost because they were not included in bibliographies found in monographs or articles can be rediscovered. Keyword searching allows researchers to combine different concepts and find where ideas may or may not overlap: searches like "women and science fiction," "landscape and urban and watercolor*," and "choreograph* and modern dance" allow researchers to tailor their search strategies to meet their specific needs. Librarians can discover, select, collect, and make accessible sources that reinvigorate the research and creative process. By demonstrating an understanding of the research process and needs within the discipline, the librarian can illustrate how developing strong research skills will enhance and expand the knowledge base of humanities researchers and contribute to their confidence that they understand the cultural heritage in which they work.

SELECTED RESOURCES

Listed below are the resources included in this chapter arranged by discipline. All of the following are representative of the types of research tools available within the humanities; the list is not intended to be comprehensive or definitive for any of the disciplines included. In the text the tools were discussed in terms of the type of source each represented. Here, the resources are sorted and grouped together by discipline to provide a different perspective on where each fits within the humanities.

General/Interdisciplinary

Academic Search Premier. Birmingham, AL: EBSCO. search.epnet.com.

Archon Directory. www.nationalarchives.gov.uk/archon (accessed March 15, 2006).

ARTstor. New York: ARTstor, 2004–. www.artstor.org/info.

Blazek, Ron, and Elizabeth Aversa. *The Humanities: A Selective Guide to Information Resources.* 5th ed. Englewood, CO: Libraries Unlimited, 2000.

Boston Streets: Mapping Directory Data. Boston: Tufts Digital Collections and Archives. dca.tufts.edu/features/bostonstreets.

C19: The Nineteenth Century Index. Ann Arbor, MI: Proquest, 2005. c19index .chadwyck.com.

Chicano Database. Mountain View, CA: Research Libraries Group, 1995–. www .rlg.org.

Digital Schomburg. New York: New York Public Library. www.nypl.org/research/ sc/digital.html.

Early English Books Online (EEB Online). Ann Arbor, MI: ProQuest, 1999–. eebo.chadwyck.com/home.

Expanded Academic ASAP. Farmington Hills, MI: Thomson Gale. find.galegroup .com.

Fuente Academica. Ipswich, MA: EBSCO, 2003–.

Google Scholar. scholar.google.com (accessed March 15, 2006).

Handbook of Latin American Studies Online. Washington, DC: Library of Congress, 199?. rs6.loc.gov/hlas.

HAPI Online. Los Angeles, CA: UCLA Latin American Center. hapi.ucla.edu.

Houghton, Walter E., ed. *The Wellesley Index to Victorian Periodicals, 1824–1900.* Toronto: University of Toronto Press, 1966–1989. Available online at c19index.chadwyck.com.

Illustration Index. 8 vols. Lanham, MD: Scarecrow Press, 1957–1998.

Indexes and Guides to Western European Periodicals in the Humanities and Social Sciences. www.people.fas.harvard.edu/~eshierl/wess/IGWEP.html (accessed March 15, 2006).

Liu, Alan. *Voice of the Shuttle*, at vos.ucsb.edu (accessed March 17, 2006).

Making of America. Ann Arbor: University of Michigan; Ithaca, NY: Cornell University, 1995–. cdl.library.cornell.edu/moa/index.html.

National Union Catalog of Manuscript Collections (NUCMC). 1997. www.loc .gov/coll/nucmc (accessed March 15, 2006).

Periodicals Index Online. Alexandria, VA: Chadwyck-Healey. pio.chadwyck
.com.

Poole, William Frederick. *Poole's Index to Periodical Literature*. 1802–1906. 6
vols. Rev. ed. Boston: Houghton, 1891. Reprint, New York: Peter Smith, 1938.
Available online through various vendors.

ProQuest Historical Newspapers. Ann Arbor, MI: ProQuest. www.il.proquest
.com/products_pq/hnp.

The Times Digital Archive, 1785–1985. Farmington Hills, MI: Thomson Gale.
www.gale.com.

Wikipedia: The Free Encyclopedia. www.wikipedia.org (accessed March 15,
2006).

WorldCat. Dublin, OH: OCLC. www.oclc.org/firstsearch.

Art, Art History, and Architecture

Archives of American Art. Washington, DC: Smithsonian. www.aaa.si.edu.

Art Index. New York: H. W. Wilson. Available online through various vendors.

Avery Index to Architectural Periodicals. Santa Monica, CA: Getty Art History
Information Program, 1994. Available online through various vendors.

BHA: Bibliography of the History of Art. Santa Monica, CA: J. Paul Getty Trust,
Getty Art History Program. Available online through various vendors.

Grove Art Online. Oxford: Oxford University Press, 1998–. www.groveart.com.

Schmidt, Mary M. *Index to Nineteenth-Century Art Periodicals*. Mountain View,
CA: RLG, 1998. www.rlg.org.

Archaeology

L'Année Philologique. Villejuif: Société Internationale de Bibliographie Classique. www.annee-philologique.com/aph.

DYABOLA. Munich: Biering & Brinkmann. www.dyabola.de.

Crane, Greg, ed. *Perseus Digital Library*. Medford, MA: Tufts University, Classics Department, 199?. www.perseus.tufts.edu.

Lexicon Iconographicum Mythologiae Classicae. Zurich: Artemis, 1981–1999.

Literatures

Annual Bibliography of English Language and Literature (ABELL). Leeds:
Maney Publishing for the Modern Humanities Research Association, 1921–.
Annual. Available online via www.chadwyck.com.

Forster, Antonia. *Index to Book Reviews in England, 1749–1774*. Carbondale: Southern Illinois University Press, 1990.

———. *Index to Book Reviews in England, 1775–1800*. London: British Library, 1997.

Marks, Patricia. *American Literary and Drama Reviews: An Index to Late 19th Century Periodicals*. Boston: G. K. Hall, 1984.

Modern Language Association International Bibliography of Books and Articles on the Modern Languages and Literatures. New York: Modern Language Association of America, 1922–. Annual. Available online through various vendors.

Reiman, Donald H., ed. *The Romantics Reviewed: Contemporary Reviews of British Romantic Writers*. 9 vols. New York: Garland, 1972.

Twentieth-Century Short Story Explication. Hamden, CT: Shoe String Press, 1961–.

Ward, William S., comp. *Literary Reviews in British Periodicals, 1789–1797: A Bibliography with a Supplementary List of General (Non-Review) Articles on Literary Subjects*. New York: Garland, 1979.

———. *Literary Reviews in British Periodicals, 1798–1820: A Bibliography with a Supplementary List of General (Non-Review) Articles on Literary Subjects*. 2 vols. New York: Garland, 1972.

———. *Literary Reviews in British Periodicals, 1821–1826: A Bibliography with a Supplementary List of General (Non-Review) Articles on Literary Subjects*. New York: Garland, 1977.

Performing Arts

Film & Television Literature Index. Ipswich, MA: EBSCO, ca. 2006. www .ebsco.com.

International Bibliography of Theatre and Dance. Brooklyn, NY: American Society for Theatre Research. Available online through EBSCO Information Services, www.ebsco.com.

Internet Movie Database. www.imdb.com (accessed March 15, 2006).

Marks, Patricia. *American Literary and Drama Reviews: An Index to Late 19th Century Periodicals*. Boston: G. K. Hall, 1984.

New York Public Library. Dance Collection. *Bibliographic Guide to Dance*. Boston: G. K. Hall, 1975.

New York Theatre Critics' Reviews. New York: Critics' Theatre Reviews, 1943–1996.

New York Times Film Reviews. New York: New York Times, 1913–1996.

Philosophy

Bynagle, Hans E. *Philosophy: A Guide to the Reference Literature*. 3rd ed. Englewood, CO: Libraries Unlimited, 2006.

Conway, Daniel W., and Peter S. Groff. *Nietzsche: Critical Assessments*. 4 vols. New York: Routledge, 1998.

Dillon, Martin, and Shannon Graff Hysell, eds. *ARBA In-Depth: Philosophy and Religion*. Westport, CT: Libraries Unlimited, 2004.

O'Hear, Anthony. *Karl Popper: Critical Assessments of Leading Philosophers*. 4 vols. New York: Routledge, 2004.

The Philosopher's Index: An International Index to Philosophical Periodicals and Books. Bowling Green, OH: Philosopher's Information Center. Available online through various vendors.

Zalta, Edward N., principal ed. *The Stanford Encyclopedia of Philosophy*, 1995. Online at plato.stanford.edu (accessed December 12, 2004).

Religion

ATLA Religion. Chicago: American Theological Library Association. Available online via various vendors.

Breslauer, S. Daniel. *Judaism and Human Rights in Contemporary Thought: A Bibliographical Survey*. Westport, CT: Greenwood Press, 1993.

Dillon, Martin, and Shannon Graff Hysell, eds. *ARBA In-Depth: Philosophy and Religion*. Westport, CT: Libraries Unlimited, 2004.

Fenton, John Y. *South Asian Religions in the Americas: An Annotated Bibliography of Immigrant Religious Traditions*. Westport, CT: Greenwood Press, 1995.

Southard, Samuel, comp. *Death and Dying: A Bibliographical Survey*. New York: Greenwood Press, 1991.

NOTES

1. Rebecca Watson-Boone, "The Information Needs and Habits of Humanities Scholars," *RQ* 34, no. 2 (Winter 1994): 203–16.

2. Watson-Boone, "The Information Needs and Habits of Humanities Scholars," 212. "However, the humanist seems to 'graze,' rather than browse, passing 'lightly along the surface' of interesting material, rather than 'jumping from one thing to another.'"

3. Carole L. Palmer and Laura J. Neumann, "The Information Work of Interdisciplinary Humanities Scholars: Exploration and Translation," *Library Quarterly* 72, no. 1 (January 2002): 85–117.

4. Palmer and Neumann, "The Information Work of Interdisciplinary Humanities Scholars," 104.

5. Palmer and Neumann, "The Information Work of Interdisciplinary Humanities Scholars," 98.

6. Palmer and Neumann, "The Information Work of Interdisciplinary Humanities Scholars," 99.

7. David Ellis and Hanna Oldman, "The English Literature Researcher in the Age of the Internet," *Journal of Information Science* 31, no. 1 (February 2005): 29–36.

8. Ellis and Oldman, "The English Literature Researcher in the Age of the Internet," 35.

9. Ellis and Oldman, "The English Literature Researcher in the Age of the Internet," 35.

10. George Buchanan, Sally Jo Cunningham, Ann Blandford, Jon Rimmer, and Claire Warwick, "Information Seeking by Humanities Scholars," *Research and Advanced Technology for Digital Libraries*, ed. Andreas Rauber, Stavros Christodoulakis, and A Min Tjoa, 218–29. Proceedings of the 9th European Conference, ECDL 2005, Vienna, Austria, September 18–23, 2005. Berlin: Springer, 2005.

11. Buchanan et al., "Information Seeking by Humanities Scholars," 228.

12. Palmer and Neumann, "The Information Work of Interdisciplinary Humanities Scholars," 110.

13. Palmer and Neumann, "The Information Work of Interdisciplinary Humanities Scholars," 111.

14. Palmer and Neumann, "The Information Work of Interdisciplinary Humanities Scholars," 112.

15. Gloria J. Leckie, "Desperately Seeking Citations: Uncovering Faculty Assumptions about the Undergraduate Research Process," *The Journal of Academic Librarianship* 22, no. 3 (May 1996): 201–8.

16. Robert A. Schwegler and Linda K. Shamoon, "The Aims and Process of the Research Paper," *College English* 44, no. 8 (December 1982): 817–24.

17. Celia Rabinowitz, "Working in a Vacuum: A Study of the Literature of Student Research and Writing," *Research Strategies* 17, no. 4 (2000): 337–46; Ethelene Whitmire, "Disciplinary Differences and Undergraduates' Information-Seeking Behavior," *Journal of the American Society for Information Science and Technology* 53, no. 8 (2002): 631–38; and Ethelene Whitmore, "The Relationship between Undergraduates' Epistemological Beliefs, Reflective Judgment, and Their Information-Seeking Behavior," *Information Processing and Management* 40, no. 1 (2004): 97–111.

18. Roberto Delgadillo and Beverly P. Lynch, "Future Historians: Their Quest for Information," *College and Research Libraries* 60, no. 3 (May 1999): 245–59.

19. Andy Barrett, "The Information-Seeking Habits of Graduate Student Researchers in the Humanities," *The Journal of Academic Librarianship* 31, no. 4 (July 2005): 324–31.

20. Barrett, "The Information-Seeking Habits of Graduate Student Researchers in the Humanities," 329–30.

21. Tenure for humanities scholars has long been tied to the publication of monographs. This may change, however, due in part to library and university press budget cuts, which are affecting the monograph publishing industry and therefore affect the ability of untenured faculty to publish in this traditional format. For example, because junior faculty are finding it difficult to publish, the Modern Language Association has begun to respond

to the crisis in the language and literature disciplines. The organization is in the process of proposing radical changes that will allow various types of publications to be considered as demonstrating research excellence, not just monographs. Scott Jaschik, "Radical Change for Tenure," *Inside Higher Ed*, December 30, 2005, insidehighered.com/news/2005/12/30/tenure.

2

Music Research

Suzanne L. Moulton-Gertig

THE DISCIPLINE OF MUSIC: A MISUNDERSTOOD STUDY

The man on the street, when asked about the study of music on the college/ university/conservatory level would generally describe the discipline as advanced study of the instrument or voice, punctuated by many rehearsals, and culminating in recitals and concerts. After all, the media have seduced and deluded the public over the years by showing musicians engaging in just these very activities as representative of a musical education. Filmmakers are wild to show orchestral musicians in the pit, competitions and auditions onstage, and exciting and dramatic interplay between master and aspiring artist in various studio backdrops. Few see fit to show a theory, history, or music education classroom and the scholastic drama unfolding there, for it is, in the colloquial, "unsexy."[1] As a result, a great number of beginning music students and their parents have no grasp of the number of requisite curricular pieces that make up the discipline of music and are shocked when presented with the array of classes and subjects the discipline comprises.

This curricular shock of the present makes an interesting comparison with the understanding and status of the discipline as a study historically. In the medieval system of education, the discipline of music was so revered as to hold one of the four coveted places in the quadrivium as a "mathematical art," along with mathematics, geometry, and astronomy. In this arrangement, music was not viewed as an art per se, as in the modern sense, but as a science with math and physics (as studied in the acoustical sense). It is perhaps the ensuing generations and cultures that, by redefining the discipline in recognition of its artistic disposition, actually erased the generational memory of its scientific nature. While held in great esteem in some past cultures, it has tumbled quickly over the centuries from its lofty perch in the quadrivium, like a noble family in decline, begging the question, "What happened?" With the denouement of the civilizations that prized it for its mathematical and physical properties, subsequent cultures focused on the notion of music's sacred and artistic essence as it served the church, while simultaneously holding secular musical genres in lower esteem. It is understandable how over time this very artistic application, which was in large measure divorced from its scientific roots, asserted its predominance over its scientific sibling. There were, after all, many more lute players than musical scientists, and their product was much more palatable to the church, the court, and the poorly educated general populace. Quite frankly, applied music became the winner through its sonic beauty, its sheer entertainment purposes, a cultural shifting of values, and the development of different religions and their dictated practices. Such is the stuff of prolonged ratiocination and regret in some circles, and another essay altogether for someone else to compose.

MUSIC AND ITS BRANCHES

The discipline of music, like most other currently studied disciplines, has grown and mutated beyond the sight of almost all who are not abidingly engaged with it on a curricular level. Much has changed since nineteenth-century music scholars Guido Adler, Phillip Spitta, and Friedrich Chrysander endeavored to identify the various branches of musical study. Adler attempted to codify the discipline under two major divisions: *Musikwissenschaft* (historical musicology), and the remainder as a systematic field that charts the major laws that apply to the other branches of music.[2] Much has transpired since 1885. New areas of study confound the Dewey Decimal assignment of numbers and strain the current Library of Congress classification. Music's subdivisions are many, but they may be gathered into several large headings with considerable repetition and cross-pollination among them.

- Historical Musicology

  History of music, musical notation, historical performance practice, reception history, musical iconography, study of musical instruments (organology), manuscript and document archival study, social and cultural force studies, criticism, gender and music, popular music and jazz histories, and historiography.

- Ethnomusicology (systematic musicology)

  Field work, instrumental classification, history of ethnomusicology, social and cultural anthropology, ethnography, practice theory, performance practice, area studies, and world music theoretical systems.

- Music Theory

  Tonal harmony, nontonal systems, composition (both acoustical and electronically conceived), form and analysis, counterpoint, history and pedagogy of theory, orchestration, and sight singing and ear training.

- Psychology of Music

  Aesthetics of music, psychomusicology, music therapy, sociology of music, and acoustics.

- Music Education

  General music, elementary music, secondary school music, Orff and Kodaly systems, eurhythmics, instrumental and vocal pedagogy, instrumental methods, history of music education, sociological and philosophical foundations, psychology of learning, developmental psychology, curriculum, measurement and evaluation, and research methodology.

- Applied Music

  Vocal and instrumental performance study (Western and non-Western, including jazz), historical performance practice, and literature and pedagogy.

THE DISCIPLINE OF MUSIC
AND ITS RESEARCH METHODOLOGY

The More We Are Alike . . . : The Practice of Research

Music research, when empirically defined, entails a systematic investigation of a topic. It certainly coheres to recent definition when an advance in knowledge is made using a method or systematic procedure. In his *The Art of Research: A Guide for the Graduate*, B. E. Noltingk spends an entire chapter discussing historical and contemporary definitions of research.[3] The meaning and scope of the fundamental and applied nature of scientific research is discussed, debated slightly, and put into perspective when compared with traditional notions of fundamental pure research. Like science, music invites such debate and redefinition when examined over time and circumstance.

The Music Research Process: Early Topic Procedures and Pedagogy Based on Standard Source Genres

The General Tertiary Sources

For the beginner, intermediate, and, depending on the familiarity with the research topic, even some more advanced individuals, best practice still dictates beginning research by uncovering the general gestalt of the topic. In other words, lest something elusive among the important components of the query be missed, the individual will proceed from the general to the specific. Librarians will discover that music research is no exception. Like any other discipline, it follows such a *locus classicus*, or systematic procedure. The researcher should be inclusive rather than exclusive of subtopics or concepts associated with the discrete topic from the outset. Excluding irrelevant information is easier in later stages of the work when the individual has a greater grasp of the corpus of the topic and the key terminology associated with it. Then the individual will be able to make informed decisions of inclusion and exclusion. In all likelihood, the musical topic harbors relationships with cogent materials outside the narrow locus of music. On numerous occasions, an adverse effect on the quality of the research product is created by the ignorance of this contextual material and how it affects the musical topic.[4] Within the discipline itself, the amount of seemingly nonmusical information will vary. The music historical, theoretical, and educational areas are more likely to find inclusion of nonmusical information imperative or appropriate than the applied music (performance) sector. Systematically speaking, then, the music research process should begin with the study of general tertiary sources like music encyclopedias and extended-entry dictionary publications. The topic may suggest supplemental nonmusical encyclopedias and even philosophical works in order to place it in perspective historically to capture the zeitgeist, its position in contemporary artistic expression and thought. Music theoretical topics may also be considered in the context of some scientific and mathematical principles.[5] The pursuit of information from genre-analogous nonmusical sources is sometimes absent in music research, unfortunately putting music research in a vacuum instead of embracing and revealing important cross-disciplinary relationships.[6] That said, it is time to leave the music library (either physically or virtually) to discover what significant amount of cogent musical and musically related information may be gleaned from those general non–musically specific databases and database aggregates and other print-format sources that form part and parcel of the general university library.[7] Regardless of the musical topic, the awareness of cross-disciplinary sources should be remembered and subsequently applied to the research process when appropriate analogous nonmusic research tools of the same genre are mentioned in the following pages.

Like any creative process, research is a messy affair. While a systematic procedure is encouraged overall, even starting with general tertiary sources will take the individual afield, if not through the text of the given entry, then by means of the bibliography at its conclusion. If not taken to the extreme where no end product is rendered because the research is unending and desultory, side trips are intellectually and creatively beneficial. In their best aspect, despite their tendencies to spread light particles of knowledge to the universe, they may just as often have the opposite effect of helping the individual discover and understand the enormity of his subject, helping him to define his original topic more clearly, or inducing him to change the focus to something more manageable or altogether different. Many guides to research talk about this discovery. An early work that presents this situation well for music students is John Drusedow's *Library Guide to Research: Illustrated Search Strategy and Sources.* Although aimed at the undergraduate student in music, this well-written and easily digestible work is valuable to anyone not familiar with the music research process, and helpful to librarians who are not music specialists.

Advanced Scholars: Process and Aberration

For advanced scholars with an already defined area of music specialty, librarians will discover that much of the above process is usually curtailed, for the topic generation is often a result of the scholars' previous extensive knowledge. The new topic, then, is frequently an outgrowth of previous research work, continual reading, and other professional activity in that area. A study by Christine Brown in 2002 presents a music scholar's research process as a six-stage model.[8] Based on interviews with music scholars, she identifies and describes each stage in the process. The first stage, referred to as *idea generation*, identifies scholars' procedures as "internally generated processes such as their previous work or reading in their area of specialization. Of secondary importance were face-to-face discussions with colleagues, invitations or commissions for papers, and learning of a call for papers."[9]

More Standard Tertiary Source Genres: Musical Monographs

Like that in many other disciplines, the music research process generally visits historical works that broadly, or in some cases more specifically, address the research topic. Depending on the topic, historical period, or genre, monographs help to put the topic into developmental perspective. A topic in music education profits from time spent with a book on the history of music education for discovering antecedent, concurrent, and projected outcomes surrounding a discrete topic or educational practice. Compositional aspects of Gorécki's music can be succinctly defined and presented by reading the chapter "Sound Mass, Rhythm, and Microtones" in David Cope's *New Directions in Music*.[10] Mathew Shirlaw's *The Theory of Harmony* may broaden an understanding and put into historical context a harmonic or a theoretical practice.[11]

Some pedagogues are rather cagey about how they present historical monographs to their students, for too often the novice mistakes this genre as an end unto itself. Retrieving a "book about" too often aborts any further thoughts of research on their part. Library catalogs unlock these falsely believed "be-all and end-all" works too easily for the novice.[12] For them, the search is complete, and all further research is superfluous. The instructor/librarian should feel differently. The worth, however, of this tertiary source is indisputable for bestowing a cornucopia of a previously researched body of knowledge that will explain and elaborate on the scope of a given research topic and acquaint the individual with it. In its best application, it provides more sources conveniently through its citations and bibliography. In the practical and pedagogical sense, it aids the novice in understanding the enormity of a selected research topic and the need to narrow his scope.

Advanced Scholars: Monographs

In most cases, if the music scholar remains reasonably current in his field, he will have already discovered from his professional reading and associations any new tertiary monographs in the above area.

Continuing the Research Process:
Bibliographic Treasure Chests of Literature about Music

At this juncture, it can be seen that in contrast to disciplines like business and the sciences, where the most recent trends, practices, and theories are an immediate or very early link in the chain of the research procedure, music literature tends to build on the past. That is not to say that current literature is not essential, but unless the individual is already very conversant with the topic, then historical considerations are imperative building blocks for competent music research. In many ways, music research is like studying tonal harmony in music theory: learn the rules first, and once mastered, they can be broken with a competent outcome. Conversely, old business practices yield ineffective results, and out-of-date medical practices proffer danger. That having been said, the music research process, like a number of other disciplines, then seeks to gain access to more discretely defined literature using both specialized and nonspecialized[13] bibliographic tools. They may present themselves in traditional print format, being narrow in scope like a bibliography of music performance practice or a bibliography of literature on plectral instruments like the guitar and lute. These tools may also approach the topic, along with the myriad of other musical subjects, through current or annual coverage in large or comprehensive indexes to the literature in both print and database formats. Within the discipline of music, articles, conference proceedings, obituaries, and citations to music dissertations, along with reviews of music literature, musical compositions, and audio and video recordings, are indexed in two products that are most widely used by musicians, *The Music Index* and the *International Index to Music Periodicals* (*IIMP*). Both indexes attempt to address every aspect of the classical and popular world of music. Both are categorized and organized by means of an internal subject list that includes both subject and geographic headings.

Where some of the online music databases are primarily citation only, some provide selected links directly to other databases providing full text to complete back files of core journals, reviews, and other writings.[14] Others are a combination of citation and full text, and still others take the form of an abstracting service to articles, essays in books and in Festschriften, reviews, selected dissertations, or conference proceedings. Where *The Music Index* and *IIMP* try to be as inclusive as possible, music scholars and students looking solely for abstracts of scholarly literature in music will turn to *RILM Abstracts of Music Literature* (*Répertoire international de literature musicale*). Sadly, like landing upon the catalog entry that yields "the book about," indexes and abstracting services are other places where a novice will try to begin his research, especially if they are available as online products. Not having a solid foundation in the general area of his proposed topic, he can be especially confounded by his lack of knowledge of appropriate search terms, subject headings, and the controlled language used in these indexes. This is an area where the music librarian can be particularly helpful by performing a reference interview, the same way general reference professionals would with a user unfamiliar with index products, to capture the relevant subjects and keywords associated with the proposed research.

By this time, the individual will have identified specialists associated with his topic of research, if only by the frequency with which their names are mentioned in the source materials the student has discovered. Depending on the nature of the project, the student may look for websites and even attempt contact with these specialists and interview them about their work.[15]

For some topics, bibliographies of music are necessary to identify as comprehensively as possible the actual music of a specific genre, like a bibliography of medieval tonaries, seventeenth-century French harpsichord music, or pre-1800 popular secular music in America. In some cases, identifying important collections of music or materials directly related to the topic using directories of music research libraries is crucial to the study. This is where the systematic approach to music research can be of particular benefit. Somewhere in the earlier stages, either through textual matter or accompanying footnotes and bibliographies, various writers will identify these important collections.

Some research demands the use of early editions or manuscripts of works, and even of early writings about music that are held in libraries and archives throughout the world. To address this research need, the International Association of Music Libraries and the International Musicological Association began *RISM* (*Répertoire international des sources musicales*) in 1960. This enormous project, which continues today, attempts to present a comprehensive bibliography of primary musical sources organized into various broad subject series containing multiple volumes. Each subject series has its own instructions for gaining access to the particular information it covers. Other included bibliographic tools are bibliographies of discographies, printing and publication information, and other miscellaneous tools like composer or musical genre thematic catalogs and musical directories and yearbooks that may have relevance to the topic. A monumental bibliography that addresses the thousands of research materials in music is the Vincent Duckles and Ida Reed *Music Reference and Research Materials: An Annotated Bibliography*, 5th edition, published in 1996. While this most current edition is now a decade old and many new materials have made their way to library shelves, have been published as online resources, or have appeared on the Web, this 812-page volume still remains an essential bibliography in any university library collection and an invaluable reference to both the music specialist and the general reference librarian.

Finding Specific Musical Scores

While identifying bibliographies of music and collections of music may be an important step in the research process, often the individual needs to find specific musical scores not available to him in his home library or locally through any existing library consortia. Like so many disciplines, the subscription database *WorldCat* and the *Library of Congress Online Catalog* are invaluable not only for locating the elusive musical score, but for identifying particular formats or editions of the same work.

Advanced Scholars: Archives to an End

The analogous activity to that identified in the preceding paragraphs is referred to in Brown's model as stage two: the *background-work stage*, or *archival work*. The music scholar, having formulated an idea or topic for research, makes a logical activity of testing its viability. The risk is higher for the proven scholar; his academic credibility (and self-esteem) is at stake. In Brown's words, "These activities consist of identifying, locating, and consulting materials or people that will be used to support or defend the idea."[16] The student understandably has less at risk.[17]

To this end, Brown's respondents identified source materials used by the scholars (1) from their personal collections, (2) from their campus library collections and from browsing the shelves of their campus library, and (3) from other campus library collections. In addition, but less frequently, they traveled to other libraries or archives, used specialized online resources, and searched the Web. Other activities included correspondence or interviews, workshop participation, presentations, using the students in the music classroom as laboratory subjects, or listening to music.[18]

In the Brown study, music scholars identified their seven most important research sources and ranked them in importance. Not surprisingly, the materials from most to least important of the seven appeared as follows: primary materials,[19] journal articles, recordings, monographs, interviews, dissertations, and reference materials. Surprisingly, but perhaps a result of the particular sample of scholars who were the source for this study, the use of scores, the primary source in music itself, did not rank in the top seven.[20] Brown is quick to admit the small response rate generated for the final sample of scholars and posits that "the results of this study may not be representative of, or generalizable to, all North American music scholars."[21]

Many traditional topics in music research *are* dependent on the study of the music itself, that is, the study of the musical scores and listening to or viewing various audio- and video-recorded performances.[22]

The remaining stages of the research process for both the student (whether beginner or more advanced) and the music scholar are much alike. Before discussing these stages, which deal with reading, organizing, and writing, a more recent addition to the already rich store of knowledge and specialized information available in print sources and commercial databases merits immediate attention in this chapter.

THE WORLD WIDE WEB AND MUSIC

One of the more valuable contributions that the Web has made to music research is in providing access to information about online holdings of national and even international libraries and archives. A number of free-access Internet music databases and online projects are available to music scholars and students, providing practical information like the *Gaylord Music Library Necrology File*, a frequently updated list of deaths in the musical world from 1991 onward,[23] and more specialized projects like the *Beethoven Bibliography Database* or the *Kurt Weill Foundation*, a combination library, manuscript repository, and media center of materials related to the composer. Many valuable projects continue to develop and be available via the Web. Professional music association and society homepages are easily accessible, many of which contain links to internal documents generated by these groups containing specialized music research information. Another valuable Web resource is the individual composer, music scholar, or musical artist website. Many of these individuals maintain their own website or have one created by their publisher or institution if they are affiliated with a college, conservatory, or university. Where print resource material becomes dated rapidly for living composers, scholars, and artists, these sites often contain current information unavailable elsewhere.

While popular search engines like Google will identify Web addresses for these worthy sites rich in music information, many poorly researched or badly constructed sites for music also exist that lead the novice astray with false information or ephemeral materials. Discerning the difference for the student involves the critical-thinking skills developed through general or discipline-based library and research instruction.

THE RESEARCH PROCESS: MORE STANDARD METHODOLOGY

Reading and Organizing

Once the information has been gleaned from the various source materials, the reading and organization of the materials takes place. Brown identifies this stage in the music research process as *preparing and organizing*. In most cases, the topic is further defined by narrowing the approach to it. Another side benefit is the discovery of new sources revealed by reading the gathered materials, unearthing disagreements among scholars,[24] and developing new ways of looking at the research topic. It is characterized as a time for organization by constructing written outlines of the topic and creating further hierarchies of information within the outline. Brown notes well that "the type of preparation and organization music scholars do at this stage may depend on the type of research they conduct, or possibly even their area of specialization."[25] For the student, this can be one of the most difficult stages. Faced with a grand arcade of information, the decision *not* to make a decision has a deleterious effect on the subsequent stages of the research procedure. For the student who fails to deal with the topic on the macro (outline) and micro (hierarchy of parts) levels, the final writing stage can be characterized as a scattered rambling of disjointed bits of information. It follows that the next stage, "making decisions," never occurs. Depending on the institutional culture and the library's mission, the professional librarian may or may not be approached to help the student at this stage. If approached, however, the library professional can lend a dispassionate yet helpful voice by using familiar reference interview skills to help the student rediscover his study's main objectives and escape penumbral issues that have arisen, or to redefine the original study and help him be able to continue confidently.

Making Decisions

Although at this point in the research process, not all music topics render themselves easily to methods of scrutiny (Brown's next stage of *analysis*), it could be said that after reading and organizing, the individual makes decisions about his information, at least qualitatively, before he sets to writing. Using the hierarchies of information, a decision of what is good or appropriate to retain is made. Analysis of the topic may appear in a number of ways. Some studies will lend themselves to quantitative methods of analysis. In any case, there can be multiple methods of analysis depending on the nature of the topic. This is confirmed in the Brown study where 65.9 percent of her respondents indicated that their music research involved some type of analysis. In some areas of music education research—for instance, with data (source material) gathered from classroom studies or some group study—this stage of analysis is particularly crucial to the project.[26] This portion of the research process is the step that perhaps witnesses the least involvement of the library professional. It is, however, not unusual for the librarian to be involved once again in the next stage: writing and revising the work.

Writing and Revising the Work

Music scholars differ at this point in their approach to the writing process. Brown explains,

> A majority of music scholars indicated that they have "often" or "very often" done enough research to start writing but will continue to read, analyze, or consult sources throughout the writing and revision stage. A smaller number said that they have read, analyzed or looked at all the relevant sources before beginning to write.[27]

This difference in approach has a lot to do with the personality of the individual. While both approaches bespeak a goal-oriented person, the ways the goals are achieved delineate a goal-oriented versus a process-oriented personality. The student will show this same approach to writing. One personality (goal-oriented) will insist on having what he perceives to be all the relevant information he needs and will set about writing with no further desire to analyze his materials or consult further sources. The only goal now is doing the writing and being done. The process-oriented student will see the writing as a staged process to be interrupted with the ongoing discovery of new materials or different ways to analyze what he has in hand. The library professional is likely to have ongoing interviews with this personality as it returns to the library (and the librarian) for more ideas and other source materials to study. Regardless, drafts and revisions will still take place over time for both scholar and student. For many scholars, revision work transpires even after the research has been presented publicly.[28]

Much of the above description of the music research process is analogous to the research process in other disciplines, particularly in the humanities and social sciences. It is in some of the details that the discipline stands out from its sibling disciplines. It is these details of unique source use and search anomalies that help make the distinction. In these, as the novelist John Irving says, "Detail is the difference."[29]

DIFFERENT TOYS: UNIQUE TYPES
OF SOURCES USED FOR MUSIC RESEARCH

Primary and Secondary Source Considerations: Musical Scores and Their Variant Formats—One Version Does Not Fit All

There is disagreement with regard to the definition of "primary source material in music." Most narrowly defined (and in this author's definition), primary source materials include composer sketches, manuscripts, the autograph manuscript, and fair copy corrected and signed by the composer. Facsimile reproductions of any of the preceding may in many cases also qualify. Subsequently, secondary sources would include scholarly editions, urtext editions,[30] and any other editions of the work, including corrupt editions[31] and audio or video recordings of the work.

Research Using Primary and Secondary Musical Materials

In research, as well as in practical application, various formats of a discrete musical work are essential in a library collection. Full scores (fully orchestrated) in physically full-sized versions are especially necessary for the conductor for study and performance for obvious visual purposes. Miniature scores, whose pages are photographically reduced to create a volume that fits in the hand like a small paperback book, may suffice for the sake of convenience and economy. Separate parts (with a miniature full score for a music coach or remaining parts shown with one of the ensemble player's parts) are essential for chamber music. In the case of a solo work involving solo voice or instrument with ensemble accompaniment, a piano/vocal score or solo instrument/piano reduction of the ensemble version is essential. Facsimile reproductions and scholarly editions are important parts of a collection for all.

Scholarly Performance Editions

What should concern the performer (musical performing artist) is the availability of performing editions, which are scholarly but generally lack the detail with regard to the amount of included critical text and editorial notes in the score itself. The goal is an edition that is scholarly in that it represents the composer's intent, yet readable for purposes of performance. In a number of institutions, a viable example of creative research is represented by (1) the aesthetically beautiful performance of a work with the explicit aim of expressing the composer's musical intent through the use of a scholarly performance edition coupled with (2) the demonstrable knowledge of contemporary performance practice standards of the period. More will be said about the musical performing artist in the section "Musical Performing Artists and Research."

Scholarly Research Editions

In academic music research, save the necessity of using the primary source, scholarly research editions are the essential tools of the trade. Scholarly editions in their best presentation attempt to communicate what scholars in the area perceive to be the composer's intent for his music. Copious textual notes on variant printed editions, a composer's autograph manuscript version, and copyists' versions are present in these publications. Editorial interpretations of the composer's possible intent in cases of hard-to-read originals, along with performance indications for ornaments or other contemporary performance practice, are frequently included in the score itself. They are indicated with some kind of visual cue to identify them as editorial interpretations.[32] A number of historical and collected editions are published in series by scholarly musical societies and music research institutes, as well as by a small core of publishers that specialize in this type of publication. Finding these scholarly editions is most easily accomplished by using either of two bibliographic works: Anna Harriet Heyer's *Historical Sets, Collected Editions, and Monuments of Music* or George Hill's *Collected Editions, Historical Sets, and Monuments of Music*. As scholarly editions continue to be published, the currency of the printed forms of both of these two works continues to be compromised. As a result, the Hill bibliography has now been made available as an online subscription database.

In summary, with regard to score formats, music collections have the need for the following:

- full scores in full-size format (whether for instrument or voice as unaccompanied solo or entire ensemble),
- miniature scores for convenience and expense when feasible or desirable,

- works with piano reduction of original ensemble,
- works separated into individual parts for performance purposes,
- facsimile editions,
- scholarly research editions, and
- scholarly performance editions.

All of the above formats beg for the best editions available with regard to the composer's intent. Considerable and spirited argument has erupted over the years concerning the presence of "bad" (corrupt) editions in library collections. Some argue that students should not have access to bad editions, for they often do not recognize their corruptness. Others defend their inclusion, declaring the faculty's/librarian's mission to educate the user by pointing out editorial shortcomings.

When Corrupt Editions are Research Tools

In a utopian atmosphere, everything is good. It follows that if there is nothing bad or corrupt, then it is not recognized when it presents itself. Bad copyist work in manuscripts and error-ridden printed editions have infiltrated library collections and continue to appear on the purchase market in the guise of reprint editions and "new" reprint editions. Even in the age of music scores created via computer applications, mistakes due to human input are all too common and have the ability to live long after their original production, just as the engraved plates of the traditional music publisher have survived and been reused.[33] The very presence of aberrant versions of musical works provides a whole branch of music research: manuscript and edition studies. This material continues to inspire numerous published studies and thesis/dissertation documents.

DIGITAL RESOURCES

In most cases, legal online downloads of musical scores provide a convenient, but not necessarily the most appropriate, way to gain access to research materials in score format. A corrupt edition may be scanned for download purposes just as easily as an urtext or scholarly modern edition. Many musicians will not know the difference. Exceptions are made for some studies using facsimile (manuscript, sketches) and various edition score downloads. When there is a true need for the original (primary source)—for example, in the case of watermark and manuscript paper study, or any other situation when a photographic facsimile would not be appropriate—then the digital image cannot stand as a viable substitute. The use of a digital image could render a false conclusion on the part of the individual, and he must repair to the original primary source.

ONLINE ACCESS TO AUDIO RECORDINGS

While the access to online audio recordings is growing, little work is being done to discriminate between versions and interpretations of a particular work. Like digital music scores, equally corrupt performances are available to the user.

MUSICAL PERFORMING ARTISTS AND RESEARCH

Little has been said so far about the performing artist and his research practices in music. The Brown study excluded this very large group. The performer's basic undergraduate education is similar to that of the music education and music academic (BA) core study. Depending on the nature and mission of the institution, most graduate programs include a degree of core academic music study in the performance programs. The studio instructor is crucial in either encouraging and fostering the development of the performing musician as an informed artist or ignoring his development altogether. The latter course may well have a lasting and deleterious effect on the student who later accepts a faculty position in an institution whose standards of demonstrable professional excellence exceed the ability to play triple high C and teach his students to do the same over a three-week period. Historical and contemporary performance practice research is a relevant "meat and potatoes" course of the studio experience. Making and defending interpretive decisions of the musical edition, why a recording artist chose to interpret a work in a particular way, or how and why to teach a work in a particular way involves critical thinking and tangible examples in defense of the interpretation. It exceeds thoughtless acceptance of any given score, the mimic of another's performance, and the noncritical practice of teaching exactly the way one was taught in the past (akin to multigenerational "performance welfare").

STRESSORS: SOME THINGS THAT
MAKE MUSIC RESEARCH DIFFICULT FOR ALL

It is unfortunate that the most prominent gateway to library resources and the tremendous tide of information they hold is for many not a gateway at all but a narrow slit where one has to know secret passwords to get anywhere in one's quest. I speak of the library online catalog. The anger and frustration experienced in trying to remember subject headings, truncations, uniform titles, and even keywords that are contained *somewhere* in the indexed fields of the record have turned away too many incipient library users and have spawned sullen and resentful frequent users and music scholars. It is little wonder that music librarians spend so much time with the user at the catalog level of research, even with the inclusion of music-information literacy classes within the curriculum of many music departments, if only on the graduate level.[34] In an information world hospitable to both the scholar and the less sophisticated information seeker, "dumb luck" should not be an outcome of the search process for either party. Applying an information-rich design (with true relevance ranking) for each item in the collection that goes beyond the present cataloging practice can make the normal expectation of the search a harvest of better and more complete materials. For the present, however, library system vendors are continuing to offer search options based on catalog records and their chosen searchable fields. The search is held captive further by the quality of the cataloged record.

Although woefully restricted, as mentioned in the above paragraph, many records for nonmusic materials are fairly straightforward. Simple author and title searches for them generally work sufficiently well for a number of disciplines, and library systems vendors bank on this, literally. The needs of the minority are not financially expedient to address.

The understandable necessity of gathering musical works under uniform titles for cataloging purposes on some occasions makes for a particularly challenging scenario when the information is queried on the user side of the computer platform. A couple of examples follow that explain this. With the financial crises that face most libraries, the presence of a professional music cataloger has become a premium and not a perceived necessity.[35] A number of libraries have had to "make do" either by assigning music to someone who is graciously willing (but not as able as needed) to assume the responsibility, or by allowing wholesale downloading of existing records from OCLC, the Online Computer Library Center Inc., which is a major commercial provider of library cataloging services and runs the Online Union Catalog. This calls into question quality issues, which have a direct effect on the library's primary client and the process of research. In addition, it must be said that some libraries clearly suffer from old, badly cataloged materials. Not all downloaded existing records are so complete that they include English-language translations. With current workloads and fewer professional librarians on site, there is neither time nor a music cataloging specialist to examine adopted records to find those wanting searchable fields such as, for example, commonly known English-translated titles and spelling. There is often neither time nor expertise present to capture all relevant materials for a catalog record. Correction becomes a case-by-case matter when the problem is discovered with a failed search on the public side.

The following examples serve to illustrate this substantial and ongoing problem:

Case 1: Catalog Entry with Uniform Title but No Captured Field for English Translation

User searches for the two-piano transcription of Prokofiev's *Prodigal Son*.

A title search yields twenty-eight hits, none of which are the transcription. One record is a CD recording. It appears because the English translation and the French (*L'enfant prodigue*) appear in the title field. The uniform title also appears in the record: *Bludnyi syn*. How many users know Russian uniform titles?

Only then, by doing a search using the uniform title, does the user discover the existence of the desired transcription in the catalog.[36] Had the CD recording not existed in the catalog, the transcription would not have been found. Why did this happen? See the record using the uniform title as the search words in figure 2.1.

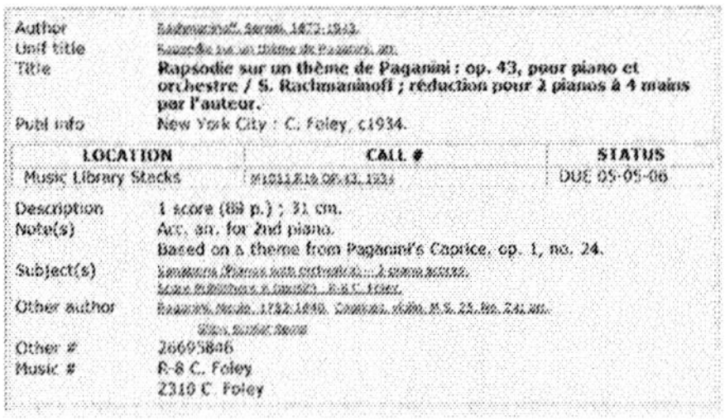

Figure 2.1. Catalog record for Proko-fiev *Bludnyi syn.*

In this case, the downloaded record had neither the English translation in the title field nor the field "Other title." Is this good service to the user? Is the user pleased about this "construction detour" in his research?

Case 2: Unusual Spellings for Familiar
Words Commonly Known by English Translations

User searches for Rachmaninoff's own version of his *Rhapsody on a Theme of Paganini* reduced for two pianos–four hands.

Unless the user already knows (and they seldom do) that *Rhapsody* is spelled in the French manner, "*Rapsodie*," then once again he will not retrieve the record in figure 2.2, for the English-language translation is not included in the searchable title field, and the "Other title" field does not exist in this downloaded record.

In both cases, given enough time, the records might have been found. Regardless of that possibility, how can institutions encourage academic and creative curiosity while simultaneously punishing the curious inadvertently by creating technical hurdles for them to overcome? Can this be fixed? In this instance, the music specialist can be of great help to those assigned to choosing downloads of records by helping them to select

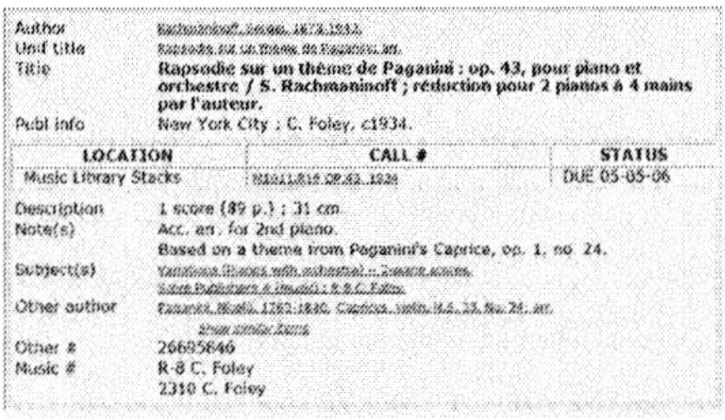

Figure 2.2. Catalog Record for Rach-maninoff *Rapsodie sur un thème de Paganini.*

reliable extant records from institutions known for excellence in music cataloging. Those catalog records will have a greater likelihood of including the necessary cataloged fields for successful searching on the public side of the online catalog already, and will need little if any massaging on the local level.

WORKING WITH COLLEAGUES

Every institution is different. Teaching and scholarship are defined by the institution, background, education, and personal preferences, prejudices, and practices of faculty colleagues. Administrators and department faculty can be strongly wedded to their own ideas of education and the direction of their departments. What is standard procedure in one department can be experimental or even radical in another. Above all, it is crucial to know the culture of the department or group with which you work. Team teaching is an option for some music librarians who are not themselves assigned to an Introduction to Graduate Studies/Music Bibliography class. Where some individual instructors or departments will welcome modules of instruction in the curriculum, others will allow single classes in a given course. Some will be amenable to online learning activities attached to a course or yearly sequence of courses. There are others, however, who express degrees of frustration with fitting anything into their syllabus, citing time constraints put on instruction by the insufficient number of meeting times in the academic quarter or semester. In any case, the instructor's individual personality and philosophy of educational outcomes for his students will be a deciding factor in his acceptance of integrating music information literacy into his classroom.

PEDAGOGICALLY SPEAKING: TEACHING INFORMATION LITERACY IN MUSIC AND ASSOCIATED LITERATURE

As the professional association most involved with information literacy in music, the Music Library Association's Bibliographic Instruction Subcommittee has patterned its March 2006 article in *Notes*, "Informational Literacy Instructional Objectives for Undergraduate Music Students,"[37] after the Association of College and Research Library's (ACRL) *Information Literacy Competency Standards for Higher Education*. In addition, it is using as its stated model another document from ACRL, *Objectives for Information Instruction: A Model Statement for Academic Librarians*. A number of excellent articles, presentations, and curricular models for information literacy in music have appeared in the last decade addressing the incorporation or integration of these objectives into the music curriculum. Some of these writings are currently cited on the American Library Association (ALA) website under "ACRL Instruction Section—Information Literacy in the Disciplines—Music."[38]

Literature is gathered from a number of areas to construct a set of writings that address music research. Included are general writings that explain the research processes.[39] As may be viewed on the ALA/ACRL website in note 38, articles dealing with information literacy, reference strategies, curriculum proposal presentations, and selected bibliographies are cited. Michael Duffy's 2004 article and excellent accompanying bibliography, "Selected Research and Writings on Instruction for Music Librarians: An Annotated Bibliography,"[40] provides a categorized bibliography of writings organized under the headings "Music Library User Instruction," "General Course-Integrated Library Instruction," "Assessment, Teaching Methods, Learning Theory, and Critical Evaluations," "Students and Library Anxiety," and "World Wide Web Resources." Other recent articles include Deborah Pierce's "Incorporating Information Literacy into the Music Curriculum: A Look at ACRL's Best Practices Initiative and Successful Music Programs."[41] Previously mentioned in note 7 is the article by Clarence et al., "'Look That Up in Your *Funk and Wagnall's!*' Music Reference Using Alternative Sources." In 2004, *Music Library Instruction*, volume 3 in the Music Library Association (MLA) Basic Manual Series, published Gregg S. Geary's "Creating Information Literacy Instruction for Undergraduates in the Music Library" and Laura M. Snyder's "Teaching the Graduate Music Research Course."[42] Two other 2004 articles address undergraduate music information literacy: "Warp, Weft, and Waffle: Weaving Information Literacy into an Undergraduate Music Curriculum"[43] and, targeting a smaller music population, "Info Lit and the Diva: Integrating Information Literacy into the Oberlin Conservatory of Music Opera Theater Department."[44]

RESEARCH SKILLS WITHIN THE DISCIPLINE

Chapter 9, "Integrating Discipline-Based Library Instruction into the Curriculum," by Carrie Forbes, addresses a number of research skills that are believed to be common to all disciplines. When approaching a research project using these skills, coupled with a solid background in music information literacy, the advanced graduate student and the seasoned music scholar will

- be able to place the subject of music research in historical context, or use historical literature to defend the validity of the study and compare or contrast it with its historical treatment in the literature;
- use thematic catalogs, special subject or genre bibliographies, discographies, and bibliographies of monuments and historical and collected editions to identify and gain access to scholarly performance and research editions of individual musical works or a particular musical repertory, or to locate primary materials;
- consult materials in historical and contemporary performance practice when making and defending interpretive musical decisions in writing, performance, or another's written or performance interpretation (whether live performance or recorded); and
- after having read and gathered materials, systematically organize, analyze, and make informed decisions of inclusion and exclusion to refine the product of the research for presentation (or performance) or publication (or recording).

CONCLUSION

In conclusion, while music appears as a small division hiding within the large group of humanities disciplines, music's sheer number of subdivisions, along with the thousands of specialized reference and resource materials, takes the uninitiated librarian, student, or incipient scholar by surprise. It is little wonder that institutions of higher education with larger and more developed music programs have separate branch libraries with subject specialists and staff to deal with the terminology, the problems of access and interpretation, and, on the very most practical level, all of those variant formats and their "pieces and parts." The complex nature of the discipline is not apparent to those not immersed in it daily. A number of master's programs in library science offer concentrations in music librarianship that, along with higher divisional elective music courses, combine to train professional librarians to deal with the discipline's complexities and challenges.

The basic music research process, however, to a significant extent mirrors its sibling disciplines in the humanities. Applying the same information literacy standards, performance indicators, and outcomes endorsed by ACRL, tailored to include music-specific instructional objectives set forth recently by the Music Library Association, will set the groundwork at the undergraduate student level to support competent research at the postbaccalaureate level and beyond.

SELECTED RESOURCES

Vincent Duckles and Ida Reed's *Music Reference and Research Materials* provides citations to thousands of resources in music. While discussing the research process in music, this chapter has attempted to identify a *very* small core of basic resources helpful to most scholars and students in the discipline. Some resources have been referred to only by their genre, like encyclopedias, dictionaries, discographies, yearbooks, and guides. Others have been cited by title. The most basic resources for music research most commonly used in American colleges, universities, and music conservatories appear below. Some resources are not devoted entirely to music but are nonetheless invaluable for musical information.

Research and Writing Guides

Bellman, Jonathan. *A Short Guide to Writing about Music*. New York: Longman, 2000.

Drusedow, John. *Library Guide to Research: Illustrated Search Strategy and Sources*. Ann Arbor, MI: Pierian Press, 1982.

Wingell, Richard J., and Sylvia Herzog. *Introduction to Research in Music*. Upper Saddle River, NJ: Prentice Hall, 2001.

General Music Dictionaries and Encyclopedias

Macy, Laura, ed. *Grove Music Online*. Oxford; New York: Oxford University Press, 2005–. Includes the full text with ongoing updates of *The New Grove Dictionary of Music and Musicians*, 2nd ed., 29 vols.; *The New Grove Dictionary of Opera*, 4 vols.; and *The New Grove Dictionary of Jazz*, 2nd ed., 3 vols.

Nettl, Bruno, Ruth Stone, James Porter, and Timothy Rice, eds. *Garland Encyclopedia of World Music*. 10 vols. New York: Garland Publishers/Routledge, 1998–2002.

Randel, Don Michael, ed. *The New Harvard Dictionary of Music*. Cambridge, MA: The Belknap Press of Harvard University, 1986.

Sadie, Stanley, and John Tyrell, eds. *The New Grove Dictionary of Music and Musicians*. 2nd ed. London: Macmillan, 2001.

Shepherd, John, et al., eds. *Continuum Encyclopedia of Popular Music of the World*. London; New York: Continuum, 2003–.

General Histories of Music

Grout, Donald Jay, Peter Burkholder, and Claude Palisca. *A History of Western Music*. 7th ed. New York: W. W. Norton & Co., 2005.

Music Indexes and Abstracting Services—Periodical Literature, Reviews, Dissertation Citations, Congress Reports

Academic Search Premier. Ipswich, MA: EBSCO Publishing. Online publication.

International Index to Music Periodicals: IIMP Full Text. Alexandria, VA: Chadwyck-Healey Inc., 1996–. Online publication.

JSTOR. New York: JSTOR, 1995–. Online publication.

The Music Index. Detroit: Information Coordinators, 1949–.

The Music Index Online. Warren, MI: Harmonie Park Press, 1999. Online version of *The Music Index*.

Project MUSE: Scholarly Journals Online. Baltimore, MD: Johns Hopkins University, 1993–. Online publication.

Répertoire international de literature musicale (RILM Abstracts of Music Literature). New York: International RILM Center, 1967–.

RILM Abstracts. 1996–. Online version of *Répertoire international de literature musical*. Available through various vendors.

Locating Scores, Historical Treatises, and Writings about Music

Library of Congress Online Catalog. catalog.loc.gov.
Répertoire international des sources musicales (International Inventory of Musical Sources, RISM). Kassel: Bärenreiter, 1971–.
RISM: International Inventory of Musical Sources. Baltimore, MD: NISC International, 2002. Online version of *Répertoire international des sources musicales*.
WorldCat. Dublin, OH: OCLC FirstSearch, 1979–.

Locating Scores in Monuments, Collected Editions, or Historical Sets

Heyer, Anna Harriet. *Historical Sets, Collected Editions, and Monuments of Music: A Guide to Their Contents*. 3rd ed. Chicago: American Library Association, 1980.
Hill, George Robert, and Norris L. Stephens. *Collected Editions, Historical Series & Sets & Monuments of Music: A Bibliography*. Berkeley, CA: Fallen Leaf Press, 1997. Online version available through NISC.
Grove Music Online. Works list for individual composers.

Authority for Birth and Death Dates

Gaylord Music Library Necrology File. library.wustl.edu/units/music/necro.
Library of Congress Online Catalog. catalog.loc.gov (Author/Creator Browse).

Identifying Thematic Indexes in Music

Brook, Barry, and Richard Viano. *Thematic Indexes in Music: An Annotated Bibliography*. 2nd ed. Stuyvesant, NY: Pendragon Press, 1997.

NOTES

1. Admittedly, an exception is found in the movie *Fame* and its television progeny of the same title where there is an occasional classroom scene with the stereotypical academic instructor. These scenes, however, are used either as filler or for dramatic purposes to include soulful exchanges between teenage main characters and not really to convey the true subject content of the classroom meeting.

2. Adler, Chrysander, and Spitta started work on a quarterly journal in 1884, the *Vierteljahrsschrift für Musikwissenschaft*. Adler wrote the lead article in the first issue, which

appeared in 1885, "Umfang, Methode und Ziel der Musikwissenschaft," which codified the study of Musikwissenschaft and its subdivisions.

3. B. E. Noltingk, *The Art of Research: A Guide for the Graduate*, chap. 1, "What?" (New York: Elsevier Publishing Co., 1965), 1–29.

4. For instance, a study of German composers between 1900 and 1938 is incomplete without an understanding of the politics of the Weimar Republic and the radical changes brought about by the National Socialists.

5. Consider, for instance, the study of musical works based on the Fibonacci series or the Golden Section.

6. Consider disciplines like ethnomusicology, women in music, gender and music, music and art/architecture/mathematics/psychology, and a myriad of others.

7. See Judy Clarence, Paula Elliot, Stephen Landstreet, and Howard Rodriguez's outstanding article on this subject, "'Look That Up in Your *Funk and Wagnall's*': Music Reference Using Alternative Sources," *Music Reference Services Quarterly* 8, no. 3 (2004): 25–36.

8. Christine D. Brown, "Straddling the Humanities and Social Sciences: The Research Process of Music Scholars," *Library & Information Science Research* 24, no. 1 (2002): 73–94. Brown goes further in this article to compare existing models of the research process of other humanities scholars and looks at the implications of the processes for library professionals.

9. Brown, "Straddling the Humanities and Social Sciences," 77.

10. David Cope, *New Directions in Music*, 7th ed. (Prospect Heights, IL: Waveland Press, 2001).

11. Matthew Shirlaw, *The Theory of Harmony: An Inquiry into the Natural Principles of Harmony, with an Examination of the Chief Systems of Harmony from Rameau to the Present Day* (New York: Da Capo Press, 1969).

12. Unfortunately, because of constraints in the cataloging system, more and relevant information may not be unlocked and may not be the fault of anyone. See further comments on this problem in the section "Stressors: Some Things That Make Music Research Difficult for All."

13. Database products like *JSTOR*, *Project MUSE*, and *Academic Search Premier* contain titles not indexed in the music databases, with relevant articles to some music research topics.

14. Reviews of books, music reviews, premières of musical compositions, and audio- and video recordings are invaluable for some studies for unearthing contemporary criticism, reception, and attitudes toward creative output.

15. This is a particularly valuable activity for individuals whose topics are related to the work or style of living composers; attitudes toward performance practice and style of performing artists; and connections for further research as a result of interviewing a performing artist, composer, or writer.

16. Brown, "Straddling the Humanities and Social Sciences," 79.

17. Exceptions to this would be theses or dissertations, student papers to be delivered at a professional meeting, and the like, where academic accountability will be judged by others in the field in a very public way.

18. Brown, "Straddling the Humanities and Social Sciences," 79.

19. Brown does not define further what primary materials include.

20. Brown, "Straddling the Humanities and Social Sciences," 80.

21. Brown, "Straddling the Humanities and Social Sciences," 76.

22. This activity may come earlier in the research process and, in some cases, may be the impetus or inspiration for the original topic of research. Brown's sample respondents mention the importance of music listening in the early part of stage two: background work.

23. This database is alphabetically arranged by last name of the deceased, giving a brief identification of his or her connection to the musical world, date and place of death, and source(s) of the information. For currency, this database is well ahead of the Library of Congress's authority file, which can be years behind in entering a death date for a composer, musical artist, or writer in music.

24. Famous disagreements have arisen, for instance, on the use of *notes inégales* in French Baroque music. Another interesting article discussed composer Dufay's use of the architectural proportional formula of Brunelleschi's famous dome on the Florentine cathedral of Santa Maria del Fiore for devising the *talea* and *color* formula of his isorhythmic motet *Nuper rosarum flores*. It was debated several years later in two subsequent articles.

25. Brown cites scholars who conducted controlled experiments in music education and computer applications for music composition.

26. For instance, many published studies in music education are interpretations of data gathered measuring student musical achievement, preferences, musical perception, and variants on classroom or rehearsal experience.

27. Brown, "Straddling the Humanities and Social Sciences," 82. Brown continues to say that music theorists used this phase in the process to select musical examples for incorporation in their writing to help structure their writing and illustrate their points.

28. In Brown's sample, all but three of the scholars who shared their research at a conference later revised it either for publication or for presentation elsewhere.

29. John Irving, *Setting Free the Bears* (New York: Random House, 1968), 309.

30. Printed musical editions without editorial additions to the score.

31. Printed editions may enjoy a certain period of being considered good until proven to be aberrant from the composer's intentions.

32. These editorial notes can appear, for instance, above the score line itself in smaller font, in a different ink color, or set off by brackets. This indicates to the individual an aberration or editorial decision made by the creator of the scholarly edition.

33. Whole publishing companies are founded on producing reprint editions. Due to their availability and, in some cases, attractive price, they have populated library shelves everywhere. Some are actually reprints of urtext editions, others the direct use of other publisher's original plates.

34. It is common to have a formal course on the graduate level. An equivalent course on the undergraduate level is rare, however. It is puzzling that, despite NASM's (National Association of Schools of Music) many course requirements, music information literacy is left out. Do the undergraduate students have critical-thinking skills that they lose immediately upon becoming graduate students? In defense of the undergraduate, music librarians find themselves "sneaking into" their colleagues' classrooms (often at the latter's request) to deliver bibliographic instruction in time-sensitive little bits so that the students may develop the critical-thinking skills for going beyond the lecture in order to fulfill the expectations of NASM's general guidelines for baccalaureate degrees in music (which are strikingly vague with regard to their actual meaning). NASM curiously is more definitive in its expressed standards for graduate students. Such standards are expressed as "scholarly competence in the organization, interpretation, and evaluation of knowledge." Is this to say

that the undergraduate degree bespeaks *incompetence* in the aforementioned approach to knowledge?

35. As a result, the practice of outsourcing has become a popular and financially expeditious way of addressing the problem. Good, solid catalog records are for purchase from music catalogers who choose to work in this manner. This practice, however, has its professional price. In an administration's effort to keep its employees, longtime music catalogers are finding themselves reassigned to public areas of the library like information commons and reference desks, or other access points where they may have mixed success and job satisfaction.

36. The user may also use the French equivalent, but only if he knows it in the first place. Using *L'enfant prodigue*, the user gets a large set to search, including many versions of the Debussy oratorio by the same name.

37. Paul Cary and Laurie J. Sampsel, "Informational Literacy Instructional Objectives for Undergraduate Music Students: A Project of the Music Library Association Bibliographic Instruction Subcommittee," *Notes: Quarterly Journal of the Music Library Association* 62, no. 3 (March 2006): 663–79.

38. www.ala.org/ala/acrlbucket/is/projectsacrl/infolitdisciplines/music.htm (accessed December 19, 2005).

39. I speak of works like the cited Noltingk in note 3. Where Noltingk is focused on scientific research, other works like Wayne Booth, Gregory Colomb, and Joseph Williams, *The Craft of Research* (Chicago: University of Chicago Press, 1995) approach the research process without a particular audience in mind other than, in their words, "student researchers, from the newest beginners to graduate and professional students" (ix).

40. Michael J. Duffy IV, "Selected Research and Writings on Instruction for Music Librarians: An Annotated Bibliography," *Music Reference Services Quarterly* 8, no. 3 (2004): 37–61.

41. Deborah L. Pierce, "Incorporating Information Literacy into the Music Curriculum: A Look at ACRL's Best Practices Initiative and Successful Music Programs," *Music Reference Services Quarterly* 8, no. 4 (2004): 57–76.

42. Gregg Geary, Laura M. Snyder, and Kathleen A. Abromeit, *Music Library Instruction*, ed. Deborah Campana, MLA Basic Manual Series, No. 3 (Lanham, MD: Scarecrow Press, 2004). The remaining chapter by Abromeit provides an overview of a model program for teaching student assistants in the music library, "Reference Assistants on the Front Line in the Music Library."

43. Beth Christensen, "Warp, Weft, and Waffle: Weaving Information Literacy into an Undergraduate Music Curriculum," *Notes: The Quarterly Journal of the Music Library Association* 60, no. 3 (2004): 616–31.

44. Kathleen A. Abromeit and Victoria Vaughan, "Info Lit and the Diva: Integrating Information Literacy into the Oberlin Conservatory of Music Opera Theater Department," *Notes: The Quarterly Journal of the Music Library Association* 60, no. 3 (2004): 632–52.

3

Historical Research

Michael Levine-Clark

INTRODUCTION

To varying degrees, historians make use of humanities and social science methods.[1] In the same text, you might find a close textual analysis of sources and a statistical analysis of demographic data. According to John Tosh, "History is a hybrid discipline which owes its endless fascination and its complexity to the fact that it straddles" the humanities and the social sciences. This is true both in terms of its aims and its methodologies. Tosh notes that "the fundamental premise of [the humanities] is that what mankind has thought and done has an intrinsic interest and a lasting value irrespective of any practical implications," while "the social sciences owe their position to their promise of practical guidance."[2] History fits into both of these traditions, Tosh continues, in that "it trains the mind, enlarges the sympathies *and* provides a much-needed perspective on some of the most pressing problems of our time."[3]

History can be defined geographically, chronologically, or by theme. Generally, it is defined by a combination of these elements. Thus, a historian might define his or her research interest chronologically and geographically as early modern Britain or medieval France or twentieth-century China. And a modern Indian historian could study medical, gender, intellectual, cultural, social, economic, or any other themes.[4]

Historical methods can also cross traditional disciplinary boundaries. All disciplines make use of historical methods in some ways. For instance, business historians might study the history of marketing, while historians of science might study the history of anatomy. To do so effectively, they need to be grounded in the concepts and issues particular to those disciplines while having a thorough understanding of historical research methodologies. A librarian helping such scholars needs to understand that sources for their research can appear in resources particular to history or to their specific disciplines.

HISTORICAL RESEARCH

For their research, historians rely equally on primary and secondary sources. Secondary sources are books, articles, interviews, speeches, videos, and the like that interpret events of the past. Sources of this sort are written or compiled with the intent of furthering our understanding of the historical event in question, generally through interpretation of the original documents of the time. Secondary literature can be from any period, whether written by someone at the time of the event or thousands of years later.

Primary sources are the original documents, in whatever format, that historians use to understand the people and events of the past. Written at or near the time of the event, primary sources give the closest glimpse possible of the thoughts and intentions of the historical actors involved. Obviously, some primary source material is better than others. As John Tosh observes, "Those [sources] that carry most weight are the ones that arise directly from everyday business or social intercourse, leaving open the task of interpretation."[5] It is generally preferable to use sources that were not written for posterity, since writers can be less truthful when writing for an imagined audience. Primary sources can include diaries, journals, correspondence, interviews, or memoirs, whether written or conducted at the time or many years later by someone who participated in the event of interest. Newspaper articles or other secondary publications, written about the event in question, can be treated as primary sources as well if they can provide insight into the thoughts of contemporaries. Anything that can be used to further understanding of the event can be treated as a primary source.

Context will determine whether a source should be treated as primary or secondary. For instance, a student writing about the history of American historical education could make good use of history textbooks as primary source material. Though written originally as secondary literature, in this context they become primary literature. Conversely, though letters are almost always considered primary sources since they can provide a glimpse into the mind of the writer, a letter written by a historian to a colleague might include important interpretative passages about historical events and thus could be treated as a secondary source. Therefore, when helping someone with historical research, it is vital to understand the context of the research project in order to best determine how to search for primary and secondary source material.

SECONDARY RESEARCH

Secondary literature can help a researcher understand the context of a historical problem. Historians need to know what has already been written on a subject in order to determine the relevance of their topic and the scope of their arguments. All historical research therefore makes use of secondary literature to some extent. Research papers, though based on primary research, must be grounded in the existing literature, and so will make use of a large number of secondary sources. Historiographical essays do not make use of primary sources at all, aiming instead to provide an overview of the historical research and writing about a particular subject over time.[6] It is important to keep in mind that the purpose of secondary research is often to provide an understanding of a particular research methodology. For instance, someone interested in using probate records to determine ownership of books, and thus the degree of literacy in eighteenth-century New England, would want to make sure to look for similar research in other geographic areas and time periods.

Finding secondary literature is generally easier than locating primary source material. Most libraries have access to at least some secondary sources through the library catalog or online databases and can generally borrow most others through Interlibrary Loan. When searching for secondary literature, it is crucial to think carefully about the research topic in the context of the resource used for searching. Thus, someone researching the history of the plague in early fifteenth-century York would need to consider the chances of finding books or even articles on that exact topic.

It would be wise to search more broadly, for books on the plague in England, or even in Europe, and then use the indexes and tables of contents to locate sections or chapters about York within those books, rather than to search for books on such a narrow subject. When searching for articles, however, it might make sense to search on the specific topic.

As in the humanities, history is still dependent on monographs, though this is less true than it used to be. In a 2001 study, Margaret Stieg Dalton and Laurie Charnigo found that historians cited books or chapters within books 82.2 percent of the time (as opposed to 88.2 percent of the time in a 1975 study).[7] Because of this reliance on books, searching the library catalog is a good starting point. Besides providing access to books, the catalog may help locate other materials, including videos, about the topic.

Dalton and Charnigo characterize history as "a field where vocabulary control is problematic," something that others say about the humanities in general, and they therefore stress the importance of keyword searching.[8] A worthwhile first step is to do a keyword search on the topic in question. A successful keyword search can then lead to useful subject headings that can be used themselves, or whose terms can be applied to further keyword searches. In general, when searching the catalog, it is important to think about a topic more broadly than when searching the article literature.

For history, there are two primary electronic databases of use for locating articles. *America: History and Life* (*AHL*) and *Historical Abstracts* (*HA*) are both published by ABC-CLIO, and together they cover the world from 1450 to the present. Though the primary purpose of the ABC-CLIO databases is to index article literature, both also include information about books and dissertations. *AHL* indexes and abstracts articles written since 1964 and covers the entire period of United States and Canadian history, from prehistory to the present. *HA* covers the rest of the world, indexing and abstracting articles written since 1954. Unfortunately, though, *HA* does not cover the period before 1450.

Historians, more than most researchers, are concerned about periods of time. An article about economic conditions in fourteenth-century Cairo, though perhaps useful from a methodological perspective, will not be helpful to a historian looking for information about economic conditions in nineteenth-century Cairo. In many cases, this need for specific time-period coverage is true even down to the decade. In most article indexes, it is difficult or even impossible to search by subject date. This is not so, however, in the ABC-CLIO databases, which allow searchers to specify centuries or decades of coverage. From the advanced-search screen, you can search by time period, using the term *1900D* to search for material about the decade from 1900 to 1909, or *1900H* to search for material about the twentieth century.

The ABC-CLIO databases are very useful for the time periods and regions they cover. However, there is a large period of time (pre-1450) for which there is no electronic coverage. For premodern history outside of the region that became the United States and Canada, it is necessary to consult other sources, in some cases searching several databases for a single topic.

European history is generally well served by the *International Medieval Bibliography* and *Iter: Gateway to the Middle Ages and Renaissance* for the medieval period, and *L'Année Philologique* for the classical period. The *International Medieval Bibliography*, published by Brepols, covers the European Middle Ages from 400 to 1500, indexing articles, conference proceedings, and book chapters published in all languages since 1967. The University of Toronto's *Iter* covers a slightly longer period, from 400 to 1700, and indexes books, articles, chapters, and other formats published in some cases as far back as 1784. Neither is as easy to use, and neither offers the degree of time-period specificity that the ABC-CLIO databases do, though the *International Medieval Bibliography* does allow searchers to limit by century.

L'Année Philologique has been published annually since 1928 by the Société Internationale de Bibliographie Classique. Volumes 30 (1959) to the present are available online as part of a database. This is the most comprehensive index to scholarly work in the classics, covering a broad range of materials in all languages. It is important to keep in mind that *L'Année Philologique* is not limited just to historical topics, so searches may need to be adjusted as appropriate. It is not easy to use and requires some time to get used to the interface and the concepts. The database can be searched by "modern author"; "ancient author"; "full text," of the record, not of the article; "subjects and disciplines," which allows browsing or searching within the tables of contents; "date"; or "other criteria," including words in the title and language. Though these are all separate sections of the interface that must be searched individually, they can be combined postsearch.

The *International Bibliography of Historical Sciences*, published annually since 1926, is a classified listing of books and journal articles covering all areas of historical research. Though stronger for Europe, each volume does contain relatively small sections for other areas of the world.
This is a multilingual text, indexing materials in a wide range of languages. Sponsored by UNESCO, it has had a variety of publishers, with
recent volumes published by K. G. Saur.

Another print source that covers all historical topics is *C.R.I.S.: The Combined Retrospective Index Set to Journals in History, 1838–1974.*[9] This
eleven-volume set provides very brief entries from 243 English-language
journals arranged in 342 subject categories followed by a two-volume author index. Its coverage of publications well back into the nineteenth century makes it a valuable resource.

Locating recent non-European sources covering the period before 1450
is much more difficult. Because there are no history-specific resources,
researchers will need to make do with either interdisciplinary or related-
subject sources. Obviously, these will vary depending on the subject at
hand. For many topics, a good general database such as EBSCO's *Academic Search Premier* or Thomson Gale's *Expanded Academic ASAP* will
provide a range of relevant sources. Since these are interdisciplinary databases, you will almost certainly locate much more than just history-related
sources, so keywords should be adjusted accordingly. When searching
Historical Abstracts or one of the medieval databases, it would be appropriate to search on a simple term such as *plague*, since everything located
would have something to do with the history of the topic. In a general-
coverage database, however, the same search would locate dozens of articles from medical and other nonhistory perspectives. Therefore, when
searching nonhistory databases, it is usually necessary to add *history* as an
additional keyword.

Because history is often an interdisciplinary subject, interested in the
events of the past in terms of another discipline, subject-specific databases
will help find related historical material.[10] This is true both for the areas
covered well by the history databases and for those that are neglected. For
example, someone studying the history of the book—an interdisciplinary
research area that encompasses the histories of printing, publishing, dissemination of books, and reading, with an aim of understanding what
books and the book trade can tell us about the societies and individuals

who produced and used them—would likely want to include sources such as H. W. Wilson's *Library Literature & Information Science*; EBSCO's *Library, Information Science & Technology Abstracts* (*LISTA*); *LISA: Library and Information Science Abstracts* (published by the Chartered Institute for Library and Information Science Professionals (CILIP); and *MLA International Bibliography* (published by the Modern Language Association), any of which might provide access to perspectives not found in the history literature. And *EconLit* (published by the American Economic Association) might provide additional information on the book trade, or even trade in general, not found in any of the other sources.

PRIMARY RESEARCH

Primary literature allows the historian to get as close as possible to the original event. Though some literature, such as published memoirs, is constructed and disseminated as such, most primary literature is created for other purposes. Because of this, there is no single place to look for primary literature; it truly can be found anywhere. Unfortunately for many students, particularly undergraduates who generally have a very brief time to complete an assignment, much of it is unique and available only at one library or archive. This means that in many cases, students will need to define a topic based on locally available primary source material. Luckily, with the advent of the Web and the digitization of collections worldwide, the definition of "locally available" has expanded tremendously in recent years.

As with secondary literature, a good starting point for identifying locally held primary source material is the library catalog. The following terms, appended to a keyword search, can often help to locate primary sources in the library: *diaries, personal narratives, correspondence, interviews, sources, archives, manuscripts,* and *document**. All but the last of these are subheadings that appear frequently in Library of Congress Subject Headings (LCSH). The first two apply to published memoirs, and the next two to collections of sources. None of these terms necessarily means that the source was published specifically as a primary source, though they all can be used as such. The next term, *sources*, applies to collections of materials, of whatever nature, that have been compiled specifically as anthologies of primary source materials. These could include collections of correspondence, articles, excerpts from longer publications, or anything else that might be useful for study of the subject. *Archives* and *manuscripts* are often used to designate collections of materials held in original manuscript format by the library. The last term, *document**, truncated here to search for any word beginning with "document," does not necessarily appear in LCSH. It is useful as a keyword, however, since compilations of primary source material, published as such, often have titles that include the terms *documents* or *documentary*.

Examples of Library of Congress Subject Headings with terms indicating primary source material italicized:

Subject (s):   World War, 1939–1945 — Naval operations, Japanese —
           Sources
           Japan. Kaigun — History — World War, 1939–1945 —
           Sources
           Japan. Kaigun — Officers — *Diaries*
           Kido, Kȳichi, 1889–1977 — *Diaries*
           Nomura, Kichisaburȳ, 1877–1964 — *Diaries*
           World War, 1939–1945 — *Personal narratives,* Japanese

Keep in mind, too, that for many research projects, monographs on the subject written at the time of the event can make useful primary source material.

Moving beyond the library catalog, indexes can generally point to important primary source material. Government documents and newspaper or popular magazine articles from the time of the event are often readily accessible through a variety of indexes in the library. These include historical indexes to newspapers, H. W. Wilson's *Reader's Guide to Periodical Literature* (available electronically as *Reader's Guide Retrospective*), *Poole's Index to Periodical Literature* (available electronically as part of Chadwick-Healey's *C19*, available through ProQuest, or Paratext's *Nineteenth Century Masterfile*), indexes to U.S. government hearings or the *Serial Set*, and specialized indexes on any number of subjects. A lot of these are now available electronically, though many are available only in print.

When using older indexes to locate primary source material, make sure to consider the time when the index was created, and craft your search strategy appropriately. For instance, if searching for popular movie stereotypes of African Americans in the 1920s, *Reader's Guide* or the *New York Times Index* (or the full-text *Historical New York Times*, available from ProQuest) would both be valuable resources, since each indexes the movie reviews necessary for such a project. However, neither *African American* nor *movie* was a term generally in use at the time that these indexes were created, so it would be crucial to identify the correct terms, *Negro* and *moving picture*.

Every week, it seems, something new and wonderful and important is digitized and offered freely over the Internet. Most major research libraries, including many national libraries, have contributed to this global digital library of primary source material. Unique resources that once necessitated a special trip to the owning library are now available for anyone to use. So much is now accessible that for many projects a significant portion of the needed primary source material is offered online, and for the lucky few, everything is accessible this way. Though a great deal is available, it is not always easy to find.

Because strategies for locating primary source material on the Internet will vary by topic and by type of source, a general overview of historical research can offer only a cursory outline of strategies for locating such material. As with most Internet research, a search of Google or some other search engine will often turn up the very thing for which you are looking. This is particularly true if you are looking for a particular unique source, which would allow a search on a distinctive phrase from the title. If, however, you are searching more broadly for a subject, a good digital library will often come up at or near the top of a search result list. A search on *slave narratives,* for instance, brings up digital collections of narratives at the University of Virginia, the Library of Congress, and the University of North Carolina as the first three results.

Sometimes, though, a topic is too broad to bring up results on early pages. Searching on *plague*, for instance, results in a good deal of secondary literature, as well as current information about disease. Sometimes adding terms to the search can locate useful primary source material. Adding *primary sources*, *papers*, *diaries*, or *diary* will change the results, bringing different but worthwhile primary sources near the top of the results. If this does not work, another strategy that can sometimes help is limiting the search to just .edu or .gov sites. There is no consistent way of designating institutions of higher education outside the United States, other than .ac.uk in Great Britain, .ac.nz in New Zealand, and .edu.au in Australia, so this method will not work for all countries. Instructions on how to do this are generally available on the search sites.

Sometimes search engines will not yield useful results. In these cases, it is of course possible that there is nothing out there, but sometimes the apparent lack of results is because there are sources hidden within databases or in other structures not searchable by the engines. It can therefore be a worthwhile strategy to go directly to the site where you expect to find such material. Obviously, to do this requires that you know what sites are likely to house particular subjects. Having this knowledge beforehand may sound hopeless, but it is sometimes fairly simple to determine. One thing to consider when looking for digitized material is where such resources might be housed in print form. Think in terms of language, country of origin, and institutional strengths. When looking for English-language materials, consider whether they would be more likely to be held by an American, British, Canadian, Australian, or some other library or museum. Then consider whether particular institutions have strengths in the area you are researching. Use sources such as *Subject Collections: A Guide to Special Book Collections and Subject Emphases as Reported by University, College, Public, and Special Libraries and Museums in the United States and Canada*, compiled by Lee Ash and William G. Miller, or *Subject Collections in European Libraries*, compiled by Richard C. Lewanski, to determine in which areas libraries collect heavily.[11] Chances are good that if they have strong collections in a particular subject, they may have digitized some of that material.

A similar strategy is to look at archival and manuscript holdings to determine what may have been digitized. Most of these sorts of things may turn up through the strategies outlined above. If not, follow the suggestions offered later in this chapter to determine print archival holdings and then check those websites to see if anything has been digitized. With some luck, you may be able to find some or all of the needed primary source material for a particular project through these methods. This is more likely for small undergraduate-level projects that may not need a comprehensive collection of primary source material, but sometimes it will suffice even for graduate and faculty research.

REFERENCE SOURCES

As with most disciplines, there is a wealth of print resources available for all sorts of historical topics. In a brief space there is no room to describe more than a handful of these volumes. Besides, there is an invaluable tool available that does just that. *The American Historical Association's Guide to Historical Literature*, edited by Mary Beth Norton and Pamela Gerardi,[12] is a comprehensive guide to the literatures of a wide range of historical topics. Divided by geographical region and time period as well as by type of history, each section of the set begins with a brief historiographical essay about the field and then features a detailed annotated bibliography, divided into subtopics, listing the important works in the area. This is a useful source for cases when you are having trouble identifying books through the library catalog. And since there is always a section annotating reference books, *The AHA Guide* can be a worthwhile starting point when looking for bibliographies, encyclopedias, or other reference sources. Because it is now a decade out of date, however, it is not useful for identifying the most recent publications.[13]

Frequently, students need to write on a topic about which they have only vague knowledge. They know, for instance, that they want to write about the American Civil War or slavery or some other impossibly broad topic. In these cases, encyclopedias and dictionaries often can be quite helpful. Using a source such as *The Dictionary of American History*, edited by Stanley I. Kutler,[14] you can find a twelve-page article on the Civil War, which leads, through "see also" references, to dozens of related topics including a brief article on the Freedmen's Bureau, the federal agency responsible for handling African Americans' transition from slavery to freedom. By looking at these brief articles and getting an overview of the topic, a student could narrow down a topic or identify a related subject. In both cases, these articles provide brief bibliographies, but it is often more useful to move on to the library catalog for keyword searching, or in some cases, to a more specialized reference book. A logical next step in this case might be the *Encyclopedia of the American Civil War*, edited by David S. Heidler and Jeanne T. Heidler.[15] This source has a slightly longer entry on the Freedmen's Bureau, but it also has numerous entries in the index. A similar process could be used for any subject.

CITATION SEARCHING AND BROWSING THE STACKS

A crucial strategy for locating both primary and secondary literature is to follow citations from a known and relevant source. Closely related to this is the tactic of browsing the stacks for groupings of related materials. Both have long been an important part of research in all disciplines, but they are particularly important in the humanities, with their reliance on often obscure primary sources and the relatively "fuzzy" language used in these disciplines. In this context, history fits into the humanities. As Rebecca Green has shown, this approach to finding information is often more successful than more formal methods of searching, particularly so with primary source material, with interdisciplinary research, and when "(portions of) the relevant literature are not captured by a well-defined vocabulary."[16] All of these factors impact historians greatly. Primary source material is often difficult to locate through bibliographic tools but can be found through the citations in relevant literature. Similarly, interdisciplinary material has traditionally been missed in many subject-specific indexing and abstracting tools (though this is much less true today than it used to be). Finally, because humanities language tends to be "'fuzzy,' often metaphorical," the controlled vocabulary needed for successful searching is less fully developed than in the social sciences and sciences.[17] For all of these reasons, footnote tracking is, as one of the historians surveyed by Dalton and Charnigo indicated, "THE KEY."[18]

ARCHIVAL RESEARCH

For many historical projects, the most important resources will be available only in archives, generally requiring a lengthy trip to study the materials. Though impractical for brief research papers, especially for undergraduates, a research trip of this nature is often required for advanced researchers. Though much of the research can only be completed once the trip has been made, a good deal can be done beforehand.

The first step is generally to identify likely archival repositories for a given subject. The best source for identifying repositories in the United States is *ArchivesUSA*, a directory of the holdings of over 5,500 repositories and almost 155,000 collections of primary source material across the

United States. *ArchivesUSA* combines the complete *National Union Catalog of Manuscript Collections* (*NUCMC*) from 1959 to the present, the *National Inventory of Documentary Sources in the United States* (*NIDS*), and descriptions of collections submitted directly from repositories. Using *ArchivesUSA*, you can be reasonably certain of identifying any archival and manuscript collections held in the United States. The "collection search" option allows you to locate collections by keyword, date range, and location. Results will include the name of the collection; a brief description, including dates of coverage and number of items; and a link to information about the repository.

A keyword search in *ArchivesUSA* for *publishing*, limited to the dates 1700 to 1750, brings up forty-two records, including the papers of William Bradford, a Philadelphia printer (and an important Revolutionary War figure), housed at the Historical Society of Pennsylvania. These papers are not identifiable via a Google search and so would be missed by anyone relying on Internet searching. Another search, for *book collecting*, brings up thirty-four records, including the papers of Holbrook Jackson, author of *The Anatomy of Bibliomania* and other works on book collecting, housed at Columbia University's Butler Library. Though relatively easy to find on Google, appearing near the end of the second page of search results for *Holbrook Jackson*, these might be missed by someone interested in the broader topic of book collecting and unaware of Jackson as a possible source. Occasionally, detailed finding aids or even digitized materials can be located by searching *ArchivesUSA* and then checking the repository's website.

ArchivesUSA is available through *Chadwyck Healey* (*ProQuest*). For libraries that do not subscribe, it is possible that they have access to *NIDS* on microfiche (*ProQuest UMI*), likely that they have the print volumes of the *NUCMC*, and certain that they have access to the freely available post-1985 *NUCMC* online at www.loc.gov/coll/nucmc. The *NUCMC* was published in print from 1959 to 1993, and most academic libraries have the set. For those that do not, the Library of Congress sells the volumes on microfilm.

Another source that allows one to search for finding aids in libraries and archives around the world is *ArchiveGrid*. This resource is available from the Research Libraries Group (RLG) at archivegrid.org/web/jsp/index.jsp and includes nearly one million collection descriptions. As of early 2006, this is a free resource. RLG is seeking funding to keep it free but may need to begin charging for it.

The United States National Archives and Records Administration (NARA) is a valuable resource and one that is sometimes overlooked by researchers not studying the history of the U.S. government. Though the mission of NARA is to collect the records of the nation's government, government business can be defined broadly enough that there are records of interest for many topics. For instance, there are twenty-five record series located through the *Archival Research Catalog* (*ARC*), NARA's online database, having to do with Louis Armstrong. Someone searching for information about Armstrong's music and his life might not think to check the National Archives and would miss some invaluable material. Though many of the finding aids for NARA records are available only in print at the archives, about 42 percent of these guides have been made available online through the freely available *ARC*, at www.archives.gov/research/arc. *ARC* searches holdings in the Washington, D.C., area; at presidential libraries; and at NARA sites around the country.

Locating archival and manuscript collections outside the United States is not as straightforward. There are many guides to manuscript collections by country or by topic, though certainly not for every country or for every subject. To identify guides by country, use the Library of Congress Subject Heading "Manuscripts—*Country*—Catalogs," entering the relevant country name. For guides to manuscript collections on particular topics, use the subheadings "Manuscripts—Catalogs" or "Sources—Bibliography—Catalogs." For example, you might use the headings "Ireland—History—16th century—Manuscripts—Catalogs" or "Brazil—History—Sources—Bibliography—Catalogs." These guides can often give a good idea of the general utility of the records for a given project, but books can go out of date as collections are lost or damaged. It is therefore never a good idea to rely on the book's information alone in planning a research trip.

Once you have identified a repository to visit, check its website for more detailed information about the collection. If you are lucky, you will find a comprehensive finding aid that may help you determine whether a visit would be worthwhile. If this information is not available, contact the repository, briefly explaining your project, and ask if the collection you have in mind has material of interest to you and whether other collections might also have helpful material. Ask as well about the hours, possible closing dates, and policies before committing to a research trip. Things to consider are cost and availability of photocopying, whether the repository permits you to use a digital camera to take pictures of documents, whether you can bring a laptop into the reading room, whether you can purchase microfilm copies of records, and whether you need a letter of introduction or other special form of identification to use the collection.

INFORMATION LITERACY COMPETENCIES

In lower-level undergraduate history classes, students are often required only to synthesize the secondary literature, with perhaps some basic analysis of primary documents presented in textbooks, course packs, or document collections. Students in the classes should be able to locate secondary literature in book and article form but will seldom need to find primary source material. It is not until they reach upper-level courses that students will be required to do significant amounts of primary research. Most history students (even history majors) will graduate with only minimal exposure to primary research in history.

At the graduate level, most coursework is also historiographical. Graduate students, however, will have more research projects involving primary source materials, culminating in the master's thesis or doctoral dissertation, both of which generally involve extensive primary research.

It is important to understand students' research needs in terms of their level and assignment. Most students will not need primary source material since they will be working on some sort of synthesis of existing historical research—a historiographical essay. They will need an understanding of how to find and evaluate books and articles.[19]

RESEARCH SKILLS WITHIN THE DISCIPLINE

The following is a list of skills, discussed above in more detail, to which those conducting historical research should aspire:

- Ability to find primary source material
  - in the library catalog
  - on the Internet
  - remotely (in other libraries and archives)

- Ability to limit searches for articles by chronological period covered
- Ability to choose appropriate research tools by geographical region, chronological period, and subject covered

SUGGESTIONS FOR FURTHER READING

For those interested in reading more about historical research and writing, there are a large number of useful books available. Generally written by historians, most of these books provide minimal information, if any, about library research. However, they do provide helpful insight into the methodology used by historians and students of history.

John Tosh's *The Pursuit of History* is a useful source for learning about the different ways of conducting historical research. He does an excellent job defining and explaining the nature of history and historical research methods. This is a particularly valuable source for getting an understanding of the various sorts of history (gender, social, political, oral, etc.). Though his discussion of historical research methods is not as practical as some others, it is very useful on a theoretical level. He makes an important distinction, which may be useful for the librarian helping a student get started on a research project, in his chapter on "Using the Sources" about the difference between a "source-oriented approach," in which the historian lets "the content of the source . . . determine the nature of the enquiry," and a "problem-oriented approach," in which "a specific historical question is formulated . . . and the relevant primary sources are then studied."[20]

Ludmilla Jordanova's *History in Practice*, Mark T. Gilderhus's *History and Historians: A Historiographical Introduction*, and Martha Howell and Walter Prevenier's *From Reliable Sources* also are useful for providing good theoretical overviews of the discipline. Though each discusses research methods, they do so as well on a fairly abstract level.[21]

More practical guides to historical research methods include Anthony Brundage's *Going to the Sources: A Guide to Historical Research and Writing*, W. H. McDowell's *Historical Research: A Guide*, Jules R. Benjamin's *A Student's Guide to History*, Andrew McMichael's *History on the Web: Using and Evaluating the Internet*, and Robert C. Williams's *The Historian's Toolbox: A Student's Guide to the Theory and Craft of History*. All of these cover in great detail the processes by which historians identify, compile, evaluate, and use sources. The first three have fairly detailed discussions about library research. Particularly valuable in this regard is Brundage's chapter entitled "Finding Your Sources: The Library Catalog and Beyond." Perhaps the most practical, providing a step-by-step guide through the entire research process, is William Kelleher Storey's *Writing History: A Guide for Students.*[22]

Another body of literature, generally written by librarians, consists of studies of the information-seeking behavior of historians and history students. Through reference and citation analyses, surveys, and interviews, these studies examine how scholars use (or say they use) information. Though these studies do not generally address the practical aspects of how to locate information, they do provide valuable insight into the sorts of information that historians are likely to use.

Margaret Steig Dalton and Laurie Charnigo's recent article entitled "Historians and Their Information Sources" presents the results of a survey of historians and of a citation analysis. It is the most comprehensive and most useful of these studies, providing up-to-date guidance about how historians identify information and what sorts of information they find important. This article gives detailed answers to questions about how historians locate both primary and secondary information, as well as which databases historians generally prefer. Results of the survey and the citation analysis show which sorts of materials, both primary and secondary, are most likely to be used. All of this information can prove valuable for librarians assisting researchers.[23]

There have been several citation or reference analyses of historical literature. The most recent of these is M. Sara Lowe's "Reference Analysis of the *American Historical Review*," in which Lowe examines citations from the premier general history journal over five decades. Also valuable is "Periodical Dispersion in American History: Observations on Article Bibliographies from the *Journal of American History*," in which Edward A. Goedeken and Jean-Pierre V. M. Herubel analyze the journal articles referenced in that journal's regular bibliography of recent scholarship. Though dated, the 1972 article by Clyve Jones, Michael Chapman, and Pamela Carr Woods, "The Characteristics of the Literature Used by Historians," is still useful.[24]

Several recent articles report on surveys of historians or history students. "Future Historians: Their Quest for Information," by Roberto

Delgadillo and Beverly P. Lynch, examines how history graduate students make use of the library. Another study of graduate student information-seeking behavior is Charles Cole's "Information Acquisition in History Ph.D. Students: Inferencing and the Formation of Knowledge Structures." Donald Owen Case reports on a survey of historians of America in "The Collection and Use of Information by Some American Historians: A Study of Motives and Methods." Wendy M. Duff and Catherine A. Johnson describe the results of a survey of historians about how they use archives in "Accidentally Found on Purpose: Information-Seeking Behavior of Historians in Archives."[25]

CONCLUSIONS

History does not have a firm disciplinary home. Some place it in the humanities, while others consider it a member of the social sciences. In terms of methodology and intent, it draws from both. Historians, students of history, and the librarians helping them need to make use of a wide range of tools and resources from the humanities and social sciences. And history can range across all disciplines. Librarians need to be aware that researchers based in any discipline can take a historical approach to their work, studying, for instance, the history of science or business.

Librarians also must be aware of the distinction between primary and secondary research within history. Though primary source material is the bread and butter of the discipline, there are many cases where secondary literature is needed, whether to provide context and background for the primary research or to stand on its own in a historiographical essay. In general, because undergraduates are more likely to use secondary literature, and because much primary source material is located elsewhere, librarians will be helping researchers identify secondary material. Primary source material is much harder to find and can involve considerable expenses of time and effort to locate. Understanding these distinctions and connections (between primary and secondary, between humanities and social sciences, and across and between disciplines) is vital to history librarianship.

SELECTED RESOURCES

This list of resources includes all of the history-related tools recommended in this chapter. It does not include any of the resources used purely as examples. Nor does it include resources from other disciplines that historians might wish to consult for interdisciplinary research.

America: History and Life. Santa Barbara, CA: ABC-CLIO. serials.abc-clio.com/active/start?_appname=serials&initialdb=AHL. Covers literature written since 1964 about the history of the United States and Canada.

The American Historical Association's Guide to Historical Literature. 3rd ed. Edited by Mary Beth Norton and Pamela Gerardi. 2 vols. (New York: Oxford University Press, 1995). A guide to books on historical topics from all periods and areas.

L'Année Philologique. Paris: Société Internationale de Bibliographie Classique. www.annee-philologique.com/aph. Issued annually since 1928. Volumes from 1959 forward are online. Covers all aspects of scholarly research in the classics.

Archival Research Catalog (ARC). Washington, DC: National Archives and Records Administration (NARA). www.archives.gov/research/arc. The online catalog of NARA holdings in Washington, at regional archives, and at presidential libraries.

ArchiveGrid. Available from RLG (archivegrid.org/web/jsp/index.jsp). Provides access to almost one million collection descriptions.

ArchivesUSA. Available from ProQuest (www.proquest.com). A directory of over 5,500 repositories representing over 154,500 collections. For more information, see www.proquest.com/products_pq/descriptions/archives_usa.shtml.

C19: The Nineteenth Century Index. Available from ProQuest (www.proquest.com). A collection of indexes to nineteenth-century books, periodicals, and official documents.

C.R.I.S.: The Combined Retrospective Index Set to Journals in History, 1838–1974 (Washington, DC: Carrollton Press, 1977).

Historical Abstracts. Santa Barbara, CA: ABC-CLIO. Available at serials.abc-clio.com/active/start?_appname=serials&initialdb=HA. Covers literature written since 1954 about post-1450 history, excluding the United States and Canada.

International Bibliography of Historical Sciences. Internationale Bibliographie der Geschichtswissenschaftern. Bibliografia International de Ciencias Historicas.

Bibliographie Internationale des Sciences Historiques. Bibliografia Internazionale delle Scienze Storiche. UNESCO. Various publishers, most recently K. G. Saur. Published annually since 1926. A classified listing of books and journal articles on all areas of historical research.

International Medieval Bibliography. Turnhout, Belgium: Brepolis. Available at www.brepolis.net. Covers materials written since 1967 on the European Middle Ages from 400 to 1500.

Iter: Gateway to the Middle Ages and Renaissance. Toronto: University of Toronto Libraries. www.itergateway.org. Covers materials written in some cases as far back as 1784 on European history from 400 to 1700.

National Inventory of Documentary Sources in the United States (NIDS). Ann Arbor, MI: ProQuest. A microfiche collection of archival finding aids. Also part of *ArchivesUSA*.

National Union Catalog of Manuscript Collections (NUCMC). Washington, DC: Library of Congress, 1959–1993. Post-1985 volumes available online at www .loc.gov/coll/nucmc. The entire set is available as part of *ArchivesUSA*.

Subject Collections: A Guide to Special Book Collections and Subject Emphases as Reported by University, College, Public, and Special Libraries and Museums in the United States and Canada, 7th ed., compiled by Lee Ash and William G. Miller (New Providence, NJ: R. R. Bowker, 1993).

Subject Collections in European Libraries, 2nd ed., compiled by Richard C. Lewanski (New York: R. R. Bowker, 1978).

NOTES

1. For a good discussion of the influences of humanities and social sciences methods on historical research, see Martha Howell and Walter Prevenier, "New Interpretive Approaches," in *From Reliable Sources: An Introduction to Historical Methods* (Ithaca, NY: Cornell University Press, 2001), 88–109. There are many other detailed analyses on the place of history in relation to the social sciences, for example W. H. McDowell, "History and the Social Sciences," in *Historical Research: A Guide* (New York: Longman, 2002), 15–26; W. Spohn, "History and the Social Sciences," in *International Encyclopedia of the Social and Behavioral Sciences*, ed. Neil J. Smelser and Paul B. Baltes (New York: Elsevier, 2001), 6829–35 (there are many additional useful articles on the relation of history to the social sciences throughout this source); and Christopher Lloyd, "History and the Social Sciences," in *Writing History: Theory & Practice*, ed. Stefan Berger, Heiko Feldner, and Kevin Passmore (London: Arnold, 2003), 83–103.

2. John Tosh, *The Pursuit of History: Aims, Methods, and New Directions in the Study of Modern History*, rev. 3rd ed. (New York: Longman, 2002), 50–51.

3. Tosh, *The Pursuit of History*, 52.

4. Tosh gives a more complete picture of the different sorts of historical research throughout his book, but especially in *The Pursuit of History*, chap. 5, "The Themes of Mainstream History," 108–37. This source and Berger, Feldner, and Passmore, *Writing History*, will help explain the various major types of historical research such as cultural history, economic history, intellectual history, political history, and social history.

5. Tosh, *The Pursuit of History*, 59.

6. For a clear discussion about the different sorts of historical writing, see Anthony Brundage, *Going to the Sources*, 3rd ed. (Wheeling, IL: Harlan Davidson, 2002), 48–86.

7. Margaret Stieg Dalton and Laurie Charnigo, "Historians and Their Information Sources," *College & Research Libraries* 65, no. 5 (September 2005): 406.

8. Dalton and Charnigo, "Historians and Their Information Services," 410. See also Helen R. Tibbo, *Abstracting, Information Retrieval and the Humanities: Providing Access to Historical Literature* (Chicago: American Library Association, 1993), 5; and Rebecca Green, "Locating Sources in Humanities Scholarship: The Efficacy of Following Bibliographic References," *Library Quarterly* 70, no. 2 (2000): 201–29.

9. *C.R.I.S.: The Combined Retrospective Index Set to Journals in History, 1838–1974.* (Washington, DC: Carrollton Press, 1977).

10. For a detailed discussion of the range of databases used by historians, see Dalton and Charnigo, *Abstracting Information Retrieval and the Humanities*, 409–11.

11. Lee Ash and William G. Miller, comp., *Subject Collections: A Guide to Special Book Collections and Subject Emphases as Reported by University, College, Public, and Special Libraries and Museums in the United States and Canada*, 7th ed. (New Providence, NJ: R. R. Bowker, 1993); Richard C. Lewanski, comp., *Subject Collections in European Libraries*, 2nd ed. (New York: R. R. Bowker, 1978).

12. Mary Beth Norton and Pamela Gerardi, ed., *The American Historical Association's Guide to Historical Literature*, 3rd ed., 2 vols. (New York: Oxford University Press, 1995).

13. Though there are no recent guides devoted specifically to history, several books that cover reference sources in general can be used to identify history-related materials: *American Reference Books Annual*, published yearly by Libraries Unlimited, reviews most reference books published each year; Robert Balay, ed., *Guide to Reference Books*, 11th ed. (Chicago: American Library Association, 1996); and Alan Day and Michael Walsh, ed., *Walford's Guide to Reference Material*, vol. 2, *Social and Historical Sciences, Philosophy and Religion*, 8th ed. (London: Library Association Publishing, 2000); these are American and British guides respectively to the most important reference sources in given subjects.

14. Stanley I. Kutler, ed., *Dictionary of American History*, 3rd ed., 10 vols. (New York: Charles Scribner's Sons, Thomson Gale, 2003).

15. David S. Heidler and Jeanne T. Heidler, eds., *Encyclopedia of the American Civil War: A Political, Social, and Military History*, 5 vols. (Santa Barbara: ABC-CLIO, 2000).

16. Green, "Locating Sources in Humanities Scholarship," 226.

17. Tibbo, *Abstracting, Information Retrieval and the Humanities*, 5.

18. Dalton and Charnigo, "Historians and Their Information Sources," 410.

19. The Association of College and Research Libraries (ACRL) has compiled a list of information literacy standards for the various disciplines. The history standards can be found at ACRL/ALA Instruction Section, "Information Literacy in the Disciplines: History," ACRL, www.ala.org/ala/acrlbucket/is/projectsacrl/infolitdisciplines/history.htm (accessed January 3, 2006).

20. Tosh, *The Pursuit of History*, 84.

21. Ludmilla Jordanova, *History in Practice* (London: Arnold, 2000); Mark T. Gilderhus, *History and Historians: A Historiographical Introduction*, 5th ed. (Upper Saddle River, NJ: Prentice Hall, 2003); Howell and Prevenier, "New Interpretive Approaches."

22. Brundage, *Going to the Sources*, 28–47; McDowell, "History and the Social Sciences"; Jules R. Benjamin, *A Student's Guide to History*, 9th ed. (Boston: Bedford Books, 2004); Andrew McMichael, *History on the Web: Using and Evaluating the Internet* (Wheeling, IL: Harlan Davidson, 2005); Robert C. Williams, *The Historian's Toolbox: A Student's Guide to the Theory and Craft of History* (Armonk, NY: M. E. Sharpe, 2003); William Kelleher Storey, *Writing History: A Guide for Students*, 2nd ed. (New York: Oxford University Press, 2004).

23. Dalton and Charnigo, "Historians and their Informational Sources." This study updates Dalton's (then Stieg's) earlier study reported in Margaret F. Stieg, "The Information Needs of Historians," *College & Research Libraries* 42 (1981): 549–60.

24. M. Sara Lowe, "Reference Analysis of the *American Historical Review*," *Collection Building* 22, no. 1 (2003): 13–20; Edward A. Goedeken and Jean-Pierre V. M. Herebul, "Periodical Dispersion in American History: Observations on Article Bibliographies from the *Journal of American History*," *The Serials Librarian* 27, no. 1 (1995): 59–74; Clyve Jones, Michael Chapman, and Pamela Carr Woods, "The Characteristics of the Literature Used by Historians," *Journal of Librarianship* 4, no. 3 (July 1972): 137–56.

25. Roberto Delgadillo and Beverly P. Lynch, "Future Historians: Their Quest for Information," *College & Research Libraries* 60, no. 3 (May 1999): 245–59; Charles Cole, "Information Acquisition in History Ph.D. Students: Inferencing and the Formation of Knowledge Structures," *Library Quarterly* 68, no. 1 (1998): 33–54; Donald Owen Case, "The Collection and Use of Information by Some American Historians: A Study of Motives and Methods," *Library Quarterly* 61, no. 1 (1991): 61–82; Wendy M. Duff and Catherine A. Johnson, "Accidentally Found on Purpose: Information-Seeking Behavior of Historians in Archives," *Library Quarterly* 72, no. 4 (2002): 472–96.

4

Research in the Social Sciences

Nonny Schlotzhauer

INTRODUCTION

What we hope for from social scientists is that they will act as interpreters for those with whom we are not sure how to talk. This is the same thing we hope for from our poets and dramatists and novelists.[1]

—Richard Rorty, philosopher

The aim of this chapter is to address the elements of library research as it pertains to the broad array of disciplines that make up the social sciences. This chapter is intended to provide relevant and useful information on the tools of scholarship and the various approaches to research undertaken by social scientists. As with the accompanying sections of this book, this chapter aims to familiarize librarians, as well as students and others, with how social scientists gather materials, develop research arguments, think critically about them, and ultimately disseminate that information for the benefit of the public.

This discussion of social science research applies to the scholar as well as the practitioner and attempts to include those from the novice to the advanced researcher. In short, this chapter is designed to provide strategies of social science research, resources for the individual disciplines, and a broad methodological framework for readers about how social scientists conduct research. While individual disciplines each have unique aspects of library-based research, much of the information presented here can be applied broadly across all of the social sciences.

A discussion of the variety of fields, some seemingly disparate, begs the question, What exactly are the social sciences? And what makes them unique? It would seem after a century of institutional research that the boundaries of individual disciplines would be clearly established, yet there remain genuine academic disagreements as to whether or not a particular field of inquiry (or its approach) constitutes a social science. For example, are psychologists who are concerned with physiological influences on behavior scientists, or do they belong in the social science camp? Are historians chiefly humanists, or are some of them social scientists too? And where do we place professions like education and communication?

Rather than make an effort to resolve this debate, I have included those disciplines with which I am most familiar. Likewise, of the scores of research methods and strategies employed by social scientists, I have chosen to focus on only a select few. Taking into account the present situation as well as the increasingly interdisciplinary nature of research, this chapter focuses on what are generally considered the "core" social science subjects of anthropology, economics, political science, social work, and sociology, together with related fields that are deemed to have a social aspect: communication, education, geography, and psychology.

One discipline that at times fits into the realm of the social sciences, history, is addressed in greater depth in chapter 3 by Michael Levine-Clark, and so is not treated here. Also, because of its rather unique research requirements, law is excluded altogether, though criminal justice, often aligned with law, is considered a social science for its methodological approach. Interdisciplinary fields such as area studies, ethnic studies, and women's studies are included as they pertain to the broader disciplines of the social sciences.

INFORMATION SEEKING IN THE SOCIAL SCIENCES

Even in this time of increased interdisciplinarity, there still exists a general tendency to generalize about the *metadisciplines*—the sciences, social sciences, and humanities—that can shed light on the workings of researchers.[2] Over the years there have been many attempts to review the information-seeking habits of individuals in the three categories.

A particularly serious effort to gauge the differences was undertaken in a series from the Research Libraries Group.[3] The three studies assessed the information needs in the humanities, the social sciences, and the sciences. The series pointed out that there are strong habits and preferences among researchers, and certain mechanisms of information seeking between the disciplines. In the study focusing on the social sciences, the authors Constance Gould and Mark Handler discovered that, among economists, political scientists, and psychologists, journals served the major part of their information needs, whereas anthropologists made very little use of secondary literature and relied on personal collections and attendance at conferences. Gould and Handler also found that informal networks of communication were highly valued; unpublished work was often sought, usually in the form of working papers; and up-to-date material was seen as essential.

Another important distinction among the metadisciplines that has been posited is the degree to which books and journals are consulted during the research process. The conclusion that Donald Owen Case states in his study is that the primary literature of science is in journals, whereas researchers in the humanities are more likely to use books and archives.[4] In another study, J. Michael Brittain noted that journal literature, as with scientists, is highly important to social scientists, yet the latter rely heavily on institutional data (such as statistics gathered from government census) for research purposes.[5]

Among the studies on the information needs and use among social scientists, several stand out. A comprehensive review was undertaken by Huberta P. Hogeweg de Haart in 1983 that summarizes the literature prior to 1980.[6] Peter Hernon, in 1984, took a somewhat narrow view, focusing on how historians use government documents.[7] A more recent article by Lokman Meho and Stephanie Haas in 2001 took a similarly narrowed examination. They conducted a survey via questionnaire, citation analysis, and follow-up interview into the information-seeking needs of social scientists studying the Kurdish people. This study focused specifically on how these scientists located government information and on factors that influenced their information seeking.[8]

One comprehensive study of research about social scientists is by David Ellis. He conducted interviews with forty-seven social scientists: twenty psychologists and the rest from eight other departments. Ellis revealed six characteristics of information-seeking behavior: starting, chaining, browsing, differentiating, monitoring, and extracting.[9] Several years later, Ellis followed up this study, joined by Deborah Cox and Katherine Hall, and compared the earlier findings with new observations of scientists.[10] While they found no major differences between the research of scientists and social scientists, the authors did note some unique verifying behavior among chemists to track down errors that was not seen previously among social scientists.

There are clearly some gray areas when attempting to distinguish among the various disciplines, and preferences and habits are often hard to define as belonging to one group or another. Nonetheless, with some understanding of the important processes of research and a better understanding of the information needs of researchers, librarians can develop strategies that allow users to navigate the complex decision making they often face within the library.

THE ROLE OF RESEARCH IN THE SOCIAL SCIENCES

Research, in short, is the systematic effort to secure answers to questions. Research questions deal with issues requiring reference to data and information. (For the purposes of this book, research is not confined to the "academy" but rather includes the practical efforts by a diverse set of individuals seeking answers to questions.) Regardless of the sources of information, all research involves gathering information that goes beyond hunches, and it requires careful work and analysis.

In its simplest form, social science research, like all research, can be divided into two types: basic and applied. Basic research is completed to learn about relationships among variables, regardless of any immediate application. What is often called "pure" scientific research falls into this category. Though most researchers hope that their work will make a lasting contribution to knowledge, no payout is imminent. Applied research is undertaken as a service, to solve practical needs of a community or organization. The support of policy-related decision making is common to much of applied research, though with some fields, such as in the sciences and engineering disciplines, there exists a rather straightforward correspondence between information generation and application. Within the social sciences, things tend to get a bit messier. Practitioners make highly variable use of knowledge generated by academic disciplines, with some (psychologists, for instance) more tightly linked to formal channels and others (school teachers) making little use of research findings.

A clear example of how research can be used for applied purposes is found in the field of economics, where economists employ differing research strategies depending on the intended outcome. Marydee Ojala quotes the *U.S. Occupational Outlook Handbook*, stating that "economists study how society distributes scarce resources such as land, labor, raw materials, and machinery to produce goods and services. They conduct research, collect and analyze data, monitor economic trends, and develop forecasts. They research issues such as energy costs, inflation, interest rates, exchange rates, business cycles, taxes, or employment levels."[11] The information needed may be related to the United States, it may be international in nature or about a specific country or countries, or it may be a mix. The research may focus on the "branch of economics that deals with large-scale economic factors; the economics of a national economy as a whole" (macroeconomics) or that which "deals with small-scale economic factors; the economics of the individual firm, product, consumer, etc." (microeconomics).[12]

Any and all research requires a planned and systemic approach. One of the keys to successful research, however, is allowing a degree of flexibility in response to changing circumstances while maintaining a coherent overall strategy. Within the social sciences, research methods will vary greatly depending on the subject area, discipline base, and intent. The social science research process can be divided into six elements: *objectives, design, methods, management, analysis,* and *presentation*.

The setting of research objectives is crucial since they guide the research process. Since most research aims to provide answers or solutions to some kind of "problem," it must be adequately formulated. Problem formulation, or "problem finding," plays a vital role in the initial stages of setting research objectives. Three main components of research objectives can be identifying a subject area, identifying the research question, and identifying key concepts.

Once research objectives have been established, the next step is to design a project that enables you to attain them. The purpose of research design is to test and eliminate alternative explanations. Good research design collects data that allow one to test alternatives; the more alternatives that are then eliminated, the stronger the final conclusion will be.

The means of collecting data are common to all social sciences. They include making observations and measurements, performing experiments, building models, and making predictions. The methodology varies, depending on the circumstances and the answers being sought. Among the many methods that the social sciences often use are documentary analysis, questionnaires, personal interviews, field observation, and quantitative or qualitative research.

After acquiring the requisite data in the course of research, they must be managed in a way that preserves their utility over time and across users. Data as such can be defined in two ways: primary data, which are collected, and secondary data, which can be reused. Among social scientists, the most common types of data are survey data and records data.

There are others, of course, such as video or audio recordings, as well as findings derived from laboratory settings. Whatever the means, all data require management of one sort or another. There are a variety of data management applications, though most social scientists tend to manage their data with software such as SAS, SPSS, or Stata.

The element for the social scientist is the analysis stage, the process or technique of synthesizing research results by using various methods to retrieve, select, and combine results from previous separate but related studies.

Finally, a researcher's primary goal is the successful completion of his or her work, and its dissemination is the culmination of the elements of the research strategy—objectives, design, methods, management, and analysis. The presentation of the findings is the end product of the whole research process.

RESEARCH STRATEGIES IN THE SOCIAL SCIENCES

As mentioned above, there are many types of research strategies used by social scientists, far too numerous to discuss here. Nonetheless, in keeping with this chapter's purpose of providing a general introduction to the broad range of disciplines in the social sciences, it is helpful to include a few of the prevalent methods employed by researchers. The kinds of studies listed were chosen because they are well represented in the social science literature and are common to books, journal articles, and research tools at most libraries.

Qualitative Research

Qualitative research is an overarching term for an array of strategies for conducting inquiry into how humans understand, experience, and interpret the world.[13] These are generally observations in predominantly nonnumerical terms that aim to describe or interpret social processes or the human condition. Qualitative researchers tend to use narrative descriptions of persons, events, and relationships.

Though qualitative research is often contrasted with quantitative research (which employs statistical methods), it is not a unified form of inquiry but rather can be characterized by activities that require multiple perspectives, cultures, and world views. Researchers in social work, sociology, psychology, education, and other disciplines in the social sciences use a variety of qualitative research methods: *grounded theory, ethnography, participant observation, field research, phenomenology, case study, discourse analysis*, and *action research*.

Quantitative Research

Quantitative research involves techniques that are used to generate scientific knowledge about various social phenomena. Quantitative research differs from qualitative research in that it is more data centered than individual centered, and it is generally free of bias and the researchers' values and ideologies.

The three main quantitative techniques are *surveys, data analysis*, and the *experiment*. Surveys are designed to elicit small amounts of information about attitudes and behaviors of individuals from a representative sample of the population. From this statistical sample, a researcher can use methods of statistical inference to draw conclusions. This is referred to as a *sample survey*.

The second common quantitative technique is the analysis of existing or secondary data to investigate various topics. Economists often use available data, frequently from government sources such as the *United*

States Census and employment and earnings data, while sociologists and criminologists employ *Uniform Crime Reports* data and may apply some new theoretical or statistical reanalysis.

The least commonly used quantitative technique is the experiment. Experiments usually have two groups for analysis, one group who receive some sort of stimulus and another group, often called the *control group*, who do not receive the treatment, to allow for a comparison with the experimental group. Among social scientists, psychologists are perhaps the most likely ones to undertake research using experiments.

For students in the social sciences, qualitative and quantitative research is highly sought, especially by graduate students. Oftentimes, they are specifically instructed to find articles that employ either method. Fortunately, within the electronic environment, *keyword* searching can yield results simply by searching for the words *qualitative* or *quantitative*, together with the research topic. Many times, the abstract that accompanies the citation indicates whether the study was qualitative or quantitative.

Case Studies

The defining characteristic of the case study is that it focuses on a single case. That case may be an individual, a family, a small group, or a large organization or community. The main emphasis is on understanding the single case through extensive research. Virtually all fields within the social sciences conduct case study research.

Case studies have clearly defined boundaries; that is, the researcher sets the features that are within the case and those that are not. Case studies are valuable because they help explain the complexity of human behavior by placing the research wholly within a specific social, economic, or historical context. The case study is often contrasted with other research designs, such as the social survey and the questionnaire, which are broad in scope. Social surveys and questionnaires study a large number of cases (or individuals), providing breadth, but they usually gather a small amount of data about each case. In the case study, by contrast, large amounts of information are collected about a single case or a few cases, providing considerable depth.

Ethnography

Ethnography is the description and interpretation of a cultural or social group or system. Simply put, "an ethnography is a written representation of a culture (or aspects of a culture.)"[14] The method most often used to create ethnography is *fieldwork*, where a researcher goes "into the field" to study a group of people and events in their natural setting. Fieldwork was originated by anthropologists in the late nineteenth and early twentieth centuries, who visited and often lived among indigenous societies.

Ethnographic fieldwork has gained more prominence as a method of research across all social sciences. Studies of ethnography are used by sociologists to study social problems in different locations, such as urban or rural settings, and by educators looking at certain populations within classroom settings or teaching practices among diverse communities.

Interviewing

Interviewing is one of the most frequently used research methods in the social sciences. Interviews may be of two types: the *unstandard interview*, in which the general nature of the questions are specified in advance, but the questions are not; and more commonly, the *structured* or *standardized interview*, in which an interview schedule is established, and specific questions are predetermined and standard for all. Interviews can be conducted face to face, via survey, or over the telephone. They can involve individuals or more than one person at a time. One type of face-to-face interview well known to librarians is the reference interview.

The social science literature contains a great deal of group interviews. One type of group interview is the focus group interview. This type of interview is commonly used by market researchers studying the opinions of consumers, or by political parties interested in voter reactions and preferences.

These, along with many additional research methods and techniques, can be studied by students and others wanting an introduction to the world of the social sciences by consulting two recent reference sources by major publishers: *The SAGE Encyclopedia of Social Science Research Methods*, released in 2004, and the *Encyclopedia of Social Measurement*, published in 2005.[15] Both titles are three-volume sets with an impressive list of authors and contributors. Together they convey the full scope of research undertaken by social scientists in sufficient detail for all to understand.

EARLY FOUNDATIONS OF
SOCIAL SCIENCE LIBRARY RESOURCES

> One essential characteristic of [the] social sciences is that they deal with the social relations between human beings, that is, with those relationships between human beings in which they interact with one another not as physical objects merely but on the basis of mutually attributed meanings.[16]
>
> —Bernard Barber, sociologist

Toward the latter part of the nineteenth century, the social sciences began to emerge as a unified concept. This stemmed from ideas throughout the Western world that human society could be studied "scientifically." The application of the scientific method to enable us to understand ourselves and bring our affairs under some sort of rational control was given its earliest and most influential formulations by European thinkers—especially Auguste Comte of France and John Stuart Mill of Great Britain. Yet it was in the United States that the study of the "science of society," that is, the social sciences, flourished.[17]

Associations intended to advance specialized research were established, among them the American Economic Association, founded in 1885; the American Psychological Association, in 1892; the American Anthropological Association, in 1902; the American Political Science Association, in 1903; and the American Sociological Association, in 1905. Also during these early years, three vital institutions that serve as a forum for research across the spectrum of the social sciences were founded: the American Academy of Political and Social Science, in 1889; the Russell Sage Foundation, in 1907; and the Social Science Research Council, in 1923.

Growing up side by side with these associations were many academic departments, and in turn scholarly journals were launched as the primary medium to disseminate the findings. Some early journals in which social science research could be published were the *American Journal of Psychology*, 1887; the *American Anthropologist*, 1888; the *Annals of the American Academy of Political and Social Science*, 1890; the *American Journal of Sociology*, 1895; the *American Political Science Review*, 1906; and the precursor to the *American Economic Review*, 1886.[18]

Outside the academy, the major source of growth of the social sciences was the hope that so-called experts would be able to solve many of the social problems that arose in the aftermath of the industrial revolution. During the Progressive Era, public discussion of social science emphasized this potential contribution as a rationale for organized public policy within the government. The historian Theodore Porter argued in his influential book, *The Rise of Statistical Thinking*, that the effort to provide a synthetic social science is a matter of both administration and discovery combined, and that the rise of social science was, therefore, marked by pragmatic needs as much as by theoretical purity.[19] Simply put, managing the new multinational enterprises, private and governmental, in the emerging industrial society required more data. More data required a means of reducing them to information upon which to make decisions. Numbers and charts could be interpreted more quickly and moved more efficiently than long texts.[20]

With the growth of knowledge and the increasing literature available, a method of codifying the information for scholars and others to gain access was needed. Bibliographies were established to gather the expanding literature in a usable format. Among the earliest bibliographies specifically focused on the social sciences were the *Psychological Index*, from the American Psychological Association, in 1894; the *Bulletin of the Public Affairs Information Service* (now known as the *PAIS International* database), founded in 1915; and *Studies in Economics and Political Science*, from London, in 1931. Another early index was H. W. Wilson's *International Index*, which attempted to cover a wide range of literature spanning the humanities, social sciences, and general sciences. This resource changed over the years and eventually split to form the *Humanities Index* and the *Social Sciences Index*. These and later publications were the precursors to today's abundant resources that allow students, scholars, and the general public to gain access to the full spectrum of social science information.

The foundations of social science thought and research are explored in depth in the *International Encyclopedia of the Social Sciences*, an eighteen-volume masterwork begun in 1968 that continues to be the standard-bearer for the comprehensive coverage it gives to a complex set of disciplines.[21] This publication has been supplemented in recent years by the twenty-six volume *International Encyclopedia of the Social & Behavioral Sciences*.[22] Published in 2001 by Elsevier, this reference source supplements the earlier work, adding additional information and providing a good picture of how the social sciences have evolved over the years. A third publication that offers concise, authoritative coverage of the social sciences is *The Social Science Encyclopedia*, edited by Adam Kuper and Jessica Kuper.[23]

APPROACHING RESEARCH MATERIALS

> History is not the foundation, but the verification of the social science; it corroborates, and often suggests, political truths, but cannot prove them. The proof of them is drawn from the laws of human nature; ascertained through the study of ourselves by reflection, and of mankind by actual intercourse with them.[24]
>
> —John Stuart Mill

Research involves sifting through materials to make cases. Though it is often said that the social sciences are concerned only with the here and now, any seasoned researcher knows that looking at past work helps build research arguments. Past research can be used as a premise for new research arguments, a process of advancing conclusions based on reasons and evidence. Of course, though the reasoning does not prove the conclusions to be true, it does provide some possible directions for future research.

Many issues—even in fields as wide open as in the social sciences—have been studied successfully in the past. A look at the results and theories that have guided past research is a means by which to test the limits of an argument or theory, and to learn from the successes of others. A review of the literature provides different opinions and gives a broad look at the ways researchers and scholars have conceptualized, justified, studied, and interpreted a research area.

Research is conducted with a goal or purpose, and getting to know the specialized language of a subject is most productive. Thus, a well-grounded library research process should involve intensive use of library reference resources. These pieces provide either discrete pieces of information such as background, definitions, or factual data, or they refer the researcher to other materials, such as books or articles on a subject. To understand and focus the topic, the researcher should consult encyclopedias, handbooks, and general books on a subject; relevant terminology should be explored in thesauri and dictionaries.

As the research process unfolds, these reference resources can be comprehensively mined for useful information. As Antony Simpson notes in his book *Information-Finding and the Research Process*, this is not, however, a linear step-by-step process where the search strategy and literature needed are determined at the beginning and followed throughout the search process.[25] It is an interactive process where the topic becomes more clearly understood and focused as the researcher progresses through the books, articles, handbooks, and so on. Both the topic and the research strategy may be repeatedly modified based on a better understanding of the subject matter.

The process of doing research is affected by the nature of the literature being searched and by the communication methods used within a particular field. Yet, considering that the body of literature in the social sciences is so voluminous and interdisciplinary, the researcher must think expansively. More often than not, one reference tool alone will not suffice to cover the current research material in a given field of study.

As we have seen from the information presented above, and indeed from the other chapters of this book dealing with various fields of study, research takes many forms. The research problem, the intended audience, and the means by which the research findings will be employed all influence the methods and techniques of library research.

Common research methods and techniques employed by social scientists at the library are

1. Analysis of historical records, that is, primary records such as letters, diaries, and field notes, and also secondary interpretations of events.
2. Analysis of statistical and nonstatistical documents.
3. Literature search for theory and previous research in books, journals, and monographs.

The question that inspires research can come from a variety of sources, but most often it comes from the researcher's innate desire to explore the topic, and this requires some sort of historical analysis of the research that preceded his or her own undertaking. For any formidable research, a search of the scientific literature is paramount. It is a way for any research to build upon past research to validate a theory or hypothesis and increase the accumulation of knowledge for future generations.

Among the common research methods listed above, the literature search can be conducted from a researcher's local library. Even for those items not held by the library, many services are in place to obtain materials from other institutions in a timely manner. The first two methods, using historical records and analyzing statistical data, can pose a challenge for many researchers, especially if they are in an isolated area or if their library simply does not have the resources necessary to fulfill their research needs.

While a lot of local libraries contain a wealth of historical matter, from diaries to letters to material culture, many researchers are placed in the position where there arises a need to reach beyond their local environs to adequately do research. Most academic libraries do have special collections or archives that can be mined, and public libraries and historical societies can serve as valuable repositories for an assortment of materials. Librarians, equipped with knowledge and know-how to find information near and far, should always be tapped by researchers, especially students encountering the research process for the first time.

To a large degree, libraries have become victims of their own success. The abundance of databases, coupled with the growth of the Internet, makes finding heretofore unknown resources increasingly possible. Knowing that no one library can hold every item needed can alleviate much frustration, while being aware that sources exist that can identify where wanted items reside improves a researcher's success. Sources such as *Subject Collections: A Guide to Special Book Collections and Subject Emphases as Reported by University, College, Public, and Special Libraries and Museums in the United States and Canada* can be used to determine which libraries are strong in certain areas.[26] While most historical items are not lent out, making a visit to use the materials may be an option for many. And in today's dynamic environment, many archived collections are now digitized and can be viewed via the Internet.

For those in need of statistics or numerical data, the Internet has emerged as a central research instrument. In chapter 6, which discusses government documents, Christopher C. Brown covers in detail the wealth of state and federal data now accessible via the Web free of charge. For social scientists requiring data beyond the local, the Inter-university Consortium for Political and Social Research (ICPSR), established in 1962, is an integral part of the infrastructure of social science research. ICPSR is a vast archive of social science data available through institutional membership to provide researchers with access and support for data use.[27]

ICPSR is of course not the only data source that is now widely accessible via the Internet. In fact, collections of social science data have existed since the early days of computing. Today, among many academic, large public, and other research libraries, there is an ever-growing digital collection of social science data. These specialized social science data centers, often staffed by librarians (as well as social scientists), help users access and manipulate the data. Apart from numerical data, many libraries now house Geospatial Centers, employing tools for geographic information system (GIS) research and other related computer-based techniques. Librarians are well suited to the role of overseeing these repositories by performing the coordinated activities of identifying, acquiring, and preserving the digital information. The structures and systems they have developed address the needs of bibliographic discovery, in-depth access, and the interrelated nature of the collection during periods of technological change.[28]

In addition to the works cited in the literature review above, several other studies written on the social scientist's use of the library reveal a heavy reliance on journals.[29] Reasons for this vary, though currency (considerably more important for social scientists than among humanities scholars) and an exposure to a greater variety of viewpoints are essential factors. But the diverse research needs of social scientists, and the different demands of the disciplines, point to a wide variety of materials that are mined for research. Indeed, among anthropologists, it has been shown that there is a heavy reliance on fieldwork data, information that, unless it is one's own, is often obtained through personal contact.[30] Practitioners whose work is formulating policy do not necessarily have the same needs as scholars, so specialized reports are critical for their work. Overall, researchers develop methods of determining which materials will most likely be valuable. The most important factor is relevance to the research topic.

Reference Resources

A careful survey of background information on the discipline, or subject, helps define the problem and bring it into focus. It lays the groundwork for quality and will lead to more efficient research. General background information can be found in encyclopedias, handbooks, and general books on the topic. These items can be general in nature (covering all fields) or limited to a particular subject. Further, many reference sources focus on particular aspects of a subject, subfield, or emerging concept. Aside from providing background information, particularly helpful with encyclopedias or handbooks are the bibliographies that many contain, listing important writings and leading to further dimensions of the topic.

There are many kinds of sources of background material. Comprehensive encyclopedias exist for all fields of the social sciences, such as the new *Encyclopedia of Anthropology*, a five-volume set released by Sage in late 2005; the *International Encyclopedia of Public Policy*; and the *Encyclopedia of Sociology*, a core title now in its second edition.[31] For those wishing to consult more specialized works, options include the *Encyclopedia of Violence, Peace, and Conflict*; the *Encyclopedia of Homelessness*; and the *Routledge International Encyclopedia of Women*.[32]

Other resources that offer background information and serve as preliminary points of inquiry are the ABC-CLIO series *Contemporary World Issues*.[33] The titles in the series cover the hot-button topics that students often choose to write about and that general readers want to know more about. Exploring such diverse subjects as abortion, tobacco, terrorism, affirmative action, and urban sprawl, this series provides historical background, contemporary context, and resources for further research. In addition to this and similar series by other publishers, there are several titles that are good for analysis and overviews of topics. *Annual Reviews*, which offers comprehensive, timely collections of critical reviews written by leading scholars in many fields, and *CQ Researcher*, a weekly report that presents in-depth, nonbiased coverage of political and social issues, are but two of the publications available.[34] Both can be used by students and other researchers who need to complete an assignment, prepare for a debate, or become familiar with an issue of the social sciences.

Other reference works that can be useful, and that for some fields are essential, are works that review the terminology or concepts of a particular field. Terminology may be critical when using print or electronic sources, since many are dependent on *controlled vocabulary* (essentially, established subject headings). For example, many resources in the field of human services use the term *family violence* as opposed to *domestic violence* or *conjugal violence*. Knowing the terminology for a particular resource will ensure that the information on the literature needed is retrieved in a more efficient manner. Several well-established thesauri are associated with a particular source, such as the *Thesaurus of Psychological Index Terms* (the thesaurus for the print *Psychological Abstracts* and the database *PsycINFO*) and the *Thesaurus of ERIC Descriptors* (a list of education-related terms used by ERIC to organize database materials by subject).[35]

The Library Catalog

Familiarity with terminology will help researchers employ the proper terms when searching a library's catalog, which is essentially the record of material held by a particular library. Most catalogs nowadays default to a *keyword* search, thus enabling the user to conduct the broadest possible search for materials. Thus, if one were interested in finding books or reports in the field of education that used evaluation as a research method, a keyword search for "education" and "evaluat*" (truncated to pick up both the terms *evaluation* and *evaluating*) would return records where those words appear in combination.

But the pitfall for many novice researchers is that sometimes the research topic is too broad and can lead to information overload. (The flip side of this is that sometimes the topic is too narrow, with very few results.) Scrutinizing the subject headings of the records, derived from the Library of Congress Subject Headings (LCSH), is an efficient method for focusing in on the materials best suited for a given topic. With our examples of "education" and "evaluat*," searching by keyword returns over one thousand entries in a local catalog, whereas using the subject heading "Education—Research—Evaluation" yields twenty-seven hits, a much more manageable, and probably more targeted, number of items to assess for their usefulness.

It is important that the catalog, like a journal database, be fully utilized by researchers; it is the window into the world of knowledge and contains attributes that provide users with an array of options. In the online environment, linking features are extremely important, acting as springboards for further explorations of a topic. Links are provided for authors, book series, call numbers, and subject headings. The latter is of particular importance, as explained above with the unique terminology used by the Library of Congress. It allows one to move from the general to the specific rather seamlessly. For example, those wanting works covering research methods within the social sciences will find broad subject headings, such as "Interviewing," "Social Surveys," or "Social Sciences—Research—Methodology." Since records generally contain more than one subject heading, these broader subjects may be accompanied by more specific, or focused, descriptions, such as "Children—Longitudinal studies"; "Body, Human—Social aspects"; or "Social work with older people."

The catalog also provides access to the many *types* of resources held by libraries, not just the subject of the book or report. The accompanying chapters list some of the types of sources that can be located in the library, among them *personal narratives, correspondence, documents, market reports, manuscripts, music scores,* and *archives.* Some common requests that librarians receive from library patrons, such as "What journals do you have in women's studies?" or "I need to find a reference book on criminology," are format-based questions. Again, knowing the terminology and structure of subject headings can be helpful. Thus, knowing the following headings, "Feminist theory—Periodicals" and "Criminal justice, Administration of—Encyclopedias," will lead to the appropriate resources.

Another critical step for researchers is to get to know how the library arranges its materials. Becoming familiar with where materials are housed provides researchers with the highly valuable opportunity to browse the shelves for books, journals, and documents on a particular subject. Most libraries are organized by either the *Library of Congress Classification Schedule* or the *Dewey Classification System* (there are exceptions), so educating oneself with one or both, depending on the library, is indispensable for researchers. Tables 4.1 and 4.2 show the schedule of classes for the social sciences in each system.

Table 4.1. Library of Congress Classification Outline

BF	Psychology.
GF	Human ecology. Anthropogeography.
GN	Anthropology.
H	Social sciences (general).
HA	Statistics.
HB	Economic theory. Demography.
HC	Economic history and conditions.
HD	Industries. Land use. Labor.
HM	Sociology (general).
HN	Social history and conditions. Social problems. Social reform.
HQ	The family. Marriage. Women.
HS	Societies: secret, benevolent, etc.
HT	Communities. Classes. Races.
HV	Social pathology. Social and public welfare. Criminology.
HX	Socialism. Communism. Anarchism.
J–JZ	Political science.
L–LJ	Education.
P	Linguistics. Communication.
PN	Journalism.

Anyone considering serious research at a library needs to familiarize oneself with the organizational structure of the library. This will make the research experience more productive, since, aside from actually finding the material, it allows for serendipitous browsing among subject matter that is highly profitable yet often overlooked in the research process.

Table 4.2. Dewey Decimal System

100	Philosophy and psychology
150	Psychology
300	Social science
310	General statistics
320	Political science
330	Economics
340	Law
350	Public administration
360	Social problems and services
370	Education
380	Commerce, communications, transport
390	Customs, etiquette, folklore
900	Geography and history
910	Geography and travel

While designed to provide pivotal access to the enormous array of subjects that form the body of knowledge within the world, the classification system has its shortcomings. As seen above, the outline for the social sciences appears neat and tidy and implies that the material you seek will be within the appropriate range. Yet the system is limited by the simple fact that there can only be one call number assigned to one book, and this can sometimes appear arbitrary. For instance, take the following book, *The Quest for Peace in Africa: Transformations, Democracy and Public Policy*, edited by Alfred G. Nhema.[36] From the title, the words *peace*, *democracy*, and *public policy* all seem to fit squarely within the realm of the social sciences. Perhaps it should fall in the range between J and JZ? In fact, this book is assigned the call number DT30.5.Q47 2004, placing it in the area of history, and specifically African history.

Finding Articles

Moving beyond the catalog, finding articles can be challenging without some degree of knowledge of the indexing methods. As mentioned above, the journal literature is profoundly important for any and all fields, but particularly so with the social sciences. Whether in print or online, journals are the single best source of current research in the field. There are generally two kinds that are consulted, each one for varying reasons and by different researchers. *Research journals*, often referred to as *peer-reviewed* journals, publish articles by scholars that detail their original research or synthesize the work of others, and are scrutinized by peers with subject expertise in the field. *General interest* journals (in nonlibrary jargon, magazines), though they differ in content and lack the rigorous academic criteria found in research journals, can nonetheless serve an immensely important role for social scientists by disseminating research that can be of practical use by the public, governments, or others.

The social sciences are not unique in that many journals and other resources, such as databases, are published by professional or scholarly associations.[37] In fact, for some fields, the publishing and indexing go hand in hand. A good example of this can be found in psychology, where the American Psychological Association (APA) and its many sections publish approximately forty-two journals. The APA also produces the main indexing tool, *Psychological Abstracts*, and its online equivalent, *PsycINFO*. The APA in recent years has also developed its own database that specifically indexes and contains the full text of its journals, and others from affiliated associations, called *PsycARTICLES*. Another example of an association playing a major role in publishing can be found in social work, where the National Association of Social Workers (NASW) publishes several journals, including *Health & Social Work* and *Social Work Research*; some core reference works, such as the *Encyclopedia of Social Work* and the *Almanac of Social Work*; and the key indexing resource for the field, *Social Work Abstracts*.

There are a number of methods, both formal and informal, for finding relevant articles. Among the informal methods is personal communication or examining footnotes from other articles. The most common method of finding articles, though, involves utilizing indexes and abstracts (often referred to as databases in the online environment) and performing a citation search. Increasingly, libraries are offering journals in full-text format either through individual subscriptions; aggregated databases, such as EBSCO's *Academic Search Premier*; or packages, like *JSTOR* or *Project MUSE*. Suffice it to say, online journals are the preferred method among social scientists.[38]

The options for finding articles have developed immensely since the advent of electronic databases. In fact, it can be downright dizzying for the first-year student or for the patron simply wanting a little information on a topic of interest. Most libraries provide guidance for the researcher by placing the appropriate resources under "Subject Guides," a listing of the tools best suited for a particular discipline. This still may not be enough, and so an approach that takes into account a wide range of resources may be most beneficial.

For students, starting with comprehensive databases like *Academic Search Premier* or the similarly broad-based *ProQuest Research Library* can be effective tools for preliminary research. Both feature a diversified mix of scholarly journals, trade publications, magazines, and newspapers. Both databases index key social science publications, such as the long-standing journals *Social Forces* and *Child Welfare*, as well as titles in area studies, ethnic studies, women's studies, and popular culture. Beyond these all-inclusive databases, more specialized sources such as *Alternative Press Index* and *GLBT Life* can get at articles not found elsewhere. Graduate students will want to search *Digital Dissertations* (the electronic version of *Dissertation Abstracts*) to peruse past research in their field of study.

Major databases for identifying articles (and other information sources) in the social sciences are many and varied. The list of resources at the end of this chapter includes core databases that can be found in many libraries serving students and scholars in the social science disciplines. It includes general resources that provide access to the broad array of social sciences as well as subject-specific databases.

Research Skills within the Social Sciences

A general understanding of the information process is essential for productive library research. Anyone attempting to wade through the literature in today's electronic environment must know how the flow of information is produced and distributed in order to utilize the appropriate resources. Knowing the landscape minimizes frustration, and cutting corners will only prolong the goal of acquiring the right materials needed for the research paper or to solve the research problem.

At the moment, there are no ACRL (Association of College and Research Libraries) information literacy standards for the social sciences as a whole. Some attempt has been made to formulate guidelines, but these are by no means comprehensive. The *ACRL IS Teaching Methods Committee* has gathered links and citations to information literacy standards and curricula developed by accrediting agencies, professional associations, and institutions of higher education.[39]

In order to achieve success in the provision of library services in the social sciences, some basic competencies must be obtained. These are as follows:

- A general understanding of the social sciences as a whole and the various methods of research.
- A working knowledge of particular subject areas within the social sciences and of fields that are related.
- Knowledge of professional associations or organizations in the social sciences. In addition to the journals and databases mentioned above, many organizations publish and produce resources that are highly valuable but are sometimes neglected (the so-called gray literature). Many organizations don't have regular distribution methods and are sometimes overlooked by libraries. Most professional associations or

organizations have an Internet presence that can be searched for information about the field or for resources.

- If possible, acquire some basic understanding of statistical methods and know how to use a statistical tool for analysis (SPSS, SAS).
- Keep current of the latest trends or research findings in the social sciences. This can be done by reading magazines, journals, and newsletters; visiting websites; attending conferences; or talking with peers and faculty members.
- Finally, maintain an awareness of the social issues that are part of our everyday existence. The social sciences are ubiquitous, and there is a great deal of invaluable information that is generated on a daily basis in newspapers, general interest magazines, television, and on the Internet.

CONCLUSION

The social sciences are a rich set of individual disciplines that share a common interest in the exploration and understanding of human society. Collectively, they are dynamic specialties pushing the boundaries of research and influencing new avenues of research. More and more, the fields increasingly overlap, and together with technological development and intellectual advancements, the social sciences continue to evolve to generate new knowledge for students, faculty, researchers, and librarians to confront, synthesize, and disseminate.

Some of the basic elements presented in this chapter attempt to bring to bear the many facets of what exactly constitutes *the social sciences*. New developments in theory, coupled with established methods of research, make the information-seeking behaviors of librarians and others an ever-changing process that is as abundant as it is rewarding.

SELECTED RESOURCES IN THE SOCIAL SCIENCES

This list includes resources mentioned in this chapter, as well as additional sources that can be consulted by social scientists, students, librarians, and other researchers. It is not intended to be exhaustive but rather to provide a general reference point for conducting research in the social sciences.

These are but a few of the deep assortment of research tools now available that will provide a thorough literature search.

General/Comprehensive

ASSIA: Applied Social Sciences Index and Abstracts. Bethesda, MD: Cambridge Scientific Abstracts.

A database providing information on the social sciences. It deals with social services, sociology, psychology, health, economics, politics, race relations, criminology, and education. Coverage is from 1987 onward.

IBSS: International Bibliography of the Social Sciences. London: London School of Economics and Political Science.

IBSS is a key resource for social science and interdisciplinary research. It includes nearly two million bibliographic references to journal articles and to books, reviews, and selected chapters dating back to 1951. It has broad coverage of international material and incorporates over one hundred languages and countries. Over 2,700 journals are regularly indexed, and some 7,000 books are included annually.

Social Science Abstracts. New York: H. W. Wilson.

International index to English-language periodicals in sociology, anthropology, geography, economics, political science, and law. Provides abstracts for articles. Coverage is from 1983 to present.

Social Sciences Citation Index. Philadelphia: Institute of Scientific Information.

Begun in 1956 and now part of a suite of databases called *Web of Science*, this allows cited reference searching for particular authors, articles, or publications. This is invaluable for those wanting a means to track past and future research in their field of study.

Anthropology

Anthropology Plus. Mountain View, CA: Research Libraries Group.

An index of bibliographic materials combining *Anthropological Literature* from Harvard University and *Anthropological Index*, Royal Anthropological Institute, from the UK. It provides worldwide indexing of journal articles, reports, commentaries, edited works, and obituaries in the fields of social, cultural, physical, biological, and linguistic anthropology, as well as ethnology, archaeology, folklore, material culture, and interdisciplinary studies. Coverage is from the late nineteenth century to the present for all core periodicals in the field, in addition to lesser-known journals.[40]

AnthroSource. Berkeley, CA: University of California Press.

Produced by the American Anthropological Association (AAA) and the University of California Press, *AnthroSource* is an online resource serving the research, teaching, and professional needs of anthropologists. It includes access to the electronic archive of all AAA journals (some complete with access via JSTOR), newsletters, and bulletins in the field of anthropology.

The Human Relations Area Files (HRAF). New Haven, CT: Human Relations Area Files Inc.

HRAF files are designed to facilitate the cross-cultural study of human society, culture, and behavior. Two *HRAF* databases are available: Ethnography *Collection* and *Archaeology Collection*. They provide full-text access to source material on a wide variety of cultures around the world, as well as a cultural summary and bibliography for each culture covered.

Communication

Communication Abstracts. Thousand Oaks, CA: Sage.

A comprehensive source of information about communication-related publications on a worldwide scale, with indexing of articles, reports, chapters, and books from a variety of publishers, research institutions, and information sources.

Communication and Mass Media Index (CMMI). Birmingham, AL: EBSCO Publishers.

CMMI contains bibliographic records from *CommSearch*, formerly produced by the National Communication Association, bibliographic records from *Mass Media Articles Index*, formerly produced by Penn State University Libraries, and records for 285 "core" journals for all major communication and mass media fields.

Economics

EconLIT. Nashville, TN: American Economic Association.

AEA's electronic bibliography of economics literature throughout the world. *EconLit* contains abstracts, indexing, and links to full-text articles in economics journals. It abstracts books and indexes articles in books, working-papers series, and dissertations. It also provides the full-text of *Journal of Economic Literature* book reviews.

National Bureau of Economic Research (NBER). Cambridge, MA: National Bureau of Economic Research.

NBER is a comprehensive database that disseminates unbiased economic research among public policy makers, business professionals, and the academic community.

Education

Education Abstracts. New York: H. W. Wilson.
Journal database that encompasses all areas of education, including critical thinking, teaching methods, curriculum, and legal issues in education. The database provides comprehensive abstracting and indexing of over 475 international English-language periodicals, yearbooks, and monographic series covering all areas of education from preschool to postgraduate.

ERIC. Washington, DC: Office of Educational Research and Improvement, U.S. Department of Education.
The Educational Resource Information Center (ERIC), sponsored by the U.S. Department of Education, is the world's largest source of education information, encompassing journal articles and education-related documents. Many libraries receive ERIC documents on microfiche arranged by the ERIC document accession number.

Political Science

CIAO: Columbia International Affairs Online. New York: Columbia University.
This database is a comprehensive source for research in international affairs. It includes full text of selected books on international affairs, working papers from university research institutes, occasional-papers series from NGOs, foundation-funded research projects, and proceedings from conferences. It also contains abstracts and some full texts of selected journal articles.

International Political Science Abstracts. Montréal: International Political Science Association.
Authoritative database that provides abstracts of political science articles published in scholarly journals and yearbooks worldwide. Topics include method and theory; political thinkers and ideas; political and administrative institutions; political processes (public opinion, attitudes, parties, forces, groups, and elections); international relations; and national and area studies.

Worldwide Political Science Abstracts. Bethesda, MD: Cambridge Scientific Abstracts.
Provides citations, abstracts, and indexing of the international serials literature in political science and its complementary fields, including international relations, law, and public administration/policy.

Psychology

Mental Measurements Yearbook (MMY). Lincoln, NE: Buros Institute.
  MMY contains full-text information about and reviews of all English-language standardized tests covering educational skills, personality, vocational aptitude, psychology, and related areas. Each entry includes test author, publication information, scoring information, an overview of the test, a description of the test materials and time needed, and one or more reviews of the test.
PsycARTICLES. Washington, DC: American Psychological Association.
  Complements the *PsycINFO* database. This database contains more than twenty-five thousand searchable full-text articles from forty journals published by the APA and nine from allied organizations. It contains all journal articles, letters to the editor, and errata from each of the forty-nine journals. Coverage spans from 1988 to the present.
PsycINFO. Washington, DC: American Psychological Association.
  This is an important database for all social sciences. It covers professional and clinical literature in psychology and related disciplines, such as education, medicine, social science, and organizational behavior. It provides indexing to over 1,500 journals, dissertations, book chapters, books, technical reports, and other documents.

Social Work

Social Services Abstracts. Bethesda, MD: Cambridge Scientific Abstracts.
  Provides abstracts of the literature on the fields of social work and human services, including social welfare, social policy, and community development. Indexes over 1,500 journals, including most of the core titles in social work.
Social Work Abstracts. Washington, DC: National Association of Social Workers.
  This is the core database for social-work-related articles. It provides abstracts of the literature on the fields of social work and human services. It covers more than 450 journals in all areas of the profession, including theory and practice, areas of service, social issues, and social problems.

Sociology

SocINDEX. Birmingham, AL: EBSCO.
  New database that features records for more than 620 core journals dating as far back as 1895 and priority coverage of more than 500 journals, as well as selective coverage of more than 1,070 additional journals. Indexing for books, monographs, conference papers, and other sources is included. Searchable cited references also are provided.

Sociological Abstracts. Bethesda, MD: Cambridge Scientific Abstracts.

Provides abstracts to the latest research sponsored in sociology and related disciplines. The database draws information from an international selection of over 2,600 journals and other serial publications, plus conference papers, books, and dissertations. Major areas of coverage include community development, culture and social structure, demography, evaluation research, family studies, gender issues, methodology and research, policy studies, social development, social psychology, and social welfare.

Additional Databases for the Social Sciences

Ageline. Washington, DC: American Association of Retired Persons.

Summarizes journal articles, books and chapters, research reports, disertations, and gray literature on social gerontology as well as aging-related research from psychology, sociology, social work, economics, public policy, and the health sciences. It covers aging-related issues for professionals in aging services, health, business, law, and mental health. Coverage is from 1978 to the present, with selected coverage from 1966 to 1977.

Contemporary Women's Issues. Beachwood, OH: Responsive Database Services.

This database provides access to full-text sources covering global information on women. The sources include periodicals, newsletters, reports, fact sheets, and pamphlets. Topics covered range from human rights to health and reproductive issues to legal information. Coverage is from 1992 to the present. Includes nearly 1,500 titles.

Criminal Justice Abstracts. Thousand Oaks, CA: Sage.

Provides abstracts of articles from the major journals in criminology and related disciplines, as well as books and reports from government and nongovernmental agencies. For each document, an informative summary of the findings, methodology, and conclusions is provided. Topics include crime trends, prevention projects, corrections, juvenile delinquency, police, courts, offenders, victims, and sentencing.

Ethnic NewsWatch. Stamford, CT: Softline Information Inc.

ENW is a full-text database of the newspapers, magazines, and journals of the ethnic, minority, and native press. Searchable in both English and Spanish, with titles in both languages and more than one hundred thousand articles in Spanish, *ENW* offers in-depth coverage of a wide range of current and retrospective topics easily accessed using free-text and fielded searching. An average of 7,500 new articles are added each month.

GEOBASE. Amsterdam: Elsevier.

This is a multidisciplinary database supplying bibliographic information and abstracts for the geosciences, but for social scientists its coverage of the literature for human geography and international development studies is unmatched. The database provides current coverage of over 1,800 journals and archival coverage of 2,000 additional titles from 1980 onward.

Linguistics and Language Behavior Abstracts (LLBA). Bethesda, MD: Cambridge Scientific Abstracts.

LLBA covers all aspects of the study of language, including phonetics, phonology, morphology, syntax and semantics, hearing and speech pathology, philosophy of language, and applied linguistics. It indexes journals in the field from 1973 to present and is updated monthly. Currently 1,246 journals are monitored for inclusion in the database.

PAIS International. Bethesda, MD: Cambridge Scientific Abstracts.

PAIS, acronym for Public Affairs Information Service, contains references to more than 460,000 journal articles, books, government documents, statistical directories, gray literature, research reports, conference reports, publications of international agencies, microfiche, Internet material, and more.

NOTES

1. Richard Rorty, "Method, Social Science, and Social Hope," *Canadian Journal of Philosophy* 11 (1981): 569–88.

2. Donald Owen Case, *Looking for Information: A Survey of Research on Information Seeking, Needs and Behavior* (San Diego, CA: Academic Press, 2002), 238.

3. Constance C. Gould, *Information Needs in the Humanities: An Assessment* (Mountain View, CA: Research Libraries Group, 1988); Constance Gould and Mark Handler, *Information Needs in the Social Sciences: An Assessment* (Mountain View, CA: Research Libraries Group, 1989); and Constance C. Gould and Karla Pearce, *Information Needs in the Sciences: An Assessment* (Mountain View, CA: Research Libraries Group, 1991).

4. Donald Owen Case, *Looking for Information*, 239.

5. J. Michael Brittain, *Information and Its Users: A Review with Special Reference to the Social Sciences* (New York: Wiley, 1970).

6. Huberta P. Hogweg de Haart, *Characteristics of Social Science Information* (Budapest, Hungary: Hungarian Academy of Sciences/International Federation for Documentation, 1981).

7. Peter Hernon, "Information Needs and Gathering Patterns of Academic Social Scientists, with Special Reference Given to Historians and Their Use of U.S. Government Publications," *Government Information Quarterly* 1, no. 4 (1984): 401–29.

8. Lokman I. Meho and Stephanie W. Haas, "Information-Seeking Behaviour and Use of Social Science Faculty Studying Stateless Nations: A Case Study," *Library and Information Science Research* 23, no. 1 (2001): 5–25.

9. David Ellis, "Modeling the Information-Seeking Patterns of Academic Researchers: A Grounded Theory Approach," *The Library Quarterly* 63, no. 4 (1993): 469–83.

10. David Ellis, Deborah Cox, and Katherine Hall, "A Comparison of the Information Seeking Patterns of Researchers in the Physical and Social Sciences," *Journal of Documentation* 49, no. (1993): 356–69. For a more recent study, see Lokman Meho and Helen Tibbo, "Modeling the Information-Seeking Behavior of Social Scientists: Ellis's Study Revisited," *Journal of the American Society for Information Science and Technology* 54, no. 6 (2003): 570–87.

11. Marydee Ojala, "Searching for Economics; Joking with Economists," online, March–April 2005, 42.

12. *Oxford English Dictionary Online*, dictionary.oed.com/entrance.dtl (accessed January 6, 2006).

13. Jennifer Mason, *Qualitative Researching* (Sage: London, 1996).

14. John Van Maanen, *Tales of the Field: On Writing Ethnography* (Chicago: University of Chicago Press, 1988).

15. Michael S. Lewis-Beck, Alan Bryman, and Tim Futing Liao, eds., *The SAGE Encyclopedia of Social Science Research Methods*, 3 vols. (Thousand Oaks, CA: SAGE, 2004); and Kimberly Kempf-Leonard, ed., *Encyclopedia of Social Measurement*, 3 vols. (Amsterdam: Elsevier, 2005).

16. Bernard Barber, *Science and the Social Order* (New York: Free Press, 1952).

17. The social sciences were well established in Europe prior to their rise in the United States. There were several societies, such as the Ethnological Society of London (now the Royal Anthropological Institute of Great Britain and Ireland) and the French Société d' Économie et de Science Sociales, as well as "schools" dedicated to the advancement of human study. In the United States, many library resources were developed that led to the rapid expansion of study and scholarship.

18. The first three volumes of the journal (1908–1910) carried the title *The Economic Bulletin*.

19. Theodore M. Porter, *The Rise of Statistical Thinking: 1820–1900* (Princeton, NJ: Princeton University Press, 1986).

20. In the 1930s, this new model of managing decision making became cemented with the New Deal in the United States, and in Europe with the increasing need to manage industrial production and governmental affairs. Institutions such as the New School for Social Research, the International Institute of Social History, and departments of "social research" at prestigious universities were meant to fill the growing demand for individuals who could quantify human interactions and produce models for decision making on this basis.

21. David Sills, ed., *International Encyclopedia of the Social Sciences*, 18 vols. (New York: Macmillan, 1968–1991).

22. Neil J. Smelser and Paul Baltes, eds., *International Encyclopedia of the Social and Behavioral Sciences*, 26 vols. (Amsterdam: Elsevier, 2001).

23. Adam Kuper and Jessica Kuper, eds., *The Social Science Encyclopedia*, 3rd ed., 2 vols. (London: Routledge, 2004).

24. John Stuart Mill, "Sedgwick's Discourse," in *Collected Works of John Stuart Mill*, vol. 10 (Toronto: University of Toronto Press, 1969).

25. Antony Simpson, *Information-Finding and the Research Process: A Guide to Sources and Methods for Public Administration and the Policy Sciences* (Greenwich, CT: Greenwood, 1993).

26. Lee Ash and William G. Miller, comp., *Subject Collections: A Guide to Special Book Collections and Subject Emphases as Reported by University, College, Public, and Special Libraries and Museums in the United States and Canada* (New Providence, NJ: R. R. Bowker, 1993).

27. The facilitation of statistical data is now a feature of many libraries. These are sometimes specialized units within libraries that serve populations needing to gather data and to perform analysis. Data from ICPSR, government sources, international organizations, and local researchers often make up the bulk of the collection, with a librarian serving as data specialist.

28. Richard C. Rockwell, "Using Electronic Social Science Data in the Age of the Internet," in *Gateways to Knowledge: The Role of Academic Libraries in Teaching, Learning, and Research*, ed. Lawrence Dowler (Cambridge, MA: MIT Press, 1997); and Wendy L. Thomas, "Social Science Data and the Digital Library," in *Libraries, the Internet, and Scholarship: Tools and Trends Converging*, ed. Charles Franklin Thomas (New York: Marcel Dekker, 2002).

29. Patricia F. Stenstrom and Ruth B. McBride, "Serial Use by Social Science Faculty: A Survey," *College & Research Libraries* 40, no. 5 (1979): 426–31; and Hannah Francis, "The Information-Seeking Behavior of Social Science Faculty at the University of the West Indies," *The Journal of Academic Librarianship* 31, no. 1 (2005): 67–72.

30. Jonathan Hartmann, "Information Needs of Anthropologists," *Behavioral & Social Sciences Librarian* 13, no. 2 (1995): 21–22.

31. H. James Birx, *Encyclopedia of Anthropology*, 5 vols. (London: Sage, 2005); Jay M. Shafritz, ed., *International Encyclopedia of Public Policy and Administration*, 4 vols. (Boulder, CO: Westview Press, 1998); and Edgar F. Borgatta, ed., *Encyclopedia of Sociology*, 2nd ed., 5 vols. (New York: Macmillan Reference USA, 2000).

32. Lester Kurtz, ed., *Encyclopedia of Violence, Peace, and Conflict*, 3 vols. (London: Academic Press, 1999); David Levinson, ed., *Encyclopedia of Homelessness*, 2 vols. (Thousand Oaks, CA: Sage Publications, 2004); and Cheris Kramarae and Dale Spender, eds., *Routledge International Encyclopedia of Women: Global Women's Issues and Knowledge*, 4 vols. (New York: Routledge, 2000).

33. Santa Barbara, CA: ABC-CLIO Inc.

34. *Annual Reviews*, published since 1932, are collections published each year for thirty-two disciplines within the biomedical, physical, and social sciences. *CQ Researcher* is one of the many publications from Congressional Quarterly Press.

35. Both thesauri are now integrated into the online databases.

36. Addis Ababa, Ethiopia: OSSREA, 2004.

37. Some scholarly associations have their own publishing houses, while others contract with commercial publishers such as Blackwell Publishers, Cambridge University Press, and Sage Publishers, among others.

38. For recent articles highlighting the changing nature of research in the electronic environment, see Eric Klinenberg and Claudio Benzecry, "Cultural Production in a Digital Age," in *Annals of the American Academy of Political and Social Science*, vol. 597,

January 2005; John M. Budd and Corrie Christensen, "Social Sciences Literature and Electronic Information," *Portal: Libraries and the Academy* 3, no. 4 (2003); and Richard W. Meyer, "The Library in Scholarly Communication," *Social Science Quarterly* 77, no. 1 (1996): 210–17.

39. ALA/ACRL Instruction Section, *Information Literacy in the Disciplines*, www.ala .org/ala/acrlbucket/is/projectsacrl/infolitdisciplines/index.htm.

40. RLG's online products are to be integrated with OCLC's. As of this writing, details are yet to be finalized.

5

Business Research

Esther Gil

INTRODUCTION

Business research tends to be practical in nature as it is generally conducted in order to make business decisions or solve business-related problems. The strategies and sources one uses for business research vary depending on the type of information one needs, the timeframe of the information needed, and the type of research paper being written. Business research can focus on a wide range of subjects, including accounting, economics, finance, industry, management, and marketing, each of which has different information requirements and thus requires different types of strategies.

In an academic environment, an accounting assignment might require that students find and analyze a company's annual report. This is more challenging if students have to obtain historical reports published before companies were required to submit them electronically to the Securities and Exchange Commission, where they are available through the EDGAR (Electronic Data Gathering, Analysis, and Retrieval) Dissemination Service. "Live filings on the operational EDGAR system began July 15, 1992."[1] This type of research may also involve obtaining information for the industry the company is in. A management course might call for students to identify what the literature says about a particular management topic, such as human resource policies or organizational behavior, and compare and relate the findings to the policies and behavior of an actual

company. This company might be one of the thousands of public companies with readily available information, making the business research
much easier than if the company being studied is a small private local
company. A marketing assignment might require that students develop an
idea for a business and go through the entire process of obtaining both primary and secondary information. Industry research is usually focused on
trying to find information about a specific industry, from broad to niche
categories. For example, it can be research in the hospitality, restaurant,
software, or transportation industries. Or it can be research in a subgroup
of these industries, such as hot dog stands, or a shuttle service to take
tourists up to the mountains during the skiing season.

Timeframe requirements have an effect on the types of resources used
and the actual availability of the information. For example, marketing students as well as those who want to set up an actual business often want
current data. Yet it takes time for a publisher like the United States Census Bureau or a trade association to gather and publish statistical data.
Thus the information will often not be as current as a researcher wants.
Researchers have to supplement any reports published by commercial and
government agencies with information from trade journals; national, regional, and local newspapers and newswires; and primary research. On
the other hand, economic researchers or business historians may want data
sets spanning back decades that may be hard to obtain because of the age
of the desired material.

Finally, the strategy used also depends on the type of document one
plans to write. For example, a researcher who wants to write a business
plan in order to obtain funding to start a new business will use a different
strategy from one who plans to report the findings of a literature review
on how to deal with employee acceptance of new technology implementation in an organization.

Business research can also involve more in-depth study as a social science discipline because of the interrelationship of business with society.
Textbooks written about business research tend to describe it within this
context of social science research. They discuss developing the business
proposal, development of the research design, quantitative and qualitative
methods, the need to include a literature search, survey development, data
analysis, and writing the research paper. Academic faculty and students
working on doctoral and master's theses tend to use this framework when

doing research. Economic research also generally falls within this context. The reader should refer to chapter 4, in which Nonny Schlotzhauer discusses the social science research process, to get a better understanding of what is involved.

Business research can also lean heavily on historical research strategies. For example, someone might be researching the history of a university business school's academic department. This might require the researcher to look at original departmental documents in an institution's archives. Or a researcher might be doing research on the entire history of a company. The researcher may need to look at historical annual reports kept in a library's microfiche collection or visit the company and search its archives. In this case, the process uses many of the historical research strategies presented in chapter 3.

This chapter provides an overview of strategies and sources for doing the practical side of business research for the United States, recognizing that there are other types of research. Commercial Web-based databases and Internet sites are listed alphabetically at the end of the chapter. Bibliographic information for print resources is provided in the notes section of the chapter. Those wanting to learn more about the sources mentioned should refer to other publications that cover them in greater detail. Such publications include *Business Research Sources: A Reference Navigator*;[2] *Business Information: How to Find It, How to Use It*;[3] *Strauss's Handbook of Business Information Researchers*;[4] the *Small Business Sourcebook*;[5] and the *Encyclopedia of Business Information Sources*.[6] In addition, one should refer to a book like Mary Ellen Bates's *Building & Running a Successful Research Business*[7] for alternate strategies to use if conducting complex business research. There are also many business research guides or pathfinders on library websites worldwide that can be used to help identify strategies and sources. Librarians and researchers should refer to these sources to begin or expand their business research.

RESEARCH STRATEGY

In academia, the business curriculum is often project based or practical in nature. For example, students may have to develop a business or marketing plan for a business start-up, identify a new market for a product, or prepare a strategy to introduce a new product or service. A project may be either an idea that students have come up with or a field study for an actual company. This type of assignment tends to reflect what businesspersons have to do in the real business world. In both the academic and the actual business environment, researchers have to conduct secondary research in which the library plays a major role. According to the Small Business Administration, "Secondary research exploits published sources like surveys, books, and magazines, applying or rearranging the information in them to bear on the problem or opportunity at hand."[8] Secondary research for this type of project can be broken down broadly into the following categories:

- finding industry information to determine current or past trends,
- doing a competitive analysis that requires identifying competitors and finding information about them, and
- finding information about the market.

Within these broad categories, other types of research may be needed. For example, industry research may require discovering whether there are any regulations that affect the industry. Competitive analysis may require determining whether someone else has already patented a product. And market research may require finding out what type of promotional strategies competitors use to reach their target market.

Another project that is typical in the business curriculum is a company financial analysis. This type of research can also occur in the real world where the researcher needs the information for personal investment purposes. In either case, the starting point is finding information about the company. This includes finding current and historical stock prices for the company and possibly its competitors, and information from investment analysts or advisory services. It is also important to find information about the industry in order to understand why the company and its competitors are performing as they are. Finding information about the market may or may not be necessary when doing only a company or competitive analysis.

The research strategies presented in this chapter for finding business information use a conceptual framework along the lines written about by Julie O'Keefe, who introduced students to basic company and industry data by helping them "build a mental construct, or framework, of business sources by demonstrating the content and inter-relatedness of specific core sources in a systematic way."[9] Thus, the business research strategy focuses on the interconnectedness of the information being sought and the resources, rather than focusing on the type of resource. That is, the focus isn't on whether the items are book catalogs, indexes, encyclopedias, or handbooks, but rather on the type of information being sought.

SIC AND NAICS CODES

SIC and NAICS codes are concepts that one should be aware of when doing business research. *SIC* stands for Standard Industrial Classification and is an industry classification system upon which federal economic statistics are based up through 1996. NAICS, or North American Industry Classification System,

> was developed as the standard for use by Federal statistical agencies in classifying business establishments for the collection, analysis, and publication of statistical data related to the business economy of the U.S. NAICS was developed under the auspices of the Office of Management and Budget (OMB), and adopted in 1997 to replace the old Standard Industrial Classification (SIC) system.[10]

A standard method for obtaining these codes is by using the NAICS search interface on the census website.[11] There are many cases, however, where one will not obtain an exact code. For example, mountain transportation will not have a specific SIC or NAICS code, and the researcher may have to use various transportation-related codes such as those related to shuttles or buses.

One reason that researchers should be aware of these codes is that the U.S. government regularly gathers statistics on business and economic activity. The data are then published and grouped by NAICS code in sources such as the *Business Expenses Survey*, *CenStats*, and the *Economic Census*. These types of statistics are very important when one is doing industry research. The codes are also important when researchers need to analyze companies and compare their ratios to those of the industry. SIC and NAICS codes are critical to obtain information from sources such as Dun and Bradstreet's (D&B) *Industry Norms and Ratios*[12] or *RMA Annual Statement Studies*[13] because they organize the data by these codes.

Although one needs these codes to obtain data from certain sources, there are times when they are not critical to the process. For example, various databases provide other search mechanisms in addition to SIC and NAICS codes search fields, such as industry keywords, yellow-page headings, and full-text searching fields that allow one to pull up potentially relevant industry information. *Business & Company Resource Center (BCRC)* is such a database. It has an advanced feature whereby one can search the full text of its industry overviews using keywords. And while one can search *ReferenceUSA* by SIC and NAICS codes, sometimes it is more effective to use a yellow-page heading search. For example, one might use a yellow-page heading search in this database if one wants to find the number of Chinese restaurants in a city. Other databases with industry information do not even offer SIC or NAICS code searching, including Standard & Poor's (S&P) *NetAdvantage*.

In addition, there are often cases when the codes are ambiguous because of a lack of standardization across publishers in assigning SIC and NAICS codes. For example, assume the researcher wants to find information for the industry in which Franklin Covey participates and wants to use SIC or NAICS codes. A strategy one can take to identify them is to search for the company in a subscription-based database. If we use *Mergent Online*, we discover that they have used 8742 (Management Consulting Services) as this company's SIC code and 541611 (Administrative Management and General Management Consulting Services) as its NAICS code.[14] Searching on *Hoover's Online*,[15] we discover that it uses SIC codes 2782 (Blankbooks), 5112 (Stationery and office supplies), and 5961 (Catalog and mail-order houses), and it uses NAICS codes 32223 (Stationery Product Manufacturing); 323118 (Blankbook, Looseleaf Binders, and Devices Manufacturing); 453210 (Office Supplies and Stationery Stores); 45411 (Electronic Shopping and Mail-Order Houses); and 611430 (Professional and Management Development Training).[16] It is evident that there are times when publishers use different codes and thus have different business descriptions from one another for the same company. Thus, searching by such codes in databases that allow SIC or NAICS code searching may not yield precise results. We are left to use our best judgment on which codes to use.

SIC and NAICS codes are an important part of business research. Users should be aware of them and how to use them, keeping in mind that there will be times when codes may not exactly match the industries and companies they are researching.

INDUSTRY RESEARCH

The business researcher needs to find out what is going on in the industry, including determining whether there are any competitive, economic, social, regulatory, or technological trends affecting it. This information can be found in industry overviews; statistics; articles from trade journals, newspapers, regional/state/local publications, and newswires; market research reports; and association websites. As the researcher gathers industry information and data from these sources, other information that answers other parts of the research should be recorded, such as information about the market and competitors. For example, this could include how much is being spent in a particular industry, demographics about those consumers, or major players in the industry.

For industry overviews, there are numerous sources that can provide this type of information. Some of these sources include S&P's *Industry Surveys*,[17] Datamonitor's industry reports,[18] Gale's *Encyclopedia of American Industries*,[19] OneSource's *US Business Browser*, Plunkett's almanacs,[20] and market research databases.

A classic source for obtaining industry information is S&P's *Industry Surveys*. This source is available in print as well as through the online service S&P's *NetAdvantage*. The surveys provide extensive information for approximately fifty-five major U.S. industries and fifty-two global industries. The source is weak, however, for niche and local industries. For example, it is excellent for obtaining information about the airline industry, but not particularly helpful for someone doing research on the soft-skills management industry. Even so, unless one is very familiar with the coverage included in this source, a researcher should start with it to obtain whatever information may be in the surveys and proceed to other sources.

Gale's *Encyclopedia of American Industries*[21] provides over one thousand industry overviews in the U.S. manufacturing, service, and non-manufacturing industries. It has significantly more coverage than S&P's

Industry Surveys and includes essays on niche industries, such as life coaching. None of the overviews in this source go into the same depth as *Industry Surveys*, and some of them may consist of only a few paragraphs. This particular source is available in print and is also integrated into *BCRC*.

Other sources for obtaining industry overviews are Plunkett's almanacs, which cover twenty-nine industries to date. These almanacs also include a directory section of companies in an industry.

In addition to providing information that answers questions like what is going on in an industry, there are other pieces of information that can be obtained from these overviews. Here are some examples:

- S&P's *Industry Surveys* identify major companies, associations, and trade publications for the industry. Associations and trade publications should be pursued for further research. Usually the links to websites are provided, but if not, one can use an Internet search engine to determine whether the association has a website. Researchers tend to go directly to the trade-publication websites, where they are usually required to pay for articles they might want. Consequently, as part of instruction or the reference desk transaction, it is important to point out to the researcher that an article may be available from a subscription-based business database. For example, *ABI/Inform Global, BCRC, Business Source Premier, PROMT*, and Responsive Database Services' (RDS) *Business and Industry* are rich sources for trade publications. Many libraries subscribe to these and other databases.
- *Industry Surveys* and the overviews in *BCRC* provide bibliographies or refer to publications within their content that allow one to pursue further sources.
- The reports in *Industry Surveys* and *BCRC* include charts of data. Researchers should make note of the charts' sources and pursue them for further information.

There are many times when the information one is looking for is not available in these overviews. This is often the case for niche industries. In such instances, researchers have to rely primarily on articles from trade journals or newspapers and on information gathered through primary research.

Statistical sources are critical for doing industry research. Often the statistics are provided only in raw form, requiring statistical analysis. Depending on the source and the data provided, statistics can be used to determine whether there are any trends by virtue of looking at consumption data, industry forecasts, sales figures, manufacturing volume, spending trends, or changes in the number of establishments in an industry throughout time, to name a few examples. Researchers should refer to books like Paula Berinstein's *Business Statistics on the Web*[22] for strategies and sources for finding data.

Publications and databases that provide either statistical information or sources for obtaining statistics include the United States Census Bureau website (census), *LexisNexis Statistical*, the *Statistical Abstract of the United States*,[23] and *Tablebase*.

The census website is a very rich resource for industry statistics. Industry data from 1997 forward are categorized by NAICS code. Prior data are categorized by SIC code. Examples of industry-related information available on this website include the *Annual Survey of Manufacturers*, the *Business Expenses Survey*, *CenStats*, *Construction Statistics*, the *Economic Census*, and *Monthly Sales for Retail and Food Services*.

Statistics published by the government are so rich and relevant to business research that entire books have been written about how to use them. One such publication is *Industry Research Using the Economic Census: How to Find It, How to Use It*.[24]

A subscription-based database that includes industry statistics is *Tablebase*. These industry statistics are taken from numerous trade publications and sometimes from market research reports. The currency of the data varies. *Tablebase* presents the statistics in tabular form pulled from charts included in a wide range of articles; the articles are also provided. The *Statistical Reference Index (SRI)*,[25] also available as one component in *LexisNexis Statistical*, indexes data published in trade journals, by state governments, and by associations. If one finds a citation in *SRI* that is of interest, the information can be obtained from the *SRI* microfiche if a library subscribes to it. Another strategy for retrieving the full text of an *SRI* citation is to go to the trade source, such as an annual issue from a trade journal, using a database that indexes the journal. Such databases include *ABI/INFORM Trade & Industry*, *BCRC*, *Business Source Premier*, *PROMT*, and RDS's *Business & Industry*. If one finds that the citations in *LexisNexis Statistical*,

SRI, or *Tablebase* are more than two years old, and after reviewing the citation one determines that the statistics are published annually in a trade journal, then one can go to a database that indexes the trade journal to search for a more current article updating the statistics.

Trade and association publishers also publish statistics in industry-specific sources. A library might purchase such a publication if it has consistent demand for information about an industry. Researchers should search a library's catalog to identify such holdings. Examples of publications from association or trade publishers include *Superstudy of Sports*[26] from American Sports Data Inc., *National Coffee Drinking Trends Through . . .*[27] from the National Coffee Association, and *Restaurant Industry Forecast*[28] from the National Restaurant Association.

Researchers and the librarians helping them should always check out an association's website to find out what is published on that industry. As noted, libraries may purchase these sources. Other times, these association websites offer tidbits of information for free. One should be careful about using this information, as it might not provide the whole picture or the data provided may be older than desired. If a researcher is doing a project for an actual company, that company, or someone in it, may have an association membership that allows the researcher to access the membership portion of the association's website. The membership portion usually has more information than what is provided freely. Sources for identifying associations include *Associations Unlimited* (and its print version, *Encyclopedia of Associations*)[29] and Internet search engines like Yahoo! and Google.

In addition to finding statistical and other types of information on association publications or websites, these associations may sponsor trade shows or conferences. If a researcher is doing a project for an actual company, the company may be willing to provide funding for one to attend such events where some information useful for the project may be discovered.

The industry research strategy should also include searching for articles from trade publications, newspapers, regional and local publications, and newswires. Because these publications are often published daily or weekly, the articles in these sources enable the researcher to update and supplement any information obtained from industry overviews and statistical sources. Articles from these types of publications may mention the release of a recent market report or provide current statistical information about an industry. A researcher should try to determine whether such a report is available at a local library, or even search for it on the Internet. Some reports published by nonprofit entities such as the Pew Research Center may be freely available on the Web. Commercial publishers sometimes provide certain reports freely on the Web. If not, it may be possible to purchase a report.

Trade publications may also have other information, such as articles about competitive, economic, regulatory, social, or technological trends and other issues that are affecting an industry. Newspapers such as the *Wall Street Journal*[30] and the *New York Times*[31] might also provide such information. Regional or local newspapers may have information about an industry on a regional or local level. Databases rich in trade journals; national, regional, and local newspapers and other publications; and newswires include *BCRC, Business Source Premier, Factiva, Lexis-Nexis Academic, PROMT*, RDS *Business & Industry*, and *Access World News*.

Although market research databases focus primarily on the market for products or services, they also provide information about the industry. Researchers should try to determine whether a library has such sources and seek to access them. There are numerous market research databases available, including those from Forrester Research, Frost & Sullivan, Gartner, IBC, Jupiter Research, marketresearch.com, and Mintel. Unfortunately, no single market research database covers all the types of industries that researchers might want to investigate. In addition, some market research database publishers prohibit their use in academic libraries if the research is for a field study or if the information is to be provided in any way to an actual company.

COMPANY RESEARCH

Company research or competitive analysis is another step in the business research process. One should have identified some of the companies in the industry while doing the industry research. Industry sources such as S&P's *Industry Surveys* and Plunkett's almanacs help identify major companies in an industry. *BCRC* can also be used to do this. For a more comprehensive identification of companies in an industry, company-related directories and sources should be used. This is especially necessary if one is doing a competitive analysis on a local level. Sources that can help identify competitors include *Hoover's Online, Mergent Online, ReferenceUSA*, OneSource's *US Business Browser*; company directories that focus on regions or states, such as those published by InfoUSA and Cole Information Services; Internet directories like Yahoo! Yellow Pages and Google Local; and the yellow pages of the phone book.

ReferenceUSA is extremely powerful for identifying competitors in a certain industry down to a zip-code level. Consequently, it is very useful when one is doing local or regional business research. It provides estimated sales data, information about employee size, whether a company is private or public, and who the parent is if the company is a subsidiary. Google Local, an Internet directory, is also useful for identifying local competitors for specific types of businesses. For example, it is easier to find companies around Denver that provide mountain transportation using Google Local than by using *ReferenceUSA*. This is because the latter has no yellow-page heading for mountain transportation, requiring the user to use headings such as "taxi" or "shuttle," which will retrieve many companies that are irrelevant. Google Local is not tied to such headings. Consequently, when one uses it to search for mountain transportation in a particular location, the most relevant companies tend to be listed on the first page of the search results. The results for Google Local, however, will not have the estimated sales data and other information that are included in *ReferenceUSA*.

There are also specialized company directories that focus on specific industries and regions. Examples of industry-specific directories include *CorpTech Directory*,[32] *Thomas Food & Beverage Market Place*,[33] and Plunkett's almanacs. Libraries may have other directories that a researcher can identify by searching a library's online catalog.

Once the companies have been identified, the next step is to find information about them. To do this, the researcher should begin by determining whether a company is public, private, or a subsidiary. This will help establish what type of information is available and where to go to find it. A public company sells stock to the public. As a result, there is generally a significant amount of information published about it, especially financial data. A private company does not sell stock to the public, so information about its financials is not publicly available. Subsidiaries are owned by other companies, referred to as parent companies. It is often difficult to find financial data about subsidiaries. Some sources that can be used to identify whether a company is public, private, or a subsidiary are *BCRC*, *LexisNexis Corporate Affiliations*,[34] *Hoover's Online*, *Million Dollar Directory*,[35] *Reference USA*, and the company's website.

Once the researcher knows the type of company being examined, one can go to specific sources of information for them. If one determines that a company is public, then one should be able to find the following types of information:

- financial information,
- histories and profiles, and
- investment information.

Financial information can be obtained from corporate reports, such as a company's 10-K or annual reports to shareholders. "The 10-K report . . . is a detailed annual report that all publicly traded companies must submit to the SEC."[36] This should not be confused with annual reports to shareholders, which are not official SEC filings; because they are often used as public relations tools, information can be presented in a positive light. Corporate reports can be found in databases like *LexisNexis Academic*, *Mergent Online*, *Hoover's Online*, and *LIVEDGAR*, as well as through *SEC Filings & Forms* (*EDGAR*), and often the company's website. There are websites that provide a collection of annual reports, including the *Wall Street Journal Online Annual Reports Service* site. The researcher should also look for information about the industry and market that might be included in these reports.

Sources for histories or profiles include Datamonitor's company profiles,[37] *Hoover's Online*, *Mergent Online*, S&P's *NetAdvantage*, and Gale's *International Directory of Company Histories*[38] (also integrated into *BCRC*). *Hoover's Online* also has videos of CEOs for certain companies. One should listen to them and identify whether they speak to what is going on in the industry or markets, keeping in mind that the CEO is most likely speaking to the company's shareholders and is consequently focusing more on the positive and downplaying any negatives.

If the researcher is required to do a financial analysis for investment purposes, there are several strategies and sources that can be used. This includes looking at analyst reports, which are available in databases like

InvestextPlus and *Global Business Browser*. Advisement services like ValueLine and S&P also provide investment information. Value Line provides a wide range of information, including information on 1,700 stocks through its *Value Line Investment Service*.[39] S&P's *Stock Reports*[40] (also available via S&P's *NetAdvantage*) is another source for investment. Reviewing stock prices is another strategy that should be included when doing a financial analysis. There are various websites that offer current and historical stock prices, including *BigCharts*, *Yahoo! Finance*, and the various stock exchange websites. *Hoover's Online* also offers ten years of fiscal-year high, low, and closing stock prices. The in-depth financial analysis may not be necessary for the researcher who is doing a project for initiating a new business, but it certainly is when doing investment analysis.

One might compare a company's performance and those of its competitors against the industry when doing company research. One way of doing this is through a ratio analysis, comparing a company's financial ratios with those of the industry. According to Rita Moss, "Ratio analysis is the study of relationships between and among various items on financial statements. Each ratio relates one item on the balance sheet (or income statement) with another, or more often, relates one element from the balance sheet to one from the income statement."[41] An example of a ratio is the current ratio, which is the "ratio between all current assets and all current liabilities."[42] A 1:1 ratio indicates evenness between the current assets and current liabilities, while the greater the ratio, the higher the liquidity, or the "company's capacity to pay its debts as they come due."[43] The first step is to get ratios for the individual companies. Two sources for this are *Hoover's Online* and *Mergent Online*. Once these are obtained, the data can be compared to those of the industry. Sources for obtaining industry ratios include D&B's *Industry Norms and Ratios*, *RMA Annual Statement Studies*, Leo Troy's *Almanac of Business and Industrial Financial Ratios*,[44] and *Financial Studies of the Small Business*.[45] Except for *Financial Studies of the Small Business*, these sources provide the industry data arranged by SIC and NAICS codes. *Financial Studies of the Small Business* arranges the information by broad industry names (e.g., Retail Gift Shops, Services Advertising). *Hoover's Online* also includes some industry ratios as part of the information provided on a public company.

If the researcher determines that a company is a subsidiary, then its parent should be identified as well as determining whether it in turn is public or private. A subsidiary might trade independently from the parent. If so, then one can follow the same research strategy for public companies that has already been covered. Whether the subsidiary is public or not, the researcher should still look for information about the parent, as there might be information related to the subsidiary. If it is determined that the parent company is also a subsidiary, then the researcher should follow the process previously discussed.

It will be impossible to find publicly available financial information for a private company in the same depth as for a public company. Company directories often have some financial information, but it is often estimated sales data. Sources and directories that offer some data are *BCRC*, *CareerSearch*, *Hoover's Online*, and *ReferenceUSA*. If a company is a manufacturing company, one might consider looking at the *Thomas Register*[46] (formerly *Thomas Register of American Manufacturers*) to find out which particular product or products it manufactures. One can try to determine if the company has a website with information as well. In addition, there are services like SkyMinder and D&B that sell information about private companies.

Other types of sources that might help for competitive analysis include those that rank businesses and provide market share. Such sources include *Business Rankings Annual*[47] (which is also integrated into *BCRC*), D&B's *Business Rankings*,[48] special issues from *Forbes*[49] and *Fortune*[50] (which annually publish reports such as the top one thousand companies), and *Market Share Reporter*.[51]

Another important strategy for finding information not only for private companies but also for public companies and subsidiaries includes searching for articles about them in trade publications, regional trade/newspapers and publications, and newswires.

It is more difficult to find extensive information for the local small independent business, but one could try searching local newspapers. Sources that provide articles from these types of publications are mentioned above in the section covering industry research. In addition, there is a series called *Book of Lists*[52] published for over sixty metro areas that might be helpful for local research. It identifies the top companies in a metro area by various categories (e.g., "Fastest-Growing Colorado Public Companies") and industries or services (e.g., "Denver-Area Homebuilders").[53] Researchers should search their local library's catalog to determine if such a title is owned. Another strategy might include looking in a local newspaper's want-ads section to see if that company is hiring for certain types of jobs. If one discovers that a company is doing this, it may be possible to identify an industry or market in which there is growth potential because of the types of job advertisements. This strategy could also be included for a public company if one is doing local research. If researchers are doing a project on a theoretical basis (e.g., possibly as part of coursework at a university), managers of local businesses might provide some information. If they think the information gathered will be provided to a competitor, it is likely that they will not be helpful. The bottom line is that if the research is for a private company or a subsidiary, the financial information will be minimal, and more primary research will be necessary.

There are many academic and public libraries worldwide that create company research guides and make them available via the Internet. Many of these guides include both company research strategies and the sources for finding the information. If one wants to find such guides on an academic library website, one can use an Internet search engine to discover them. For instance, the following search strategy for Google would identify many of them: *company research library site:edu*.[54] If the researcher is trying to focus on a particular region, one should include the name of an institution in the region, or the name of a city, for example, *company research library boston site:edu*. Oftentimes these Web-based research guides will include more local sources than one will find in traditional business reference sources.

MARKET RESEARCH

Another step a researcher may need to take when doing business research is to find information about the market. "Potential consumers make up a market, which is people with both the desire and the ability to buy a specific product."[55] Given this, a starting point one might consider for gathering market information is to ask the following questions:

- Does the market have the ability to buy? If so, how much, and who are the customers?
- Does the market have the desire to buy? How are people spending their time and money? Who are these people?[56]

By answering these questions, a researcher may be able to determine not only whether the consumers targeted have the money to purchase a new product or service, but whether the target market might be interested in purchasing it. Sources in which one might discover this type of information include those that have data on income, spending, consumption, demographics, and lifestyles. Some of the information may have been discovered in the process of doing the industry or company research or by searching in a market research database. Even if a market report is found, more research may be required if the report is older than desired, or if the research is for a local market.

The census website provides numerous sources that include income, demographic, and consumer spending statistics. They include *American Factfinder*, the *Consumer Expenditure Survey*, and the *Statistical Abstract of the United States*. Commercial publishers, such as ESRI Business Information Solutions, produce the *Community Sourcebook of Zip Code Demographics*[57] and offer online databases that generate relevant market data.[58] Other sources produced by commercial publishers include Congressional Information Service's (CIS) *SRI*, RDS's *Tablebase*, and those published by New Strategist, including *The Baby Boom*,[59] *Best Customers*,[60] *Household Spending*,[61] and *The Millennials*.[62] These sources provide raw data, requiring the researcher to do an analysis for a project. In addition, market researchers often want more complex information such as consumer psychographics. Psychographics is

> the categorization of a market or other population groups, e.g. consumers, on the basis of psychological—as distinguished from demographic—dimensions, including activities, interests, opinions, values, attitudes, lifestyles, personality traits, such as innovativeness, sophistication, etc.[63]

A source like Standard Rate and Data Service's (SRDS) *Lifestyle Market Analyst*[64] can help with this process. Market research reports might have this information as well. In addition, researchers can use services such as Scarborough Research, Mediamark Research Inc. (MRI), and Simmons Media Group to find and analyze data and develop a report. One should be aware that services like MRI tend not to sell the current data that researchers want to academic libraries.

A very simple approach for doing market research has been presented, but market research is much more complex than herein described. To get a more extensive foundation on market research and the sources available, researchers should refer to books published on the subject, such as *Marketing Information: A Strategic Guide for Business and Finance Libraries*.[65]

OTHER BUSINESS RESEARCH COMPONENTS

Basic strategies for doing the more common types of business research have been presented. Research, however, might take a different twist. For example, there might be an international component needed that was not covered above. A researcher can apply some of the same strategies presented in this chapter if he or she is trying to introduce a new product or service into another country—that is, finding information about the industry, companies, and market. But one needs to include international sources into the strategy, for example, sources that

- provide information about international industries and markets, such as *GLOBUS & NTDB*[66] and *Global Market Information Database*;
- offer information about international companies (specific international company directories include D&B's *Principal International Businesses*[67] and the *Directory of Foreign Firms Operating in the United States*[68]);
- provide country overviews or political risk analysis, including the *CIA World Factbook*, EIU's *Country Commerce*, the Library of Congress's *Country Studies*, and *Political Risk Yearbook Online*; or
- present import and export data, such as *WISERTrade*.

Not all business research involves finding information about industries, companies, or markets as described. For example, accounting researchers may be trying to find information about tax laws or accounting principles and standards that may have been issued by an accounting body authorized to do so. In the case of tax law, a researcher might refer to various tax sources to obtain information, such as the Commerce Clearing House's

(CCH) *Standard Federal Tax Reporter*,[69] the *Internal Revenue Bulletin*,[70] and its permanent edition, the *Internal Revenue Cumulative Bulletin*.[71] Publishers of accounting principles or standards include the American Institute of Certified Public Accountants (AICPA) and the Financial Accounting Standards Board (FASB). A key fee-based database for searching accounting principles or standards is the FASB *Financial Accounting Research System (FARS)*.[72] This database "provides access and retrieval software which aids the student searching for authoritative literature. Similar products are available through vendors such as Research Institute of America (RIA) and CCH."[73] Although AICPA and FASB have websites where information is available, the use of a commercial database like *FARS* allows more effective searching for authoritative publications than is possible at the various websites.[74]

Business researchers may also be searching for articles on how to solve a particular business problem. For example, a management researcher may be trying to identify literature in organizational behavior as it relates to the implementation of new technologies in the workplace. Or an accounting researcher may be trying to find out what has been written in the literature about the application of a particular tax law or accounting principle. This type of research often requires a focus on how to find articles and books on a particular topic.

THE LIBRARY CATALOG

There is an inclination for users to favor Web-based sources over print sources; but there are many times when print sources are valuable to the research process. For example, librarians may choose print over online access when a particular source is too expensive to acquire electronically. Another case might be when a publisher does not provide online access to an item that might be of value in a library. In order to identify such sources in a library, a researcher should include searching the library catalog as part of the research process.

Other chapters in this book note that many Web-based catalogs offer keyword searching. Starting with a keyword search is generally a good strategy because most users are unfamiliar with the rudiments of Library of Congress Subject Headings (LCSH) or other controlled vocabulary. For example, if one wanted to find statistical sources in the ski industry, one could use the following keyword search:

(ski or skis or skiing) and statistics

In this example, "or" is used in the search strategy rather than "ski*." This is done to avoid retrieving many false hits that might include items such as *skin*, *skinner*, and *skinning* in the searchable fields of a bibliographic record. Furthermore, using "statistics" in the search strategy will generally retrieve relevant statistical sources owned by the library because LCSH uses *statistics* as a subheading. The level of success one has will depend on the information provided in local catalog records. For example, in this case a key source that might not be retrieved in most libraries that have it is *Kottke National End of Season Survey*.[75] This is because the bibliographic record will probably only have one subject heading: "Skis and skiing—Economic aspects—United States—Periodicals," as indicated in *WorldCat*, and it won't have statistics in any other searchable field of the record. If a reference librarian feels that other appropriate subject headings might help retrieve pertinent sources, the librarian should make the suggestion to a cataloging librarian. In cases where the reference librarian and the cataloger have good communication and the suggestion makes sense, it is not unknown for the cataloger to include a new subject heading. For example, an additional subject heading for this title in a cataloging record is "Skis and skiing—United States—Statistics—Periodicals."

The library catalog should also be used to identify sources that might have been published by an association. For example, the National Restaurant Association publishes trade-related information on the restaurant industry that librarians might purchase. A keyword search strategy to identify such sources in the library would be the name of the association, that is, "national restaurant association."

Libraries often purchase books published about companies for their collections. If the research being conducted is about a large company, libraries will undoubtedly have books about it. In this case, one can start with a keyword search using the name of the company, for example, Coca-Cola. If the researcher finds the ideal book, then he or she should use the related subject heading to retrieve other books, such as "Coca-

Cola Company—History." The bibliographic record might also reveal other subject headings in a related area of research. For example, a subject heading in a record for a book on Coca-Cola might be "Soft drink industry—United States—History." By pursuing this latter subject heading, one might identify books useful for industry research. In addition, if a researcher needs a company directory in a certain industry, a possible search strategy would be to search on the name of the industry and the additional term "directories." LCSH tends to use "directories" as a subheading for such publications.

Public libraries are inclined to buy books on how to start certain types of businesses or services that academic libraries do not acquire. Researchers who are interested in starting a business should include searching local public library catalogs to identify such handbooks.

The level of success one has in retrieving appropriate titles using the library catalog will depend not only on the search strategy but on the quality of an item's bibliographic record. With the implementation of table-of-contents notes in catalog records, the success rate will be better. The use of appropriate subject headings as well as other searchable fields—such as alternate titles—will also help. Open communication channels between catalogers, bibliographers, and reference librarians can improve the local library catalog's retrieval function.

INTRODUCING USERS TO BUSINESS RESEARCH

There are various methods that librarians employ to help users with business research. One includes purchasing books on how to do business research. Some of these books are textbooks, and others are reference books such as Michael Lavin's *Business Information: How to Find It, How to Use It*[76] and Rita Moss's update of *Strauss's Handbook of Business Information Researchers*.[77] Another strategy is providing Web-based subject research guides. Typical business research guides include those for doing company research, industry research, and market research. A number of libraries also provide Web-based guides for doing research in specific industries, as well as guides for doing research on private companies, subsidiaries, or nonprofits. Some libraries have also developed Web tutorials to help the researcher through different parts of the business research process, such as how to search a particular business database or how to do company research. Many academic libraries have developed research guides related to a course's specific curriculum. In addition to helping business researchers, these various research tools—books, research guides, and tutorials—can be useful to nonbusiness reference librarians assisting them. Finally, there are also reference librarians whose subject specialty is business research. They tend to keep up with business research trends and thus can provide extensive assistance.

In academia, librarians tend to offer library instruction on how to do business research to students and faculty. The instruction ranges from one-hour presentations of course-related information resources to in-depth implementation of business information literacy instruction.[78] More about information literacy in instruction is covered in chapter 9. Suffice it to say that there is evidence that librarians are introducing business students to information literacy, and it "is growing and continuing to develop."

RESEARCH SKILLS WITHIN THE DISCIPLINE

Business curricula do require students to find company, industry, and market information for projects, as well as articles for solving business-related problems. Consequently, in addition to the basic information literacy skills presented in chapter 9, the business researcher should also develop skills related to finding this type of information. For example, researchers should have the following abilities when doing company research:

1. Understand what the differences are among public, private, and non-profit companies, and subsidiaries, and that the type of company one is researching has an effect on the sort and quantity of information that can be found.
2. Know how to determine the type of company one is researching.
3. Know where to go to find information for the specific kinds of companies. This will include comprehending the role of print sources, commercial databases, and the Internet for locating information.
4. Know how to identify competitors and find information about them.

Some skills for doing industry research might include the following:

1. Know how to find SIC and NAICS codes and how and where to use them. Be aware of their strengths and weaknesses.
2. Be aware that there are industry overviews published by major publishers that can be used to obtain information about the competitive, economic, social, regulatory, and technological trends affecting the industry.
3. Learn to identify the sources of any charts published in these overviews, recognize associations mentioned in them, and review the bibliographies for potential leads to other information.
4. Understand that not all industries have the same level of information published about them. Consequently, it is highly likely that there won't be an industry overview published for a niche industry, and if there is, it might be very brief.
5. Be sure to search for trade journal and newspaper articles when doing industry research for either a broad or a niche industry.
6. Recognize that although market research reports are focused on providing information about markets, there will be a discussion about the industry in these reports. For example, a market research report on coffeehouses will include some discussion about the industry.
7. Be aware that although the United States government publishes a wide range of industry statistics, there are limits. For example, they are often not as current as one wants or as detailed as one desires.
8. Realize that if trade associations do gather certain types of statistics that one would like, they may only be available to its members, or one may have to pay to get them. Be aware that some libraries may buy some types of association reports.

Researchers also need to acquire analytical skills. For example, with market research, there were a few questions proposed to begin the research, such as "Does the market have the ability to buy?" When one starts to gather the information to answer this question, such as consumer spending statistics, it will be out of context. The researcher needs to relate this data back to the original question to make it useful.

As with any discipline, the business researcher in general should have discovered a great deal of information from numerous sources. Therefore, one needs to acquire the ability to evaluate sources in order to establish the validity, relevance, and quality of the information discovered. Furthermore, as students go through their business curricula and learn the different concepts presented in their textbooks, they should also be able to tie the research they have done back to these theories.

Success in obtaining business research skills is increased when students can relate these skills to actual course outcomes and where these skills have an effect on their grade. One should refer to articles written by Vicki Feast;[79] Ann Fiegen, Bennett Cherry, and Kathleen Watson;[80] and Martha Cooney and Lorene Hiris[81] to see how they have incorporated Association of College and Research Libraries' (ACRL) information literacy standards into specific courses. The ability to implement research skills in a course requires collaboration between the librarian and course faculty, as well as significant investments of time by both. Furthermore, it will take a student more than one semester or quarter to acquire the skills needed to do a well-thought-out and successful business research project. It is a lifelong process.

CONCLUSION

This chapter has focused on identifying some strategies and sources for doing the most common types of business research: finding company, industry, and market information. In addition, it has shown how some of the sources can be used in the research process.

Business research is a complex process. This is true even if one is researching a big company such as McDonald's, or a broad industry like restaurants, where one knows there is substantial information. Consequently, learning how to do business research is a continuous process, not only because of its complexity, but also because of constant changes occurring in the business environment. For example, technological advancements and globalization lead to the creation of new industries and markets that present challenges for anyone trying to find information about them. If one acquires some basic business research skills and builds on them, one should be able to perform more complex research, employing both basic and creative research strategies to obtain information.

LIST OF RESOURCES

Databases

This is an alphabetical list of the commercial business-related databases mentioned throughout the chapter.

ABI/Inform Global. Ann Arbor, MI: ProQuest Information and Learning Co., 1990s–. proquest.umi.com.

ABI/INFORM Trade & Industry. Ann Arbor, MI: ProQuest Information and Learning, 2001–. proquest.umi.com.

Access World News. Naples, FL: Newsbank, 2005–. infoweb.newsbank.com.

Associations Unlimited. Detroit, MI: Gale Research, 2003–. infotrac .galegroup.com.

Business & Company Resource Center (BCRC). Farmington Hills, MI: Gale Group, 2000–. infotrac.galegroup.com.

Business & Industry. Beachwood, OH: Responsive Database Services, 1900s–. search.rdsinc.com.

Business Source Premier. Ipswich, MA: EBSCO Publishing, 1999–. search .epnet.com.

CareerSearch. Needham, MA: CS Information Technologies, 1998?–. www .careersearch.net.

Country Commerce. New York: Economist Intelligence Unit, 2000–. www.eiu.com.

Datamonitor Business Information Center. London; New York: Datamonitor, 2003–. www.datamonitor.com.

Factiva. New York: Dow Jones & Reuters, 2002–. global.factiva.com.

Global Business Browser. Cambridge, MA: OneSource Information Services. www.onesource.com.

Global Market Information Database. London: Euromonitor, 1999–. www.gmid.euromonitor.com.

GLOBUS & NTDB. Washington, DC: STAT-USA, 1998–. www.stat-usa.gov/ tradtest.nsf.

Hoover's Online: The Business Information Authority. Austin, TX: Hoovers, 1996–. www.hoovers.com.

Investext Plus. Detroit, MI: Gale Group, 1990s. infotrac.galegroup.com/itw.

LexisNexis Academic. Dayton, OH: LexisNexis, Division of Reed Elsevier, 2002–. web.lexis-nexis.com.

LexisNexis Statistical. Bethesda, MD: Congressional Information Service, 1990s–. web.lexis-nexis.com/statuniv.

LIVEDGAR. Washington, DC: GSI, 1996–. www.gsionline.com/livedgar/index .html.

MarketResearch.com. Rockville, MD: MarketResearch.com, ?–. market research.com.

Mergent Online. New York: Mergent Inc., 1998–. www.mergentonline.com.

Political Risk Yearbook Online. East Syracuse, NY: PRS Group, 1999–. www .prsgroup.com.

ReferenceUSA. Omaha, NE: infoUSA Inc., 1999?–. www.referenceusa.com.

Standard & Poor's NetAdvantage. New York: Standard & Poor's, 1998–. www .netadvantage.standardandpoors.com.

TableBase. Beachwood, OH: Responsive Database Services, 19–. search .rdsinc.com.

US Business Browser. Cambridge, MA: OneSource Information Services, 199?–. www.onesource.com.

WISERTrade. Holyoke, MA. 200?–. www.wisertrade.org.

Websites

This is an alphabetical list of association, government, publisher, and Internet search engine websites mentioned throughout the chapter.

American FactFinder. factfinder.census.gov/home/saff/main.html?_lang=en (accessed February 14, 2006).

American Institute of Certified Public Accountants. www.aicpa.org (accessed February 27, 2006).

Annual Survey of Manufacturers. www.census.gov/econ/overview/ma0300.html (accessed February 14, 2006).

BigCharts. bigcharts.marketwatch.com (accessed February 21, 2006).

Business Expenses Survey. www.census.gov/csd/bes (accessed February 14, 2006).

CCH. www.cch.com (accessed February 27, 2006).

CenStats. censtats.census.gov (accessed February 14, 2006).

CIA World Factbook. www.cia.gov/cia/publications/factbook (accessed February 18, 2006).

Cole Information Services. www.coleinformation.com (accessed February 27, 2006).

Construction Statistics. www.census.gov/const/www (accessed February 14, 2006).

Country Studies. lcweb2.loc.gov/frd/cs (accessed February 27, 2006).

D&B. www.dnb.com (accessed February 18, 2006).

Economic Census. www.census.gov/econ/census02 (accessed February 14, 2006).

ESRI Business Information Solutions. www.esribis.com (accessed February 18, 2006).

Financial Accounting Standards Board. www.fasb.org (accessed February 27, 2006).

Forrester Research. www.forrester.com (accessed February 27, 2006).

Frost & Sullivan. www.frost.com (accessed February 27, 2006).

Gartner. www.gartner.com (accessed February 27, 2006).

Google. www.google.com (accessed February 27, 2006).

IBC. www.ibc.org (accessed February 27, 2006).

InfoUSA. www.infousa.com (accessed February 27, 2006).

Jupiter Research. www.jupiterresearch.com (accessed February 27, 2006).

Mediamark Research Inc. www.mediamark.com (accessed February 18, 2006).

Mintel. www.mintel.com (accessed February 27, 2006).

Monthly Retail Trade and Food Services. www.census.gov/mrts/www/mrts.html (accessed February 14, 2006).

Pew Research Center. pewresearch.org (accessed February 27, 2006).

RIA. ria.thomson.com (accessed February 27, 2006).

Scarborough Research. www.scarborough.com (accessed February 18, 2006).

SEC Filings & Forms (EDGAR). www.sec.gov/edgar.shtml (accessed February 16, 2006).

Simmons Media Group. www.simmonsmedia.com (accessed February 18, 2006).

SkyMinder. www.skyminder.com (accessed February 18, 2006).

Statistical Abstract of the United States. www.census.gov/prod/www/statistical abstract.html (accessed February 18, 2006).

United States Census Bureau. www.census.gov (accessed February 14, 2006).

Wall Street Journal Online Annual Reports Service. wsjie.ar.wilink.com (accessed February 16, 2006).

Yahoo! www.yahoo.com (accessed February 27, 2006).

Yahoo! Finance. finance.yahoo.com (accessed February 21, 2006).

NOTES

1. EDGAR Dissemination Service, subscriber information, www.sec.gov/info/edgar/dissemination/rel41.txt (accessed March 11, 2006).

2. Patrick F. Butler, *Business Research Sources: A Reference Navigator* (Boston, MA: Irwin/McGraw-Hill, 1999).

3. Michael R. Lavin, *Business Information: How to Find It, How to Use It*, 2d ed. (Phoenix, AZ: Oryx Press, 1992).

4. Rita W. Moss, *Strauss's Handbook of Business Information: A Guide for Librarians, Students, and Research*, 2nd ed. (Westport, CT: Libraries Unlimited, 2004).

5. *Small Business Sourcebook* (Detroit, MI: Gale Research Co., 1983–).

6. *Encyclopedia of Business Information Sources* (Detroit, MI: Gale Research Co., 1970–).

7. Mary Ellen Bates, *Building & Running a Successful Research Business* (Medford, NJ: Information Today Inc., 2003).

8. United States Small Business Administration, "Marketing Research," www.sba.gov/starting_business/marketing/research.html (accessed February 27, 2006).

9. Julie O'Keefe, "One Step at a Time: A Framework for Introducing Business Students to Basic Sources of Company and Industry Data," *Research Strategies* 16, no. 1 (1998): 72.

10. United States Census Bureau, NAICS, "Ask Dr. NAICS," www.census.gov/epcd/www/drnaics.htm (accessed February 11, 2006).

11. The NAICS search interface is at www.census.gov/epcd/www/naics.html. There will also be a related SIC code generated as a result of the search.

12. *Industry Norms and Key Business Ratios* (New York: Dun & Bradstreet Credit Services, 2004–2005).

13. *RMA Annual Statement Studies* (Philadelphia, PA: Risk Management Association, 2004–2005).

14. Franklin Covey Co., "Business Summary," *Mergent Online*, February 27, 2006.

15. The academic version of *Hoover's Online* is the one referred to in this chapter.

16. Franklin Covey Co., "Industry Information," *Hoover's Online*, February 27, 2006.

17. *Standard & Poor's Industry Surveys* (New York: Standard & Poor's Corp., 2006).

18. These reports are available directly from Datamonitor, and through aggregators like *Business Source Premier* and *BCRC*.

19. *Encyclopedia of American Industries* (Detroit, MI: Gale Research, 1994–).

20. Information about the industries covered by Plunkett's Research can be found at www.plunkettresearch.com. These sources are available in print or by subscription through the publisher's online database.

21. *Encyclopedia of American Industries* (Detroit, MI: Gale Research, 1994–).

22. Paula Berinstein, *Business Statistics on the Web: Find Them Fast—At Little or No Cost* (Medford, NJ: CyberAge Books, 2003).

23. *Statistical Abstract of the United States* (Washington: U.S. Government Printing Office, 1879–).

24. Jennifer C. Boettcher and Leonard M. Gaines, *Industry Research Using the Economic Census: How to Find It, How to Use It* (Westport, CT: Greenwood Press, 2004).

25. *Statistical Reference Index* (Washington, DC: Congressional Information Service, 1980–).

26. *Superstudy of Sports Participation* (Hartsdale, NY: American Sports Data Inc., 1999–).

27. National Coffee Drinking Trends Through . . . (New York: National Coffee Association of U.S.A., 1998).

28. *Restaurant Industry Forecast* (SI: National Restaurant Association, 1990s–).

29. *Encyclopedia of Associations* (Detroit, MI: Gale Research Co., 1961–).

30. *Wall Street Journal* (New York: Dow Jones, 1959–).

31. *New York Times* (New York: Raymond & Co., 1857–).

32. *CorpTech Directory of Technology Companies* (Woburn, MA: Corporate Technology Information Services, 1995–).

33. *Thomas Food & Beverage Market* (Millerton, NY: Grey House Publishing, 2001–).

34. *LexisNexis Corporate Affiliations* (New Providence, NJ: LexisNexis Group, 2002–).

35. *Million Dollar Directory* (Parsippany, NJ: Dun's Marketing Services, 1979–).

36. Rita W. Moss, *Strauss's Handbook of Business Information*, 280.

37. These profiles are available directly from Datamonitor, and through *Business Source Premier*.

38. *International Directory of Company Histories* (Chicago, IL: St. James Press, 1988–).

39. *Value Line Investment Survey* (New York: Value Line Inc., 1936–).

40. *Standard & Poor's Stock Reports: American Stock Exchange, New York Stock Exchange, Nasdaq and Regional Exchanges* (New York: Standard & Poor's, 1998–).

41. Moss, *Strauss's Handbook of Business Information*, 200.

42. Moss, *Strauss's Handbook of Business Information*, 201.

43. Moss, *Strauss's Handbook of Business Information*, 201.

44. Leo Troy, *Almanac of Business and Industrial Financial Ratios* (Englewood Cliffs, NJ: Prentice-Hall, 1900s–).

45. Financial Research Associates, *Financial Studies of the Small Business* (Winter Haven, FL: Financial Research Associates, 1976–).

46. *Thomas Register* (New York: Thomas Industrial Network, 2004).

47. *Business Rankings Annual* (Detroit, MI: Gale Research, 1989–).

48. *D & B Business Rankings* (Bethlehem, PA: Dun & Bradstreet Inc., 1997–).

49. *Forbes* (New York: Forbes Inc., 1918–).

50. *Fortune* (New York: Time Inc., 1930–).

51. *Market Share Reporter* (Detroit, MI: Gale Research, 1991–).

52. Information on how to purchase a "*Book of Lists*" for a particular metro area is available at www.bizjournals.com/bookoflists.

53. *Top 25 Book of Lists* (Denver, CO: Denver Business Journal, 2004–2005), 52, 130.

54. Academic libraries have the stem .edu in their URLs because they are part of an educational institution. Google locates websites with the .edu stem when the searcher uses site:edu in the search strategy.

55. Roger A. Kerin, Steven W. Hartley, Eric N. Berkowitz, and William Rudelius, *Marketing*, 8th ed. (New York: McGraw-Hill/Irwin, 2006), 13.

56. Carol Johnson, "RE: Your Powerpoint on Marketing," personal e-mail, January 3, 2006.

57. *Community Sourcebook of Zip Code Demographics* (Vienna, VA: ESRI, 2004–).

58. To date, ESRI has started offering educational packages that provide demographic and consumer spending reports at the zip code and census tract levels.

59. Cheryl Russell, *The Baby Boom, Americans Born 1946 to 1964* (Ithaca, NY: New Strategist Publications, 2004).

60. *Best Customers: Demographics of Consumer Demand* (Ithaca, NY: New Strategist Publications, 2005).

61. *Household Spending: Who Spends How Much on What* (Ithaca, NY: New Strategist Publications, 1997–).

62. *The Millennials: Americans Born 1977 to 1994* (Ithaca, NY: New Strategist Publications, 2004).

63. Wolfgang J. Koschnick, *Dictionary of Marketing* (Brookfield, VT: Gower, 1995), 490.

64. *Lifestyle Market Analyst* (Wilmette, IL: Standard Rate & Data Service, 1989–).

65. Wendy Diamond and Michael R. Oppenheim, *Marketing Information: A Strategic Guide for Business and Finance Libraries* (NY: Haworth Information Press, 2004).

66. GLOBUS stands for Global Business Opportunities, and NTDB stands for National Trade Data Bank.

67. *Principal International Businesses* (Parsippany, NJ, etc.: Dun & Bradstreet International, 1974–).

68. *Directory of Foreign Firms Operating in the United States* (Millis, MA: Uniworld Business Publications Inc., 2006).

69. *Standard Federal Tax Reporter*, loose-leaf (Chicago, IL: Commerce Clearing House, 1945–).

70. United States. Internal Revenue Service, *Internal Revenue Bulletin* (Washington, DC: Department of the Treasury, Internal Revenue Service, 1953–).

71. United States Internal Revenue Service, *Internal Revenue Cumulative Bulletin* (Washington, DC: Department of the Treasury, Internal Revenue Service, 1969–).

72. *FASB Financial Accounting Research System*, CD-ROM (Norwalk, CT: Financial Accounting Standards Board, 1996–).

73. Nancy A. Cunningham and Sherri C. Anderson, "A Bridge to FARS and Information Literacy for Accounting Undergraduates," *Journal of Business & Finance Librarianship* 10, no. 3 (2005): 10.

74. Cunningham and Anderson, "A Bridge to FARS and Information Literacy for Accounting Undergraduates," 10.

75. *Kottke National End of Season Survey* (Lakewood, CO: The Association, 1994–).

76. Lavin, *Business Information: How to Find It, How to Use It*.

77. Moss, *Strauss's Handbook of Business Information*.

78. Ann M. Fiegen, Bennett Cherry, Kathleen Watson, "Reflections on Collaboration: Learning Outcomes and Information Literacy Assessment in the Business Curriculum," *Reference Services Review* 30, no. 4 (December 2002).

79. Vicki Feast, "Integration of Information Literacy Skills into Business Courses," *Reference Services Review* 31, no. 1 (2003).

80. Fiegen et al., "Reflections on Collaboration."

81. Martha Cooney and Lorene Hiris, "Integrating Information Literacy and Its Assessment into a Graduate Business Course: A Collaborative Framework," *Research Strategies* 19, nos. 3–4 (2003).

6

Government Documents across the Disciplines

Christopher C. Brown

INTRODUCTION

Public documents are issued at every governmental level, from local to international. International documents include issuances from the United Nations and all of its principal organs, as well as other international bodies such as the League of Arab Nations, the European Union, the Organization of American States, the Organisation for Economic Co-operation and Development (OECD), and nongovernmental organizations (NGOs). Federal documents include documents from any particular national government. From the perspective of one's own nation, all other federal documents are "foreign" documents. Subnational documents, such as state documents in the United States, are of importance primarily within one's own state. Local documents, such as county, city, or special government (like regional transportation or economic entities) documents, hold interest for local areas.

This chapter focuses exclusively on federal documents issued by the United States government, although equal space could easily be devoted to documents of any of the previously mentioned governmental jurisdictions. For research on international and foreign documents, an excellent online starting point is the University of Michigan Library Document Center.[1] The works by Andrea Morrison and Peter Hajnal are print resources that provide reliable assistance.[2] Generally, librarians with expertise in one level of documents also have familiarity with other levels as well. Thus librarians with expertise in federal publications are likely also to have a degree of expertise in international, state, and local documents.

U.S. federal publications play a critical role in the research process, and they touch upon every discipline, although not in a balanced manner. There are fewer publications of interest to those in the humanities, and many more for social scientists. Scientists and engineers have a gold mine of documents available to them. Many researchers, and even many librarians, develop a "deer in the headlights" look when they realize that they need to access government documents. This chapter will have been successful if some of that fear is alleviated.

All formats are addressed in this chapter: paper, fiche, and online. While a high percentage of current documents are available online, and while there have been stunning retrospective digitization projects, federally designated depository libraries remain indispensable to researchers within any discipline. This chapter provides researchers and librarians with a general road map and a few specifics to unlock the treasures, along with the guides to find them.

DOCUMENTS IN GENERAL

Throughout the history of the United States, one of the core values has been public access to information. At various stages, government entities have recognized this need and have provided means for dissemination of that information. This section covers the three major document distribution initiatives: the *United States Congressional Serial Set*, the Federal Depository Library Program, and online access.

The Serial Set

The *United States Congressional Serial Set*, as it is now officially known, began with the first session of the Fifteenth Congress (1817)[3] and served as an early form of document distribution.[4] The numbering system started at that time and has run consecutively (serially) since then. Presently, only congressional reports and documents are published in the Serial Set, but in earlier years it contained many executive agency documents, annual reports, and other publications. While congressional hearings have not appeared in the Serial Set for many years, it is not at all unusual to find hearings from the early years of the twentieth century and before. Subjects covered in Serial Set publications include nearly every topic imaginable, including foreign relations and military conflicts, economic conditions, social issues, health and welfare, transportation and infrastructure, food and agriculture, and of course government and politics.

A retrospective collection known as the American State Papers covers the years 1789 through 1838 and includes over six thousand congressional and executive department documents.

Although one could theoretically use the Document Catalog or the *Monthly Catalog* (referenced below) to find items in the Serial Set, it is much more efficient to use the indexes published by the Congressional Information Service (CIS) that provide indexing access to all the Serial Set publications. Since the Serial Set is arranged sequentially by session of Congress, document type, and then document number, these bibliographic finding aids are essential to being able to locate materials. Although the range of document and report numbers appears on the spines of Serial Set volumes from the early years of the twentieth century, there are many exceptions to the rule, and much time can be wasted tracking down desired volumes. Earlier volumes of the Serial Set do not have document and report numbers on the spines, making the "numerical lists" essential.[5] Numerical lists give a breakdown, by Congress and session, of all Senate and House reports and documents with their respective Serial Set volume assignments. As an example, after consulting the numerical lists, we discover that the annual report for the Interstate Commerce Commission from 1914 (H.Doc.1389, Sixty-third Congress, third session) is in Serial Set volume 6873.

Finding aids for Serial Set publications include the *United States Congressional Serial Set Catalog: Numerical Lists and Schedules of Volumes*; the *Preliminary Schedule of Volumes, Reports and Documents of the . . . Congress . . .* ; *Numerical Lists and Schedule of Volumes of the Reports and Documents of the 73rd–96th Congress*; the *CIS U.S. Serial Set Index*; and the *CIS Index to Publications of the United States Congress*.

Larger academic libraries may be able to afford one of two competing full-text products providing high-resolution images of the Serial Set and the American State Papers, one produced by Readex and the other by LexisNexis. These digital collections have the advantage of being searched in one of two ways: (1) searching the bibliographic record of each publication, which allows for the full constraint provided by carefully assigned subjects (this is especially crucial for the complex corporate authors that only the federal government could produce, as well as for subject headings, which control terminology that varies over the centuries but that is able to be collocated with carefully selected subjects) and (2) searching the full text of every publication in the Serial Set. This had never been possible before the advent of the two competing digital Serial Set productions. The technology opens up new research possibilities such as frequency of word/term usage, genealogical research involving discovery of names previously buried in obscure pages of text, retrieval of statistical data, and access to rare color and bitonal maps and plates.

The Federal Depository Library Program

Throughout the history of the United States, Congress has made provisions for the printing and public distribution of the documents of the federal government.[6] The current program, called the Federal Depository Library Program (FDLP), is operated by the Government Printing Office (GPO) and distributes documents to specially designated depository libraries in all fifty states, American Samoa, the Federated States of Micronesia, Guam, the Northern Mariana Islands, Puerto Rico, and the Virgin Islands. Most of these libraries are "selective" libraries, meaning that they receive some, but not all, of the items available for selection through the FDLP. "Regional" libraries receive 100 percent of items distributed through the FDLP, and they have administrative responsibilities over the selective libraries in their respective regions. The designation of depository libraries follows a strict set of guidelines.[7]

Locating a Depository Library

The researcher will want to identify depository libraries that are large enough to suit his or her research needs.[8] Although regional libraries generally have the most complete holdings, some regionals were appointed relatively recently and have not had much time to amass large historic collections. Many larger selective depositories have excellent historic holdings. The best strategy is to contact the designated depository librarian in a given library and ask questions about the extent of the holdings.

Arrangement of Depository Materials in Libraries

Depository libraries may choose to arrange their materials in any way they see fit, provided that they provide public access and that a finding aid of some type be made available. Some depositories choose an integrated approach, where depository materials are integrated into the regular materials. For example, if a public library uses the Dewey Decimal Classification System, documents would be integrated into the stacks along with other materials on the same topic, based on the Dewey classification. Academic libraries, more likely to utilize the Library of Congress Classification System (LC classification), could integrate documents as well. This type of arrangement makes access easier for the user, since all materials are classed together, whether published by the federal government or by commercial publishers. But this approach takes a lot more time and resources on the part of those processing the documents, since materials will need to be bound (many documents are consumer pamphlets or very thin publications), and catalogers will have to assign call numbers in the appropriate classification. Thus smaller libraries are more likely to adopt this approach.

Larger depositories generally segregate government publications, usually into the Superintendent of Documents (SuDocs) classification system, which allows them to manage the collection with greater ease. The SuDocs arrangement is not a subject-based arrangement as the Dewey and LC arrangements are; rather, it is based on the agency that issued the document. As an example, environmental impact statements (EISs) might generally be classed around TD 194.6 under the LC classification. But under the SuDocs scheme, EISs issued by the Department of Agriculture would be shelved under the SuDocs classification A, those from the Environmental Protection Agency would be under EP, those from the Department of the Interior would be under I, and those from the Department of Energy would be under E.[9]

Further, a significant number of depository items were distributed in microfiche format, requiring shelving in microfiche cabinets. Since the fiche are received with SuDocs numbers already imprinted on them, there is little incentive to reclassify them to another classification system. Thus, the serious documents researcher will need to be thoroughly familiar with the SuDocs classification system and be prepared to use microfiche. Fortunately, new digital microform scanners make it more tolerable to use fiche, since documents on fiche are generally not subject to copyright and may be copied in digital format and later converted via optical character recognition (OCR) software to a word-searchable document.

The most helpful work for gaining familiarity with the SuDocs system is the *Guide to U.S. Government Publications*. Reference librarians often refer to this work as "Andriot," after the original editor, John Andriot. For historic (legacy) documents, use the *United States Government Manual* and Andriot to familiarize yourself with the years of an agency's existence, and research the SuDocs classes accordingly. Andriot serves the researcher as the best roadmap through any major federal document collection.

One of the most useful features of using Andriot is the ability to trace the history of a SuDocs stem. Take, for example, the *Annual Report of the Governor of the Panama Canal*. Andriot traces the four SuDocs stems under which this report was classed in its history:

W 79.1:   Issued under the War Dept., 1915–1947
M 115.1:   Issued under the Military Establishment, 1948
D 113.1:   Issued under the Defense Dept., 1949
PaC 1.1:   Issued under the Panama Canal Zone, 1950–51

Be aware that local policy sometimes prescribes deviation from Andriot, however, so that serial titles can be shelved together.

The researcher will want to befriend the documents librarian in his or her local depository library. If the library is a research library of considerable size, such as a regional library or a large selective library, it is very likely that large portions of the documents collection have never been cataloged electronically. One of the best-kept secrets of large federal depository libraries is that many older documents may be owned by the library but not represented in their online catalog. This happens for several reasons: (1) older card catalog entries have not yet been converted to online format, (2) large depositories have so many documents that it takes time and resources to complete the task, and (3) the U.S. Congressional Serial

Set is owned in part by many libraries but is usually not cataloged. Users will need to rely on Serial Set indexes as mentioned previously.

We will first discuss general finding aids for federal documents, and then we will focus on several specific but popular topics within the documents world. The special topics are legislative research, statistical materials, and technical reports.

Essential Finding Aids

The bibliographic record of the earliest years of federal publications is more or less adequately covered in Poore's *A Descriptive Catalogue of the Government Publications of the United States, September 5, 1774–March 4, 1881* and Ames's *Comprehensive Index to the Publications of the United States Government: 1881–1893*.[10]

The *Checklist of United States Public Documents* is a retrospective work that imputes the SuDocs classification system, developed between 1895 and 1903, to documents published from 1789 to 1909. The subject index was never published, so users need to be very familiar with the Su-Docs classification.

The *Catalogue of the Public Documents*, commonly known as the Documents Catalog, served as the comprehensive index required by the Printing Act of 1895. It provides full bibliographic details, including Serial Set numbers, but does not include any SuDocs numbers.

The *Monthly Catalog of United States Government Publications*, as it is known today, is essential to documents research, even in this day of online documents and online catalogs, and will continue to be so for years to come. The diligent researcher will want to be immersed in the *Monthly Catalog* to ensure that all resources are found.

The *Monthly Catalog* has evolved over time. When it began in 1895, the intent was that it serve as a publication list, not as a bibliographic authority. The Documents Catalog serves as a better authority during these early years. It was not until 1924 that SuDocs numbers were included, so researchers will need to consult other sources to determine the classification for documents published up to that date. The arrangement of entries varied over the years. From 1895 through August 1947, there is a hierarchical arrangement; from September 1947 through June 1976, the arrangement is alphabetical by issuing office; and from July 1976 onward, the arrangement is in SuDocs order.[11] The title of the *Monthly Catalog* has varied over the years: *Catalogue of United States Public Documents* (1895–1907); *Monthly Catalogue, United States Public Documents* (1907–1933); *Monthly Catalog, United States Public Documents* (1933–1939); *United States Government Publications Monthly Catalog* (1940–1951); and *Monthly Catalog of United States Government Publications* (1951–present).

In early 2006, the GPO released a retooled *Catalog of U.S. Government Publications* (*CGP*).[12] Unlike its predecessor, which contained only recently created catalog records, the new *CGP* is a true integrated library system. Records from July 1976 (the beginning of electronic cataloging of U.S. government publications) to present are in the *CGP*, with older records being added on a regular basis. There is reason to believe that the *CGP* will improve in accuracy and completeness as the years go by.

One other source should not be overlooked for locating older federal documents. The Online Computer Library Center's (OCLC) *WorldCat* bibliographic database serves as a union catalog and is especially useful for bibliographic verification of older documents.

Online Distribution and Access

Federal documents are increasingly available in electronic format via the Internet. This presents many conveniences as well as challenges. It is often not necessary to travel to a depository library to read and use the full text of government publications, given the high proportion available on the Internet. With this kind of ubiquitous availability, virtually any library can become a depository library if it chooses to add document records to its local online catalog.

Government entities generally post current consumer publications, annual reports, statistical data, technical reports, research publications, and serial (periodical) publications on their websites. Maps and geospatial data, searchable databases of bibliographic records, and dynamic databases of earth and space data can also be found, to mention only a few categories.

Online access does not solve all problems. The negative aspects to online distribution must be clearly understood.

1. Not all documents are online. Although a majority of documents released through the Federal Depository Library Program are online (over 90 percent), most older documents are not yet available online.
2. Not all online documents are cataloged by the GPO catalogers. Reasons for this include the ephemeral nature of some online publications, the ever-increasing number of online documents, the opaque nature of documents buried within "deep Web" or hidden Internet databases,[13] and fugitive documents (see number 4 below).
3. There are procedural impediments to some documents being available online. Congressional hearings, for example, are only published online if they are released to the GPO by the committee. Each committee establishes its own rules. Thus, many recent hearings are only available in tangible formats (paper or microfiche).
4. Some online documents are never properly identified and cataloged. These "fugitive documents" are a cause of great concern in the documents community, and much current discussion is being given to the topic. The danger is that they may disappear, never to be seen again.
5. Some depository library online catalogs are better than others. This is especially the case when discussing online availability. Most modern online catalogs allow for users to follow hyperlinks, but others make this task difficult.
6. Document URLs often change. The GPO has taken many steps to deal with this. Persistent URLs (PURLs) theoretically point to the current active version of a document. Many times, however, PURLs go bad and need to be updated. Current catalog procedures call for GPO catalogers to capture and archive the online content as they catalog it. However, there was a period of several years when this was not done, and these documents disappear at an alarming rate.

One of four approaches can be used to locate online documents:

- Research strategy number 1. Use a hierarchical list of government agencies to navigate the many agencies. The GPO provides a Web page for doing just that: www.gpoaccess.gov/agencies.html. The excellent GPO-partner site, Louisiana State University Library, is also a recommended starting point: www.lib.lsu.edu/gov/fedgov.html.

- Research strategy number 2. Use a federal government Web portal to locate information. Firstgov.gov (www.firstgov.gov) and Google Uncle Sam (www.google.com/unclesam) are examples of such portals.
- Research strategy number 3. Use a library online catalog to find online documents. The advantage here is that library catalogs employ controlled vocabulary, bringing control to the uncontrolled Web world. The disadvantage is that even the largest research library catalogs have only a fraction of online government publications represented in their catalogs. To locate a depository, start with the GPO's "Locate a Depository Library" Web page: www.gpoaccess.gov/libraries.html. This can identify selective and regional depository libraries by state, area code, or congressional district. Links are provided to library websites so that the local online catalog can be searched.
- Research strategy number 4. Use a search engine such as Google in a focused manner to locate specific online publications. First, find the Internet domain of the agency. This can be done using a search engine such as Google or by consulting the GPO's list of government servers: www.access.gpo.gov/su_docs/fdlp/tools/domains.html.

For example, if looking for the Biological Resources division of the United States Geological Survey, a Google search will reveal that the root URL is biology.usgs.gov. Next, do a site-specific search of this site, using Google to constrain the search to this website. To locate documents concerning global warming from this website, enter this in the Google search box: *site:biology.usgs.gov global warming*.

As another example, to find information from the State Department concerning arms control, enter this into the Google search box: *site:state.gov arms control*. This restriction on the Google results retrieves only State Department Web pages. An unrestricted search retrieves British sites (.uk), organizational sites (.org), Australian sites (.au), and dozens of others.

We will now examine three categories of documents that are of interest to many disciplines and yet have their own challenges: legislative research, statistics, and technical reports.

LEGISLATIVE RESEARCH

There are many reasons for doing legislative research. Social scientists often want to see the motivations for legislation, as well as the outcomes. Attorneys generally desire to research the legislative intent—the reason why a law was passed. As noted in the chapter on historical research, historians value this kind of information as primary source material.

The purpose of this section is not to instruct in the steps legislation takes—"how a law is made."[14] Rather, it is to call attention to the documentary trail left behind as federal legislation goes through the process. Rather than taking a time-line approach, let us take an approach that groups materials by the likely arrangement in depository libraries.

Bills

In recent years, bill text is most efficiently retrieved from one of two freely available online sources: GPO Access, www.gpoaccess.gov/bills/browse.html, with bills from 1993 (103rd Congress) onward, and the Library of Congress's Thomas site, thomas.loc.gov/home/bills_res.html, with bills from 1989 (101st Congress) onward.

Reports and Documents

Congressional reports and documents (used as technical terms, not just generic reports or documents) are handled together here because they are eventually published in the Serial Set. The reports tend to be more interesting in terms of legislative histories, since some of them give the background of the bill and the need for the legislation (legislative intent). Documents connected with legislation are very often brief presidential statements on the day of signing the bill into law, but there are some notable exceptions. In most depository libraries, a SuDocs number will be necessary if the reports and documents are kept in "slip" format (paper or fiche). In those cases, the SuDocs numbers will follow the format depicted in table 6.1.

For reports and documents appearing in the Serial Set, the SuDocs numbers as above are of little help. Since the Serial Set is a sequentially numbered set, it is helpful to have the volume number in which the report

Table 6.1.   Report and Document Series in the Serial Set

Y 1.1/3:[Congress-no.]	Senate Documents
Y 1.1/4:[Congress-no.]	Senate Executive Documents
Y 1.1/5:[Congress-no.]	Senate Reports
Y 1.1/6:[Congress-no.]	Senate Executive Reports
Y 1.1/7:[Congress-no.]	House Documents
Y 1.1/8:[Congress-no.]	House Reports

or document appears. To do this, you will need to use the "numerical lists" as mentioned at the beginning of this chapter.

Hearings and Committee Prints

These two publication types are treated together because they do not generally show up in the Serial Set. In most depository libraries, they are shelved in the "Y 4" SuDocs classification. Hearings are important because they may contain background testimony relevant to topics within the legislation, as well as statistics, maps, submitted research, and many other relevant materials. They are among the most heavily circulated depository items, and among the most frequently accessed online.[15] Committee prints often present background studies relevant to the legislation at hand. They may not assist with legislative intent, but when they exist, they are a rich source of research.

Congressional Record

The *Congressional Record* contains a transcript of the debates on the floors of the U.S. Senate and House of Representatives. Relevant information can often be gleaned from these proceedings. The title of the *Congressional Record* has changed over the years: *Journals of the Continental Congress* (1774–1789); *The Debates and Proceedings in the Congress of the United States* (1789–1824); *Register of Debates in Congress* (1825–1837); *The Congressional Globe* (1834–1873); *Congressional Record: Proceedings and Debates of the . . . Congress* (1874–present).

To simplify the legislative history research process, there are several suggested research strategies.

- Research strategy number 5. Use Thomas. Published online by the Library of Congress, thomas.loc.gov, Thomas contains many databases relevant to legislative research. Bill summary and status information are available from the Ninety-third Congress (1973) to present. A most valuable feature is the legislative histories. Libraries and users that do not have access to the more expensive products such as *LexisNexis Congressional* will find this free resource very useful. Legislative histories can be searched by bill number, or by public law number (in cases where the legislation ended up being signed into law). It should be noted that the phrase "Bill Summary & Status" is used in Thomas, since the listing includes more than the legislative history; it includes all floor and committee actions. From the 104th Congress (1995) onward, links are provided in the summaries to congressional reports. There is generally no reference made to published hearings in Thomas. Users will need to use the Congressional Information Service Indexes to gather that information.
- Research strategy number 6. Use *LexisNexis Congressional* (or the print CIS Indexes). Thomas gives background information directly related to the bill under consideration, but *LexisNexis Congressional* provides a broader view, considering work done in prior congresses on the same topic. This is not officially connected with the formal legislative history, but the statistical submissions and even oral testimony may be highly relevant to the social climate surrounding a bill.
- Research strategy number 7. Look for legislative histories already published. Major pieces of legislation may have had entire works of legislative history completed, sitting on library shelves. For example, searching many online catalogs by keyword often yields the desired results: *superfund act and legislative history*, *civil rights act and legislative history*, or *americans with disabilities act and legislative history*.

STATISTICAL RESEARCH

As noted in their respective chapters, statistics are used by scientists, engineers, social scientists, and business researchers for various reasons. Not surprisingly, U.S. federal statistics are often sought after for their value as primary research data.[16] Statistical research is challenging for several reasons. Discovery is fully reliant on descriptive metadata. Metadata refers to the information about the data contained in the statistical series. Unlike full-text searching, which can be constrained by the use of Boolean (and/or/not) and proximity (nearness of one term to another) operators, statistical series are completely at the mercy of the existence and quality of metadata, or perhaps titles or abstracts if they are adequate. Research is also challenging because statistical series may be issued by any number of entities for various reasons. It is often unclear what governmental entity is likely to issue the needed statistics.

General Statistics

The most basic research question in any kind of statistical research is who (what entity) issues the desired kinds of statistics. For example, someone looking for the number of passengers traveling through Denver International Airport must ask the most basic of questions: Who is likely to issue these statistics? Could these statistics be gathered from public companies, such as the airlines? Or is it a better research strategy to get statistics from a governmental entity? In this case, both the Bureau of Transportation Statistics and the Federal Aviation Administration have this statistic.

In another example, if one is looking for statistics on fish production, there are potentially many entities releasing such statistics. It is helpful to think in broad categories by type of entity likely to release the desired statistics (see table 6.2).

Statistical compilations provide the best starting point for both novice users of statistics and the expert. The *Statistical Abstract of the United States*, published since 1878, is available in most libraries. Nearly all issues are available online through the Census Bureau. The historical compilation, *Historical Statistics of the United States, Colonial Times to 1970*, is also available in print and online. Compilations can also be generally found for most categories of statistics.

The Congressional Information Service publishes several indispensable indexes to statistical information. The *Index to International Statistics* (*IIS*) covers statistics issued by foreign governments or international organizations. The *American Statistics Index* (*ASI*) covers statistics issued

Table 6.2. Examples of Statistical Resources from Various Entities

Category	Fish Production Statistics Issued by (examples)
International Organizations	Food and Agriculture Organization
	World Trade Organization
Foreign Governments	Government of Japan, Ministry of Agriculture, Forestry and Fisheries
United States Government	U.S. Department of Agriculture
	U.S. Department of Commerce
	U.S. Department of Labor
Associations	American Institute of Food Distribution
Research Institutes	International Food Policy Research Institute
State Governments	Florida Department of Agriculture and Consumer Services
University Research Institutes	University of Florida, Bureau of Economic and Business Research

by the U.S. government. The *Statistical Reference Index* (*SRI*) covers statistics issued by associations, business organizations, commercial publishers, independent research organizations, state governments, and university research centers. All three of these products are available online via *LexisNexis Statistical*. For the scope of this chapter, the *American Statistics Index* is the relevant tool.

ASI indexes federally issued statistics at the table level. In other words, users can search for information contained in the tables themselves, not merely a more general level such as journal article title. *ASI* gives the SuDocs number for each item as well as full bibliographic information. This should be sufficient to locate the materials in depository libraries.

The following research strategies are suggested for tracking down federal statistics:

- Research strategy number 8. Use FedStats, www.fedstats.gov, to find current federal government statistics. This portal website provides descriptions and links to statistical programs of over one hundred federal agencies.
- Research strategy number 9. For historical statistics, try using an online library catalog to search by Library of Congress Subject Heading. It is helpful to use the free-floating subdivisions of the LC headings; in our case, "statistics" is a relevant subdivision. Examples of

use of free-floating subdivisions within LC headings include the following:

Rice—United States—Milling—Statistics

Automobiles—Statistics

Income distribution—United States—Statistics

If exact headings are not known, most online catalogs allow users to search by keyword. Using this strategy, it is possible to find statistics published by or about federal entities, for example, *works progress administration and statistics*, *work projects administration and statistics*, and *general accounting office and statistics*.

- Research strategy number 10. Don't forget about the Serial Set. The Serial Set (mentioned above) is a valuable source of statistical information. In earlier years, executive agency annual reports usually published official statistics for each year. In recent years, congressional reports often are replete with statistics related to the background of proposed legislative actions.

Census Research in Depository Libraries

Census materials are useful for varied reasons. Business students often desire the most recent statistics, only rarely requiring historical studies. Economists and other social scientists are often interested in historical censuses, studying changes in population and socioeconomic trends over time.

There are many censuses taken in the United States, but the focus of this section is on the decennial censuses of population and housing, both historic and recent. The resources mentioned here will guide the user in locating and using all census series including agriculture, manufacturing, governments, business, and industry. The Census Bureau website, www.census.gov, has some of the most helpful resources for understanding both historical and recent census materials.

At the outset, we must distinguish the two basis kinds of censuses, the decennial census of population and housing (taken in years ending in 0) and the economic census (taken in years ending in 2 and 7).

Navigating early census materials can be challenging. While the *Bureau of the Census Catalog of Publications, 1790–1972* and the *Catalog of United States Census Publications, 1790–1945*, published by the Bureau of the Census and the Library of Congress respectively, are helpful,

Dubester's U.S. Census Bibliography, a reworking of the *Catalog of United States Census Publications, 1790–1945*, is the single best source for identifying these older reports. This source provides SuDocs class numbers, as well as Library of Congress classes for most items. Reports in the Serial Set are noted as well, with reference to the Serial Set number. This reference work is indispensable for older census reports.

As mandated by the U.S. Constitution, population counts are required every ten years. Just to make research challenging, no two decennial censuses are alike because they all asked different questions. The recent work *Measuring America: The Decennial Censuses from 1790 to 2000* is extremely helpful. Several sources provide in-depth information about the differences in these censuses.[17]

Recent online data and scanning initiatives bring older census data directly to the user. The Census Bureau has digitally scanned selected historical decennial reports, which are available here: www.census.gov/population/www/censusdata/hiscendata.html. Included in this digital initiative are historical census reports in PDF format from 1790 to 1860, www.census.gov/prod/www/abs/decennial. The Historical Census Browser hosted by the University of Virginia Library, fisher.lib.virginia.edu/collections/stats/histcensus, allows users to produce customized data tables and ratios using historical decennial census data.

In terms of using census materials in depository libraries, many libraries choose to shelve their decennial census materials together, perhaps under the Library of Congress classification HA 201. But for depositories that use the SuDocs classification, the chart in table 6.3 is helpful.

Searching online catalogs of depository libraries generally yields a gold mine of print materials. Useful Library of Congress Subject Headings include the following:

United States—Census, 10th, 1880
United States—Census, 11th, 1890
Colorado—Census, 1950
New York—Census, 1790

The historic decennial censuses of population and housing have recently been digitized by the U.S. Census Bureau and are available online at www.census.gov/prod/www/abs/decennial.

Table 6.3. SuDocs Classifications for U.S. Federal Censuses

Year: Census	SuDocs Classification
1790: First Census	I 2
1800: Second Census	I 3
1810: Third Census	I 4
1820: Fourth Census	I 5
1830: Fifth Census	I 6
1840: Sixth Census	I 7
1850: Seventh Census	I 8
1860: Eighth Census	I 9
1870: Ninth Census	I 10
1880: Tenth Census	I 11
1890: Eleventh Census	I 12
1900: Twelfth Census	I 13
1910: Thirteenth Census	C 3.14–C 3.17
1920: Fourteenth Census	C 3.28
1930: Fifteenth Census	C 3.37
1940: Sixteenth Census	C 3.940
1950: Seventeenth Census	C 3.950
1960: Eighteenth Census	C 3.223
1970: Nineteenth Census	C 3.223
1980: Twentieth Census	C 3.223
1990: Twenty-first Census	C 3.223
2000: Twenty-second Census	C 3.223

Economic and business census data are not as straightforward, but the following are among the many subject headings that may be employed:

United States—Economic conditions—Statistics
Economic indicators—United States
Prices—United States
Income—United States—Statistics

Recent census data are readily available from American Factfinder, accessed via the census website. American Factfinder can retrieve data from the 1990 and 2000 censuses, recent American Community Survey data, as well as the 1997 and 2002 economic censuses.

As mentioned in the chapter on the social sciences, statistical data centers such as the Inter-university Consortium for Political and Social Research (ICPSR) can be a rich data source for government data. Full access to these data sets is limited to those from member academic institutions.

There may be limited access for nonmembers. Data sets originally published in print format, such as past decennial censuses, have been digitized for use in statistical analysis software. These data sets provide researchers with longitudinal time series data otherwise difficult to obtain in digital formats.

TECHNICAL REPORTS

As noted in the chapter on engineering, technical reports are of special interest to the engineering fields. Technical reports are challenging for a number of reasons: (1) the sheer number of reports is mind-boggling; (2) often referred to as "gray literature," many technical reports were not issued through the FDLP and are considered as "nondepository" materials, and as such, they are likely to be held in only the largest and most specialized depositories; (3) in the online environment, many technical reports are buried in the "hidden Internet" (also known as the deep Web or invisible Web); direct Web searches do not retrieve these documents, so the researcher needs to employ the indirect search techniques described below.

Because technical reports are so numerous, it is highly likely that these collections will be largely uncataloged. That is, individual titles will not be searchable in the online library catalog. To get around this, users should search major bibliographies, many of which are in print or online; identify desired reports; and then contact the documents department of a major university.

Older Technical Reports

The National Technical Information Service (NTIS) is a centralized resource for government-funded reports covering science, technology, and business. NTIS reports are indexed in the print sources noted below as well as in the NTIS bibliographic database available via subscription from numerous vendors. The official NTIS website, www.ntis.gov, also provides indexing for NTIS reports from 1990 onward, as well as the full text of selected reports. Although free, this search engine lacks the power and sophistication most users require. The print index to NTIS reports,

Government Reports Announcements and Index (GRA&I), had several previous titles since 1946, as noted here: *Bibliography of Scientific and Industrial Reports* (January 11, 1946–June 1949); *Bibliography of Technical Reports* (July 1949–September 1954); *U.S. Government Research Reports* (October 1954–December 1964); *U.S. Government Research & Development Reports* (1965–1971); and *Government Reports Announcements & Index* (1965–1996).

NTIS serves as the official repository for several defunct federal agencies. The Bureau of Mines existed under the Department of the Interior from 1910 until 1996. NTIS now maintains their entire collection of publications. If a desired item cannot be located in a nearby depository library, it may be ordered at a reasonable price through NTIS. Other such specialty collections include several Department of Agriculture agencies, EPA Superfund publications, National Transportation Safety Board (NTSB) reports, and Toxic Substances Control Act unpublished reports.

- Research strategy number 11. Check the *Government Reports Announcements & Index* (or its online equivalent, the NTIS database). Because of the broad subject coverage of the NTIS indexes, this should be the first place to check for technical reports. Subjects include administration and management, aeronautics and aerodynamics, agriculture and food, astronomy and astrophysics, atmospheric sciences, behavior and society, biomedical technology, building industry technology, business and economics, chemistry, civil engineering, combustion and propellants, communication, computers and information theory, detection and countermeasures, electrotechnology, energy, environmental pollution, government inventions for licensing, health care, industrial and mechanical engineering, library and information sciences, manufacturing technology, materials sciences, space technology, transportation, and urban and regional development.
- Research strategy number 12. Check the online catalog of a large depository library. Even though, as already noted, it is likely that not all technical reports will be cataloged, many will be. Don't overlook the obvious starting point, the research library catalog. In some cases it will be necessary to contact the depository librarian so that uncataloged holdings can be checked.

- Research strategy number 13. In the case of historical technical reports, check an index to the Serial Set. Hundreds of patents are in older Serial Set volumes. Before the digital Serial Set initiatives, it was not feasible to forage through the paper indexes to the Serial Set for technical patents, but the online projects have changed all that. Either the Readex or the LexisNexis digital Serial Set collections can be easily searched for early patents or other technical reports.
- Research strategy number 14. Check Andriot for relevant technical report series. Technical reports exist in nearly every SuDocs classification area, but major report series can be found in Andriot under the following classification sections: A (Agriculture), C (Commerce), E (Energy), I (Interior), NAS (National Aeronautics and Space Administration), TD (Transportation), and Y 3 (Congressional Commissions).

Online Technical Reports

Scientists and engineers were the early developers of Web hosting of technical reports. The Web is replete with many terabytes of technical reports. Many of these are issued by or in conjunction with U.S. government agencies.

- Research strategy number 15. Use a technical report portal to discover federal agencies that publish technical reports. SciTechResources.gov, www.scitech.gov, is a government portal that points to reports from many agencies including Agriculture, Commerce, Defense, Education, Energy, Health and Human Services, Justice, State, Interior, Transportation, Environmental Protection, NASA, and the National Science Foundation.
  Below are some of these databases:
  1. National Technical Information Service (NTIS) Reports (1946 to date) is freely available from 1990 to present from www.ntis.gov. Indexing and abstracting for previous years are available from numerous commercial vendors. NTIS reports are government sponsored and cover a broad variety of topics, not just "technology," but also many areas of social science and business interest. NTIS reports are sporadically held in many depository libraries,

very often on microfiche. Engineering libraries also generally have extensive NTIS fiche holdings.

2. Energy Citations Database, www.osti.gov/energycitations (1948 to date), contains indexing of technical reports, journal articles, and other document types from 1948, with full text more likely available in recent years.

3. NASA Technical Reports Server, ntrs.nasa.gov, provides searching across many NASA technical reports servers, with reports available in full text as far back as the early days of the National Advisory Committee for Aeronautics (NACA) (1915–1958).

4. Environmental Protection Agency (EPA) Publications page, www .epa.gov/epahome/publications.htm, can be helpful in navigating the complex EPA website.

5. Defense Technical Information Center (DTIC) Technical Report Collection, stinet.dtic.mil, provides access to the Defense Department's technical reports collections, with links to searching many other technical report collections as well.

6. The United States Patent and Trademark Office (USPTO) Patents Database, www.uspto.gov/patft, can be searched by keyword or any bibliographic item from 1976 to present. Older patents are retrievable online only if the patent or classification number is known.

7. The United States Geological Survey (USGS) Publications Warehouse, infotrek.er.usgs.gov/pubs, provides coverage from 1882, with full text more likely for recent publications.

8. E-Print Network is available at www.osti.gov/eprints. E-prints are scientific preprints online. In the scientific disciplines, it is important to vet research data and hypotheses so that they can be confirmed or contradicted by the research of others. Preprints are essential to this process.

9. The congressional Office of Technical Assessment closed in 1995, but its twenty-three-year legacy technical reports are available online at www.wws.princeton.edu/ota.

• Research strategy number 16. Use Google Scholar, scholar.google.com, to locate government technical reports. If looking for reports on soil conditions in Colorado, try one of the following searches in Google Scholar: *technical report soil colorado* or *report soil colorado site:gov*.

- Research strategy number 17. Use a "metasite" to discover technical report sites. One such example is the University of Maryland Libraries' Virtual Technical Reports Center, www.lib.umd.edu/ENGIN/TechReports/Virtual-TechReports.html. This is a fairly exhaustive listing of e-prints, preprints, and technical reports available online.

Federal documents are increasingly available online, with retrospective scanning projects providing access to many older publications. However, the researcher will be dependent on print publications and federal depository libraries for many years to come. Hopefully this chapter has assisted in making these publications more accessible to those from all academic disciplines.

CONCLUSION

Although there is a lot to know when it comes to U.S. federal publications, numerous available finding aids and helpful documents librarians are available to navigate users through the complex world of documents. The topics covered in this chapter by no means exhaust the challenges researchers face when delving into federal publications. The researcher should keep in mind that even though it is true that "not everything is on the Internet," one can usually find a Web-based guide produced by a librarian that will provide adequate instruction. This strategy is helpful for topics not covered in this chapter such as maps and geographic information systems (GIS) technologies, court cases, statutes, regulations, treaties, declassified documents, Foreign Broadcast Information Service (FBIS) and Joint Publications Research Service (JPRS) publications, and patents. Hopefully this chapter has taken some of the fear out of federal documents for some.

SELECTED RESOURCES

The resources listed below include publications mentioned in this chapter, both federal publications and commercial publications. SuDocs numbers are noted in parentheses for federal publications.

American Statistics Index. Washington, DC: Congressional Information Service. Available online through LexisNexis Statistical.

Ames, John G. (John Griffith). *Comprehensive Index to the Publications of the United States Government: 1881–1893*. Washington, DC: U.S. Government Printing Office, 1905. (58th Cong., 2nd Sess. House. Doc. 754, Serial 4745–46).

Bibliography of Scientific and Industrial Reports. Washington, DC: Office of Technical Services, U.S. Department of Commerce, January 11, 1946–June 1949. (C 35.7: and C 41.21:).

Bibliography of Technical Reports. Washington, DC: Department of Commerce, July 1949–September 1954. (C 41.21:).

Catalogue of the Public Documents of the 53d to 76th Congress and of All Departments of the Government of the United States for the Period from March 4, 1893, to December 31, 1940. 25 vols. Washington, DC: U.S. Government Printing Office, 1896–1945. (GP 3.6:).

Catalogue of United States Public Documents. Issued monthly by the Superintendent of Documents. Washington, DC: U.S. Government Printing Office, 1895–1907. (GP 3.8:).

Checklist of United States Public Documents, 1789–1909: Congressional to Close of Sixtieth Congress, Departmental to End of Calendar Year 1909. Compiled under the direction of the Superintendent of Documents. 3rd ed., rev., and enl. Washington, DC: GPO, 1911. (GP 3.2:C 41/2). www.evergreen.edu/library/govdocs/tools/1909checklist/index.html (accessed April 14, 2006).

Congressional Information Service. *CIS Index to Publications of the United States Congress*. Vol. 1–. Washington, DC: Congressional Information Service, January 1970–. Available online as part of LexisNexis Congressional. Volumes contain abstracts, indexes, and legislative histories from 1970 to present.

Congressional Information Service. *CIS U.S. Serial Set Index*. 13 vols., 40 parts. Washington, DC: Congressional Information Service, 1975–. Available online as part of LexisNexis Congressional. Volumes provide indexing of Serial Set and American State Papers contents from 1789 to 1969.

Cook, Kevin L. *Dubester's U.S. Census Bibliography with SuDocs Class Numbers and Indexes*. Englewood, CO: Libraries Unlimited, 1986.

Government Reports Announcements & Index. Springfield, VA: U.S. Department of Commerce, National Technical Information Service, 1965–1996. (C 51.9/3:).

Guide to U.S. Government Publications. McLean, VA: Documents Index; Detroit: Thomson Gale, 1973–. Published annually.

Historical Statistics of the United States, Colonial Times to 1970. Washington, DC: U.S. Department of Commerce, Bureau of the Census, 1975. (C 3.134/2:H 62/789-970/). www.census.gov/prod/www/abs/statab.html (accessed April 14, 2006).

Library of Congress, Census Library Project. *Catalog of United States Census Publications, 1790–1945*. Washington, DC: U.S. Government Printing Office, 1950. (C 3.2:P 96/8/790-945).

Measuring America: The Decennial Censuses from 1790 to 2000. Washington, DC: U.S. Department of Commerce, Economics and Statistics Administration, U.S. Census Bureau, for sale by the Superintendent of Documents, U.S. Government Printing Office, 2002. (C 3.2:M 46/2). www.census.gov/prod/ 2002pubs/pol02-ma.pdf (accessed April 14, 2006).

Monthly Catalog of United States Government Publications. Issued by the Superintendent of Documents. Washington, DC: U.S. Government Printing Office, 1951–.

Monthly Catalog, United States Public Documents. Issued by the Superintendent of Documents. Washington, DC: U.S. Government Printing Office, 1933–1939.

Monthly Catalogue, United States Public Documents. Issued by the Superintendent of Documents. Washington, DC: U.S. Government Printing Office, 1907–1933.

Numerical Lists and Schedule of Volumes of the Reports and Documents of the 73rd–96th Congress. Compiled under the direction of the Superintendent of Documents. Washington, DC: U.S. Government Printing Office, for sale by the Superintendent of Documents, U.S. Government Printing Office, 1934–1982. (GP 3.7/2:). The 1970 to current volumes are available online from the Law Librarian's Society of Washington, DC, www.llsdc.org/sourcebook/sch-v.htm (April 14, 2006).

Poore, Benjamin Perley. *A Descriptive Catalogue of the Government Publications of the United States, September 5, 1774–March 4, 1881*. Washington, DC: Government Printing Office, 1885. (48th Cong., 2nd Sess., Senate, Misc. Doc. 67, Serial 2265).

Statistical Abstract of the United States. Prepared by the chief of the Bureau of Statistics, Treasury Department. Washington, DC: U.S. Government Printing Office, 1879–. (C 3.134:). Selected years available online from 1878 to current, www.census.gov/statab/www (April 14, 2006).

United States Bureau of the Census. *Bureau of the Census Catalog of Publications, 1790–1972*. Washington, DC: U.S. Department of Commerce, Social and Economic Statistics Administration, Bureau of the Census, 1974. (C 56.222/2-2:970-972).

United States Congress. *The Congressional Globe*. Washington, DC: Blair & Rives, 1834–1873. (X:). memory.loc.gov/ammem/amlaw/lwcg.html (accessed April 14, 2006).

United States Congress. *Congressional Record: Proceedings and Debates of the . . . Congress*. Washington, DC: Government Printing Office, 1874–. (X 1.1:).

Access 1874–1876 online through A Century of Lawmaking, memory
.loc.gov/ammem/amlaw/lwcr.html (accessed April 14, 2006). Access 1994 to
present online through GPO, www.gpoaccess.gov/crecord (accessed April 14,
2006).

United States Congress. *The Debates and Proceedings in the Congress of the
United States: With an Appendix Containing Important State Papers and Public Documents, and All the Laws of a Public Nature; with a Copious Index;
Compiled from Authentic Materials.* Washington, DC: Gales & Seaton,
1834–1856. (X:). This title is also known as *Annals of the Congress of the
United States* and covers the years 1789–1824. memory.loc.gov/ammem/
amlaw/lwac.html (accessed April 14, 2006).

United States Congress. *Register of Debates in Congress: Comprising the Leading Debates and Incidents of the . . . Session of the . . . Congress.* Washington,
DC: Printed and published by Gales & Seaton, 1825–1837. (X:). memory
.loc.gov/ammem/amlaw/lwrd.html (accessed April 14, 2006).

*United States Congressional Serial Set Catalog: Numerical Lists and Schedules
of Volumes.* Washington, DC: Classification and Cataloging Branch, Library
Division, Library Programs Service, for sale by the Superintendent of Documents, U.S. Government Printing Office, 1988–. Numerical lists available
from Ninety-eighth Congress, 1983–present. (GP 3.34:).

United States Continental Congress. *Journals of the Continental Congress,
1774–1789.* Edited from the original records in the Library of Congress. Washington, DC: Continental Congress: U.S. Government Printing Office, 1904–37.
(LC 4.5:). memory.loc.gov/ammem/amlaw/lwjc.html (accessed April 14,
2006).

The United States Government Manual. Washington, DC: Office of the Federal
Register, 1935–. (GS 4.109: and AE 2.108/2:). Title varies: United States Government Organization Manual, 1949–1972. www.gpoaccess.gov/gmanual (accessed April 14, 2006).

United States Government Publications Monthly Catalog. Issued by the Superintendent of Documents. Washington, DC: U.S. Government Printing Office,
1940–1951. (GP 3.8:).

United States Superintendent of Documents. *Preliminary Schedule of Volumes,
Reports and Documents of the . . . Congress . . . .* Washington, DC: [U.S. Government Printing Office], 1915–1933. (GP 3.7/2:).

U.S. Congressional Serial Set. Bethesda, MD: LexisNexis Academic & Library
Solutions. Coverage: 1789–1969.

U.S. Congressional Serial Set. Chester, VT: Readex. Coverage: 1817–1980. They
have a separate digital collection, American state papers, 1789–1838. Chester,
VT: Readex.

U.S. Government Research & Development Reports. Washington, DC: U.S. Government Printing Office, Division of Public Documents, 1965–1971. (C 41.21: and C 51.9/3).

U.S. Government Research Reports. Washington, DC: U.S. Department of Commerce, Office of Technical Services. October 1954—December 1964. (C 41.21:).

NOTES

1. www.lib.umich.edu/govdocs (accessed April 14, 2006).

2. Andrea Marie Morrison, *International Government Information and Country Information: A Subject Guide* (Westport, CT: Greenwood Press, 2004); Peter I. Hajnal, ed. *International Information: Documents, Publications, and Electronic Information of International Governmental Organizations.* Englewood, CO: Libraries Unlimited, 1997–2001.

3. See the background information from the Library of Congress, rs6.loc.gov/ammem/amlaw/lwss.html (accessed April 14, 2006) and the related information referenced from this Web page.

4. August A. Imholtz Jr. "The Printing and Distribution of the Serial Set: A Preliminary Contribution to 19th Century Congressional Publishing," *DttP* 31, no. 1 (2003): 1–36.

5. To effectively use the various numerical lists, it is helpful to know the Congress and year in question. To assist in this, a congressional sessions table is most helpful; see www.senate.gov/pagelayout/reference/one_item_and_teasers/Years_to_Congress.htm (accessed April 14, 2006).

6. A brief but informative history can be found at www.access.gpo.gov/su_docs/fdlp/pr/keepam.html (accessed April 14, 2006).

7. See *Designation Handbook for Federal Depository Libraries*, www.access.gpo.gov/su_docs/fdlp/pubs/desig.html (accessed April 14, 2006).

8. For a basic search of depository libraries by state, telephone area code, or congressional district, this interface can be used: www.access.gpo.gov/su_docs/fdlp/tools/ldirect.html. A more sophisticated interface that allows for searching by designation year, designation type, library size, and many other features can be found at www.access.gpo.gov/su_docs/fdlp/tools/ldirect.html (accessed April 14, 2006).

9. For a thorough explanation of this classification system, see *An Explanation of the Superintendent of Documents Classification System*, available at www.access.gpo.gov/su_docs/fdlp/pubs/explain.html (accessed April 14, 2006); and *Classification Manual: A Practical Guide to the Superintendent of Documents Classification System*, www.access.gpo.gov/su_docs/fdlp/pubs/explain.html (accessed April 14, 2006).

10. Joe Morehead, *Introduction to United States Government Information Sources.* 6th ed. Englewood, CO: Libraries Unlimited, 1999.

11. *Library Resources for Administrative History: Indexes to Legislative and Executive Publications*, www.archives.gov/research/alic/reference/admin-history/publication-indexes.html (accessed April 14, 2006).

12. The CGP is available online at catalog.gpo.gov (accessed April 14, 2006).

13. The so-called hidden Internet includes databases that, because of technology barriers, are not able to be indexed by search utilities such as Google.

14. For that, the reader is referred to *How Our Laws Are Made*, thomas.loc.gov/home/lawsmade.toc.html, issued either as House or Senate documents, and Ben's Guide, bensguide.gpo.gov (accessed April 14, 2006).

15. Christopher C. Brown, "Knowing Where They're Going: Statistics for Online Government Document Access through the OPAC," *Online Information Review* 28, no. 6 (2004): 396–409.

16. See the chapter on historical research for the importance of primary research sources.

17. See, for example, *The History and Growth of the United States Census, Prepared for the Senate Committee on the Census* (Washington, DC: U.S. Government Printing Office, 1900), Serial 3356; Cindy Wolff, "Deconstructing Historical Census Publications: A Primer," *DttP* 31, no. 1 (2003): 20–25; and *Census of Population and Housing* (Washington, DC: U.S. Census Bureau), 2005, www.census.gov/prod/www/abs/decennial (accessed April 14, 2006).

7

Research in the Sciences

Joseph R. Kraus

INTRODUCTION

The landscape for scientific information is almost incomprehensibly complex. The literature is both deep in content and broad in scope, with a phenomenal amount of published scientific information. There are thousands of journals, hundreds of thousands of books, millions of articles, and millions more references. Over the course of this chapter, I will paint a picture of scientific research with a broad brush. This will be a light and thin coat as I gloss over the various subject areas. This chapter will cover library-based research methods in the sciences, and while laboratory-based research methods are important, that topic will be left for other sources to discuss. For a more complete view of the library and information needs for any section of scientific research, the reader should use one or more of the sources listed in the bibliography or in the section on guides to the literature.

As in all disciplines, scientists have seen ebbs and flows to their fields over time. In some decades, specialization has been the key to their existence. But lately, many scientists have become more interdisciplinary in their work to allow collaboration with colleagues in adjacent fields. The nature of interdisciplinary research is covered in chapter 10. Scientists also adjust their foci as they advance in their careers. As new funding areas open up in biotechnology, nanoscience, or stem cell research, for instance, many scientists may modify their career paths to chase the funding dollars. This change of focus is not just because of the availability of funding. Scientists may change their course when there is a perceived opportunity to perform groundbreaking research in a new field. As researchers, scientists are attentive to new areas of research, and as authors, they are attentive to the visibility, prestige, and overall impact of the journals and sources in which they publish.[1] This is because scientists feel that publishing a paper in a high-quality peer-reviewed journal is the culmination of a successful research project.[2]

DISCIPLINES WITHIN THE SCIENCES

Hundreds of years ago, a person involved in any branch of the sciences was called a scientist. For example, Robert Hooke (1635–1703) had interests in all of the sciences, including physics and astronomy, chemistry, biology, geology, architecture, and naval technology. One of Hooke's contemporaries was Sir Christopher Wren (1632–1723); he was an architect, a mathematician, and the Savilian chair of astronomy at the University of Oxford. Today, because the field of science is so complex, scientists categorize themselves into one of several disciplines, such as astronomy, biology, chemistry, computer science, geoscience, mathematics, medicine, or physics.

STANDARD RESEARCH METHODS
COMMON TO ALL SCIENTISTS

Journals, and the articles contained within them, are what most scientists use to learn about advances in their disciplines. Scientists are both readers of journals and authors contributing articles to those journals. Though most scientists publish in journals as a means to communicate their research to others in their field, the use of journals varies considerably from one scientific field to the next. For example, chemists are highly dependent upon journal articles for their research, while many computer scientists rely on conference proceedings and technical reports. In some areas of physics, such as high-energy physics, an Internet-based preprint server provides most of their information needs. Geologists often rely on government reports and other technical publications for their research. Despite the exceptions, in most scientific disciplines, journals are a vital and core means of communication.

Research methods vary depending on the level of the student or researcher. Undergraduate students tend to use a greater number of books and general science periodicals in their studies, while graduate students, faculty, and professional researchers use higher-level discipline-specific journals. Many undergraduate students learn mathematics by solving the problem sets given in their textbooks. Astronomy, biology, chemistry, geoscience, and physics students do the same, but they also take laboratory classes and write lab reports. In short, undergraduates learn scientific concepts by "doing." Since there is so much to learn in the sciences, lower-level undergraduate students work hard just to learn about past research; many are not expected to read the current journal literature. Graduate students and some higher-level undergraduates are expected to keep up to date in their fields by reading the journal literature. Since more and more scientists are working in interdisciplinary teams to solve problems, some scientists use lower-level books and reference sources to give them an overview of allied subdisciplines.

Higher-level researchers often use articles that have passed peer review.[3] These articles are published in refereed periodicals. Scholars offer their services and review articles written by other peers in the field. This maintains high standards for refereed journals. The peer reviewers can either reject submitted articles, accept them with required modifications, or accept them as received. Some journals and publishers use anonymous peer review, while others reveal to the author who is reviewing the work. The importance of peer review is particularly evident in the life sciences. For example, a doctor must be able to trust the information in a research article, since resulting decisions could have life-or-death implications. Whatever the field, the advanced researcher must be able to trust that the information contained in an article is accurate and reliable. The process of peer review is important to most scientists, but there can be some disadvantages. While a paper is reviewed by one or more peers, it adds a time lag between initial submission and final publication. Some authors might be suspicious that reviewers who reject their manuscripts are biased.

Instead of relying on peer review, some researchers who know their field extremely well can trust the content of an article based on who wrote the article, the institution that the author is affiliated with, what journal the article is published in, or a host of other factors. This is the case for high-energy physicists. They have been using journal article preprints since the 1970s as the core of their research. Many high-energy physicists trust the information in preprints because they know most of the authors in that narrow field. Those researchers do not necessarily need to see the final peer-reviewed article to trust the research findings. For undergraduate students who are just beginning to read about and understand the concepts and theories of their discipline, they will tend to use books, encyclopedia entries, or general scientific periodical articles to grasp the broader topic.

JOURNAL PUBLISHING, THE INTERNET, AND OPEN ACCESS

With the advent of the Internet, why do scientists continue to bother publishing articles in journals? Couldn't scientists simply post their articles on a website for the rest of the world to see? While it might be possible for the rest of the world to find and read those articles, publication in a prime journal provides much greater circulation and visibility to the author's work. Scientists are interested in publishing their articles in top-tier journals (such as *Science*, *Nature*, *PNAS*, or *Cell*) that have the widest possible readership. But those journals have a large number of submissions and only accept the best papers. Publication in one of these high-impact journals boosts the status of a scientist because the article and the author have received an official stamp of approval. William Costerson, a microbiologist at Montana State University with over five hundred publications, noted that if a scientist has "20 publications and none of them are in top-tier journals, the portfolio starts to look wrong."[4] These top-tier publications help many scientists achieve tenure at their places of employment. This professional approval would be missing if the author were to just post articles on a personal website.

With the use of the Internet as a delivery mechanism for most scientific journals, there is a movement among many scholars for more open-access (OA) journals.[5] OA journals provide online articles free of charge to the reader. Depending on the publication, authors might provide the money to cover publication costs. Open-access journals often have limited copyright and licensing restrictions.

Publishers of scientific information do not want to lose the revenue flow from journal subscriptions, so they are hesitant to post their journal articles online for free. Some publishers have experimented with an author payment system for individual articles to have open access, while other publishers have used a delayed or embargoed open-access model. With the embargo model, libraries need to subscribe to access the current content, while the older scientific articles are available to the rest of the world for free. Many of the journals located at Stanford's Highwire Press (highwire.stanford.edu) use the embargoed model with great success. Highwire Press is not a publisher but a platform that many publishers and societies use to mount the contents of their journals. The *Journal of Virology* from the American Society of Microbiology (ASM), for example, is able to provide greater access to its contents by making articles older than six months freely available to the world. It is also able to maintain library and personal subscribers who want to have access to the most recent literature in the area of virology. Another journal entitled *Nucleic Acids Research* is also on the Highwire platform, but the publisher, Oxford University Press, uses a different model. All articles are freely available, but authors must pay a variable fee to have their articles published in that journal.[6]

Challenges Finding Research in Journals

Most scientists know the journals in their narrow subject area, but some have difficulty finding journals published outside their field. Some reasons for these challenges include the fact that journal titles often change, split, merge, and change volume numbering with a new series for the same journal title. The French journal *Comptes Rendus* is so famously complex that a librarian at the University of Washington created a flowchart for it that showed thirty-five variant titles and sections.[7] Scientists sometimes provide cryptic information in their citations. Journals also move from one publisher to another. It is sometimes difficult to determine if a local library has a specific journal title because one has to follow links in the catalog to see the record for a prior or more recent title. The *Quarterly of the Colorado School of Mines* is a good example. It was under that title from 1912 through the start of 1978. At the end of 1978, it changed its name to the *Colorado School of Mines Quarterly*. It was published under that title through 1988, when the publication was suspended for several years. In 1992, it changed its title to the *Colorado School of Mines Quarterly Review of Engineering, Science, Education and Research*. That title ran through 1998, when it changed its title again to *Quarterly (Colorado School of Mines)*. As of June of 2006, this publication has been officially suspended again. In order for researchers to find the variant titles of this journal, they should use "continues" and "continued by" links within the catalog if available. They might also find the variant titles all shelved in the same area of the stacks. Many academic libraries shelve all the variant titles at a single call number, but in other libraries where bound journals are in alphabetical order, one might need to go looking through the Cs and the Qs to find the various parts of this journal.

The volume numbering of some journals can also be difficult to follow. The journal *Science* was first published in 1883. Then, in 1895, a new series was started (with a new editorial board), and another volume 1 was published. So a student looking for volume 21 of the journal *Science* might need an article from the original series published in 1893 or from the new series published in 1905.

Journals can also switch from one publisher to another. In order to know what digital platform a journal is on, it is important to know the current publisher. For example, the *Annals of Botany* was published by Academic Press through 2001, but in 2002 it moved to Oxford University Press. Depending on the volumes and years needed, researchers might have to go to more than one journal website for the content.

Many authors cite journal articles using cryptic abbreviations. Someone who does not regularly use the astronomical or physics literature would have no idea that *AJ* is short for the *Astronomical Journal*, and *PRD* is short for *Physical Review D: Particles and Fields*. There are several reference sources that can help researchers figure out the full title of a journal from an abbreviation. Volume 1 from a source entitled *Periodical Title Abbreviations* helps in many cases. For some of the more obscure scientific journals and foreign sources, the *Chemical Abstracts Service Source Index* (*CASSI*) is a good reference as well.

The Role of Societies

Scientists do not work in a vacuum. Science is a social activity, and most scientists work on projects together in teams or groups. Scientists often attend meetings and conferences to discuss topics and solutions to their problems. Because of this, scientific societies play a very important role in the careers of most scientists. Scientific societies are more than just groups of people who hold similar interests; societies often hold conferences and publish conference papers, books, newsletters, and journals in the field. In addition to these publication services, they provide a wide range of other services to the members, such as career and mentoring services, grant writing programs, job listings, and more.

Types of Journals

In general, there are two types of scientific journal publishers. The first scientific scholarly publishers were nonprofit society and university presses, but in the mid-twentieth century, for-profit commercial publishers came on the scene.

Many scientific societies have been publishing journals in their respective areas for dozens or even hundreds of years. With the explosive growth of scientific information over the last fifty years, many scientific societies were not able to keep up with demand from authors for publishing outlets. Some societies were slow to respond to the needs of researchers in interdisciplinary fields; many societies resisted publishing new journals in narrow subject areas. In the 1950s and 1960s, for-profit commercial publishers came into the scientific publishing market to start new journals.[8] During this time, many commercial publishers created niche journals that attracted respected authors by dispensing with the page-charge system used by many scientific societies.[9] During that time, societies charged authors for publication based on the number of pages in their articles. For the first couple of years for a new journal, subscription prices of commercial journals were kept to reasonable rates to attract institutional subscribers. Commercial publishers could then raise rates knowing that librarians prefer not to cancel journal subscriptions once they start. Richard Johnson explains the incentives for commercial journal publishers to inflate their prices:

> Commercial firms found there was money to be made publishing the overflow of articles that couldn't be accommodated in society journals. Many scholars in need of promotion and tenure were only too happy to be published in these commercial journals—especially when the alternative was not being published at all—and gave their research papers away to journals

for free. It didn't take long for commercial publishers to discover that demand for journals was remarkably inelastic. And since they were incen-
tivised to maximize profit, they did the rational thing—they raised institutional prices of journals dramatically and relentlessly to exploit the
elasticity curve. Institutional subscribers, accounting for the lion's share of
the revenue supporting publication of journals in most fields, paid the price
because their users demanded access.[10]

The journals published by nonprofit society presses often have the highest impact because the most scientists see and cite this literature. From a library's perspective, they also have the most "bang for the buck," since scientific societies publish their journals without the expectation of making a
large profit on sales. Because they want to disseminate the information to
as wide an audience as possible, many societies keep subscription prices
low to just cover their publication costs. Robert H. Marks found that some
societies even published at a loss during the 1970s, making up the loss by
charging more for member dues and conference fees.[11] But in the 1980s
and 1990s, societies worked to streamline their publishing program so that
they could break even or make money to support other member services of
the society. With recent advances in computers and software, many societies took advantage of new software programs to create digital publishing
systems. These systems help societies meet the demands of members and
readers for fast, low-cost, and Web-based access to scientific research.[12]

Science librarians must keep up to date with news concerning the commercial presses, since their journals absorb much of the library's budget.
Because of this tense financial relationship between libraries, publishers,
authors, and readers, the Association of Research Libraries created a
group called SPARC, the Scholarly Publishing and Academic Resources
Coalition (www.arl.org/sparc). SPARC aims to educate stakeholders about
scholarly communication issues and to create alternative cost-effective access to peer-reviewed literature.

LIBRARY-BASED TOOLS

Scientists should certainly know the major journals in their field, but they
do not know about all of the journals that publish articles important to
their research. Scientists use general and focused databases to discover

important articles in tangential journals. For example, an organic chemist will keep track of the articles published in several journals such as the *Journal of the American Chemical Society*, the *Journal of Organic Chemistry*, *Organic Letters*, *Tetrahedron*, and *Tetrahedron Letters*. But the chemist should also use general scientific databases and a chemistry database such as the *Chemical Abstracts Service* to find important articles published in other journals.

One of the most important general science databases is Thomson Scientific's *Science Citation Index (SCI) Expanded*. Many colleges and universities provide access to this database through the Web of Science interface. Another database that competes with the Web of Science is Elsevier's *Scopus*. These databases provide more than just descriptions of articles; they also provide citation tracking. Once a scientist finds an appropriate article, a useful next step is to track down the citations or references given at the end of the article, a process called *citation chaining*. More importantly, a researcher can see more recent references to a specific article using *SCI* or *Scopus*, allowing him or her to follow research forward and backward in time. *SCI* revolutionized the way scientists approached the research process because they could examine the tangled web of citations and references to various papers and authors. A book edited by Blaise Cronin and Barsky Atkins fully explores the history and significance of the *Science Citation Index*.[13]

The *SCI* database recently celebrated its fiftieth anniversary,[14] while *Scopus* was introduced in 2004. Since *SCI* has been around for so many years and is considered to be the standard cited reference-finding tool, more academic institutions have access to it in one form or another. Using citation data gathered from *SCI*, Thomson Scientific also publishes *Journal Citation Reports* (*JCR*), where scientists are able to find a journal's *impact factor*. This is a measure of the frequency with which the "average article" in a journal has been cited over a range of two years. If a journal has an impact factor of ten, then articles published over a two year span, 2003 to 2004 for example, will have been cited an average of ten times during 2005.

General Science Reference Works

While advanced researchers will use the journals of their field to learn of advances in a niche area, undergraduate students (or even higher-level researchers) will use general encyclopedias, handbooks, and textbooks when learning about a new subject. These sources provide a solid framework for a subject area. While textbooks are most heavily used by undergraduate students, handbooks are useful to scientists for the practical information they convey. For example, the *Handbook of Optical Materials* provides short chapters covering the optical and other physical properties of crystalline materials, glasses, metals, polymers, liquids, and gases. Most handbooks are single volumes, but multivolume encyclopedias can cover a much wider scope or be more in depth. The seventeen-volume set *Grzimek's Animal Life Encyclopedia* is able to provide a good amount of detail about many of the world's animal species. For someone who needs basic information on a macaw, a moose, or a mouse, this is a good place to start.

There are a great number of general reference works in the sciences, and the following are just a couple of the major sets. The twenty-volume *McGraw-Hill Encyclopedia of Science & Technology* is a standard resource in most academic and public libraries in the United States. Another commonly held eighteen-volume encyclopedia set is entitled the *Encyclopedia of Physical Science and Technology*. While the McGraw-Hill encyclopedia does cover many life science topics, the *Encyclopedia of Life Sciences*, also in twenty volumes, is much more comprehensive in that regard. Several of the guides to the literature listed in the "Science Resources" section at the end of this chapter can be used to learn about the thousands of other encyclopedias, handbooks, guidebooks, monographs, conferences, journals, and other sources used in the sciences.

General Guides to the Literature

The literature of science is both extremely deep and broad. It would be quite a lengthy list to print here all of the major reference works published in each of the scientific fields. If your library only had one guide to scientific literature, Charlie Hurt's *Information Sources in Science and Technology* should be it. Volume 1 from *The New Walford: Guide to Reference Resources* is also useful, and it has a focus on international resources. The guidebook from Constance Gould and Karla Pearce, *Information Needs in the Sciences: An Assessment*, does not go into very much depth, but it does an excellent job explaining how scientists in the various fields use the literature and perform their research. Though it is over fifteen years old, the information is still pertinent because scientists still use many of the same sources and research methods mentioned in the book.

SCIENTIFIC DISCIPLINES

Though there is much that the sciences have in common, each of the disciplines has its own unique information needs. For each of the disciplines, I indicate below the bibliographic tools and resources common to the discipline, the guides to the literature, and the major societies.

Astronomy

Many astronomers collect reams of data using traditional ground-based telescopes, space-based telescopes, and radio dishes. These data come in various forms, such as image or spectroscopic. All astronomers want to have accurate and precise data, and that depends on the quality and sensitivity of the instruments used for their observations. Astronomers use the entire electromagnetic spectrum for their observations, from high-energy gamma rays and X-rays, to ultraviolet, to the visible spectrum, to infrared, down to microwaves and radio waves. At the end of the research process, astronomers usually publish an article in a journal. There are many allied fields of astronomy such as astrophysics, astrogeology, cosmology, and astrobiology. Some of these subfields cover more theoretical aspects, and they may not be as rooted in the observational literature. Because important observations have been made in the past and reported in the older literature, many astronomers continue to use historical reports and articles.

Most astronomers in the United States belong to the American Astronomical Society. This is a small professional clique; there are only about six thousand professional astronomers in North America.[15] Most astronomers work in academia or for research institutes. Compared to the large number of chemists (ninety thousand) and medical physicians (over five hundred thousand) in the United States,[16] astronomy is a very small field of science.

The database most heavily used by astronomers is the NASA *Astrophysics Data System* (*ADS*). It is hosted by the Computation Facility at the Harvard-Smithsonian Center for Astrophysics. One of its features is the full-text linking to current and historical literature. With the permission of various core publishers, NASA scanned in articles from forty-six journals containing much of the historical astronomical literature, and the *ADS* links to those scanned PDFs. Since there is very little commercial use for older astronomical literature, the publishers did not feel they would lose any future revenue when they allowed the *ADS* to scan the back files of their journals. For access to the recently published astronomical journal literature, a library will need a current subscription. The *ADS* is now tracking "Citations to the Article" as well as references contained within the article. Many astronomers will use this in place of the *Science Citation Index*.

Some astronomers, particularly those doing research in instrumentation, astronomical optics, astrophysics, and cosmology, will use the *INSPEC* database. This covers all the core journals and conferences in the astronomical and astrophysical sciences, and it covers engineering and physics literature missed by the *ADS*. INSPEC also provides additional subject and numerical indexing not found in the *ADS*.

While there is no recent book that is a general guide to the literature of astronomy,[17] there are a number of books and articles that are useful. Andre Heck edited a set of books entitled *Information Handling in Astronomy*. Two prominent astronomy librarians, Brenda G. Corbin and Uta Grothkopf, contributed chapters for those two books.[18] Corbin and Grothkopf also edited a set of conference publications entitled *Library and Information Services in Astronomy* (*LISA*).[19] Most recently, the fifth conference took place in Boston in June 2006. The papers will be posted on the LISA V website, cfa-www.harvard.edu/library/lisa.

Biology

Gould and Pearce noted in their book that the field of biology "is an extremely diverse and varied discipline, described by biologists themselves as 'messy.' This is a feature that appeals to many biologists, who delight in devoting their energies to discovering biology's organizing principles."[20] The body of biology research is extremely large with many subareas such as animal behavior, biochemistry, biophysics, biotechnology, botany, cellular biology, developmental biology, ecology, entomology, evolution, genetics, immunology, molecular biology, and zoology. Because the field is so varied, there is no single overarching society to which most biologists belong. They join smaller focused societies such as the American Society for Microbiology or the American Society for Cell Biology.

Even though there is no main society for researchers in biology, there is a core database that provides access to the journal literature. *Biological Abstracts* (*BA*) covers over four thousand journals and has over nine million records going back to 1969. One of the features of *Biological Abstracts* is its relational indexing. This is a natural language-based indexing system that allows researchers to specify the relationship between subject terms. Some researchers use a larger database called *BIOSIS Previews*, which includes references to the conference literature, patents, and book chapters.

Many biology researchers also use the *Biological Sciences* database published by CSA. This is actually a set of smaller databases linked together. Some of the subjects include aquaculture, bacteriology, ecology, entomology, genetics, immunology, toxicology, and virology. It is not as comprehensive as *Biological Abstracts*, but it does index some journals not covered by *BA*. The *Zoological Record* is an important database covering animal research, however, it indexes many non-peer-reviewed journals, newsletters, and serials in foreign languages. Many biology students and faculty use the *MEDLINE* database to find articles in the biomedical literature.

Since the biological and life science literature is so varied, several guides to the literature are worth examining. Many are from Diane Schmidt, who either wrote or cowrote the *Guide to Reference and Information Sources in the Zoological Sciences*, *Using the Biological Literature: A Practical Guide*, and the *Guide to Information Sources in the Botanical Sciences*. Harold Wyatt's fourth edition of *Information Sources in the Life Sciences* is also useful.

Chemistry

Chemists are heavy and varied users of library and information resources. Chemists might want to find out how a chemical compound was first synthesized or to discover what its physical properties are, they could need current published research in a narrow area of interest, or they might want to become familiar with key trends in a field outside of their main specialization.[21]

There are many ways to divide up the field of chemistry. Chemists have split the field into several areas, such as organic, inorganic, and organometallic. They have also broken down the field into areas such as analytical, biochemical, biophysical, environmental, medicinal, nuclear, pharmaceutical, quantum, and theoretical chemistry. Just as chemists perform research in a subfield of chemistry, many will join the American Chemical Society (ACS) and affiliate themselves with one or more of the thirty-three discipline-specific ACS divisions.

Compared to some other scientific disciplines like astronomy or theoretical mathematics, much of the audience for chemical research rests in the corporate world. Some of the industries that rely on chemical information include pharmaceuticals, polymers and plastics, semiconductors, agriculture, and many of the manufacturing industries. Scientific publishers know that many corporate research and development libraries depend on chemistry information resources, and those resources are priced accordingly. In the academic market, some chemistry databases are priced below what a corporate library would pay, but chemistry journals continue to be expensive for both corporate and academic markets.

The *Chemical Abstracts Service* (*CAS*) is the core bibliographic resource for most chemistry researchers. It covers over 9,500 currently published journals and many patent sources. The database is provided on a number of different platforms and media; some of them are STN, SciFinder, SciFinder Scholar, print, and CD-ROM. Depending on the method of access, the database can go back as far as 1907. Most larger academic institutions provide access to *CAS* through client software called SciFinder Scholar (SFS). Using SFS, a patron can search by topic, author, journal, chemical substance registry number, or chemical structure. The software has a special "structure drawing window" that allows researchers to search for articles and substances based on the molecular structure. The book by Damon D. Ridley, *Information Retrieval: SciFinder and SciFinder Scholar*, provides much more information concerning how to take full advantage of this powerful interface to the chemical literature. This database is also useful for interdisciplinary researchers in fields such as physics, materials science, engineering, and biology.

At some of the larger libraries, one might find other databases. *Cross-Fire Beilstein*, derived from the *Beilstein Handbook of Organic Chem-*

istry, contains chemical property information from more than six million organic substances and covers the literature from 1779 to the present. *CrossFire Gmelin* was derived from the *Gmelin Handbook of Inorganic Chemistry*. *Landolt-Bornstein* contains data from all of the sciences, but it focuses on chemical data. The *INSPEC* database is also used by many chemists, and it has special chemical indexing.

In addition to the current literature, older literature continues to be very important for chemists. Until recently, students were using electronic databases and only finding references from roughly 1970 to the present. But since databases such as *CAS*, *Beilstein*, and the *Science Citation Index* have been adding back files, and journal publishers have been scanning in older articles, researchers have been finding many more citations to the older literature. After looking through the literature, a student might come across three methods to synthesize a specific organic compound, but the only description of a method using materials on hand was published over fifty years ago. The student will need to read that older article to understand the method.

Chemists also find older journal citations in reference sets such as the *Dictionary of Organic Compounds* or the *Dictionary of Inorganic Compounds*. These two reference sets are chock-full of data and references to the primary journal articles. Another single-volume reference work that contains a great deal of chemical and physical properties data is the *CRC Handbook of Chemistry and Physics*. If my library could only have one reference book, that would be it.

A very high proportion of the primary chemical research is published in the peer-reviewed journal literature. While many high-quality books are published in the chemical sciences, most faculty do not find books all that important since they are used to using the primary journal literature. In contrast, undergraduates still use books where a broad overview of a topic is needed. Most chemistry books are considered to be secondary sources since they often contain references to the primary journal literature.

Four recent guides to the chemical literature are: (1) *Chemical Librarianship: Challenges and Opportunities* by Arleen Somerville; (2) *How to Find Chemical Information: A Guide for Practicing Chemists, Educators, and Students* by Robert Maizell; (3) *Chemistry Resources in the Electronic Age* by Judith Bazler; and (4) *The Literature of Chemistry: Recommended Titles for Undergraduate Chemistry Library Collections* by Judith Douville.

Computer Science

The field of computer science was born in the 1940s when mathematicians and electrical engineers got together to develop electrical calculating machines. Since that time, the field has seen an explosive growth in the amount of published information. Because computer science is such a quickly changing field, access to current literature is more important to computer scientists than in some other scientific fields. Therefore, researchers in computer science read conference and technical report literature, even though it might not be peer reviewed, to keep up with their field. Computer scientists employ a variety of methods to gather their information. To no one's surprise, they often use online databases and the Internet. A free database originally developed by NEC called *CiteSeer.IST* is used by many computer scientists. It provides forward and backward linking through references and "cited by" links. Many of the articles indexed by *CiteSeer* are technical reports and conference papers. In some ways, computer scientists act more like engineers since many of them use technical reports, trade magazines, and conference papers to a greater extent than traditional books and journals. See chapter 8 for more on engineering resources. Undergraduate students still find books, magazines, journal articles, and manuals useful for their education.

Many computer scientists belong to the Association for Computing Machinery (ACM) or the IEEE Computer Society. These societies provide arenas for members to meet and discuss research problems, and they also provide publishing platforms and databases for the distribution of information in computer science. The Association for Computing Machinery (ACM) provides several useful tools such as the *ACM Digital Library* (*ACM DL*). In the *DL*, they provide the full text of their journals, magazines, and conference literature, in most cases back to volume 1. The ACM also publishes the *Guide to Computing Literature*, which provides abstracts to journal articles, book chapters, conference papers, doctoral theses, and technical reports in computer science. It contains more than 750,000 citations from over three thousand publishers back to 1980. A third publication from the ACM is entitled *Computing Reviews*, which allows readers to see how articles and books have been received in the computing community.

Besides the ACM, many other publishers provide access to full-text and indexing sources. The *IEEE Computer Society Digital Library* provides full-text access to their journals, magazines, and conferences back to

1994, or earlier in some cases. The *INSPEC* database covers all of the core journals and conferences in computer science and information technology. It is especially strong in the subjects of hardware and computer engineering. Many universities subscribe to the book series *Lecture Notes in Computer Science (LNCS)*. The series has over three thousand volumes, many of which are papers presented at European or Asian conferences. Some libraries subscribe to the *LNCS* as a full-text article database, while other libraries purchase individual volumes in print.

Geosciences

Geology is the core of the geoscience fields. Some of the allied disciplines include paleontology, geochemistry, geophysics, geography, hydrogeology, geomorphology, meteorology, petrology, and climatology. Many professionals belong to either the American Geophysical Union, the Geological Society of America, or the Association of American Geographers. Some geologists also join societies that focus on a niche, such as the American Association of Petroleum Geologists or the Society of Economic Geologists.

How does someone in the geosciences do research?

First, he/she looks for maps of the area—topographic, general geologic, or tectonic; or, more specifically, hydrologic, geochemical, and so on. Next, the researcher would look for field guides covering the area. Following that, he/she might perform searches in indexing and abstracting tools and add the results to citations found in the field guides. Finally, the researcher would move on to more specialized sources.[22]

GeoRef is the core geoscience database published by the American Geological Institute (AGI). Containing over 2.2 million references to geoscience journal articles, books, maps, conference papers, reports, and theses, it covers the geology of North America from 1785 to the present, and the geology of the rest of the world from 1933 to the present. It also includes references to all publications of the U.S. Geological Survey. Information from more than 3,500 journals in forty languages is covered. One of the unique search functions of *GeoRef* is the ability to search for articles concerning geological features by location between any latitude or longitude.

Geoscience researchers use a great amount of historical literature and are heavy users of U.S. government documents. For example, a researcher wanting to learn more about glaciation in the Sangre de Cristo Range of Colorado might read an article that appeared back in 1907.[23] This older article is still relevant because the geology of Colorado hasn't changed much in the past years.

Many geoscientists also use *GEOBASE*, a tool that provides information from most geographic and major geology journal articles, books, chapters, conference proceedings, and reports. It includes over one million records with abstracts. Some subjects include cartography, climatology, environment, geochemistry, geomorphology, geophysics, human geography, hydrology, meteorology, petrology, photogrammetry, sedimentology, and volcanology. Many geographers use computational tools, such as Geographic Information Systems software, to conduct their research. Concerning the area of human geography, chapter 4 on the social sciences should be consulted.

To understand the challenges and recent trends faced by geology librarians, one should read Lura E. Joseph's excellent article.[24] She noted that one of the main challenges faced by geoscience researchers concerns the confusion over journal access rights. Many researchers are not sure why they can remotely access some journals and articles but are denied access to others. She notes that librarians face challenges with journal pricing structures, journal and database licensing rights, journal cataloging issues, material storage issues, and many others. These issues are challenges for librarians in all disciplines, not just for geology librarians. To learn more about how geographers conduct research, consult the book by Mary Lynette Larsgaard, *Map Librarianship: An Introduction.* In it she notes that the term "map librarianship" is dated, but she has left the title the same for the third edition. Librarians working in the field now consider themselves to be "spatial-data" librarians.

Mathematics

The field of mathematics is international in scope. Even though a mathematician may not be able to read Russian, Hungarian, or Chinese, he or she will still be able to decipher the important parts of a mathematical theorem, since the language of mathematics is universal. Undergraduate students in mathematics do not use the journal literature very much since they learn by solving problem sets assigned in textbooks, but graduate students and other advanced researchers depend on the library for their research. While all of the other scientific disciplines can do research out in the field or in a laboratory, for mathematicians "the library is their laboratory, their meeting place, their archives, and their current awareness tool."[25] With the advent of electronic databases and journals, most mathematicians can perform much of their research remotely.[26] In order to track down important older books and journal articles, mathematicians still need to visit the library in person.

Most mathematicians belong to the American Mathematical Society (AMS) or the Mathematical Association of America. The AMS publishes a core resource called *Mathematical Reviews*, and many academic libraries access this publication through a Web-based product called *MathSciNet*. This covers the world's mathematical literature since 1940. About 1,800 journals are covered, with links to over two hundred thousand original articles.

Another database that covers the mathematical literature is a German publication called *Zentralblatt MATH*. Since it is produced in cooperation between the European Mathematical Society, FIZ Karlsruhe, and Springer-Verlag, it is often found in European libraries and larger academic libraries in the United States. It indexes more than 2,300 serials and contains more than two million records. With the recent addition of information from the *Jahrbuch über die Fortschritte der Mathematik*, it now covers the period from 1868 to the present.

Another Springer publication is *Lecture Notes in Mathematics* (*LNM*). Just like the *Lecture Notes in Computer Science* series, there are many, many volumes—in this case, over 1,800. Libraries can purchase individual volumes or subscribe to the series either online or in print as a standing order. Many volumes of the series are monographs, but some are conference proceedings.

To learn more about the mathematics literature, the book by Nancy Anderson and Lois Pausch, *A Guide to Library Service in Mathematics*, was the standard for a decade. Suddenly, two more guides to the mathematics literature came out in 2004. Martha A. Tucker and Nancy D. Anderson wrote the *Guide to Information Sources in Mathematics and Statistics*, and Kristine K. Fowler edited the book *Using the Mathematics Literature*. Both of these are worthwhile additions to academic collections.

Medicine

Medicine is a large scientific field that investigates how the human body works and why it works the way it does. Because the human body is so complex, medical doctors tend to specialize in a particular body part or function. The journals they read also focus on particular specialties or body parts, such as the *British Journal of Oral and Maxillofacial Surgery* or *Pediatric Nursing*. Just as medical specialists read journals in their sub-fields, most doctors and nurses belong to one or more of a host of medical societies based on their specialty. Many doctors are also members of the American Medical Association.

The literature of medicine is simply enormous. Thankfully, the core of the medical literature is indexed in a single database called *MEDLINE*. Produced by the National Library of Medicine (NLM), *MEDLINE* is a comprehensive international database of medicine. It contains over twelve million citations from the most important peer-reviewed medical and life science journals. Professionals in medicine are very concerned about the quality of their information, and thus the peer-reviewed journal literature is critical to their research. Doctors and other medical professionals do not rely on unrefereed literature when making medical decisions.

Concerning the *MEDLINE* database, some of the fields that are covered are medicine, nursing, dentistry, veterinary medicine, the health care system, and the preclinical sciences. Over 3,900 biomedical journals published in the United States and in seventy foreign countries are covered going back to the mid-1960s. Researchers in medicine should learn to use the thesaurus of subject headings called Medical Subject Headings, or MeSH. This provides a way for researchers to retrieve articles that may use different terminology for the same concepts.

Since the NLM is a branch of the National Institutes of Health, and *MEDLINE* is published by the federal government, it is a freely available database. Many students and researchers access *MEDLINE* through an interface called PubMed. *MEDLINE* is also available from many other commercial and nonprofit information vendors.

Because the medical and life science literature is so varied, researchers will want to search in other databases to be comprehensive. For example, patrons doing research on the avian influenza (or bird flu) will also want to check *Biological Abstracts* and the *Zoological Record*. Researchers in prosthetics or tissue engineering will also want to check some of the databases in the engineering literature. Someone needing pharmaceutical information should also look in the chemical literature. A student doing research in behavioral neuroscience should find the PsycInfo database (described in chapter 4) to be useful. To get a handle on the varied life science and medical literature, two books, *Introduction to Reference Sources in the Health Sciences* by Jo Anne Boorkman and *Introduction to Health Sciences Librarianship* by Frank Kellerman, are worth consulting.

Physics

Physics is a science that investigates matter, energy, and their interaction. The field can be broken down into the following branches: classical and relativistic dynamics, gravitation, electromagnetism, heat and thermodynamics, statistical mechanics, and quantum physics. There are some other branches that study the treatment or the scale of matter and energy involved. For example, a physicist might describe him- or herself as theoretical or experimental, high-energy, subatomic particle, molecular, nuclear, optical, or as a biophysicist, astrophysicist or geophysicist. Many physicists belong to the American Institute of Physics or the American Physical Society.

Most physicists use the journal literature quite extensively, but the monographic literature can be important for undergraduate students and for people who want to read an overview of a field. High-energy physicists in particular use an e-print server, www.arXiv.org, for the bulk of their information. Because this is a small, tight-knit community, the researchers know the reputations of the other authors in their field, so a preprint can often be trusted in lieu of the published peer-reviewed journal article.[27]

A comprehensive search in physics should include the *INSPEC* database. This is the leading bibliographic information database covering the fields of physics, electronics, computing, control engineering, and information technology, with more than seven million records taken from 3,500 technical and scientific journals and 1,500 conference proceedings. Many academic libraries have this database back to 1969, but the publisher also sells a back file to 1900. Some undergraduates might find the

INSPEC database a little too large, preferring an interdisciplinary database, such as *Academic Search Premier* (described in several other chapters), for general science topics. For an overview of the physics literature, consult David Stern's *Guide to Information Sources in the Physical Sciences.*

RESEARCH SKILLS WITHIN THE SCIENCES

Kate Manual from New Mexico State University wrote a great article concerning discipline-specific information literacy competencies for the sciences.[28] In short, researchers should know where to look for information, how to find that information, what tools to use, who to ask for advice, and why certain resources are better than others. The major information literacy skills are addressed in chapter 9 of this book, but that chapter does not address some of the specific information skills that scientific researchers should have. The following additional skills are extracted from Manual's article. Science researchers should

- Recognize the importance of "invisible colleges" in the research process. The researcher may have an appropriate question formed, but the researcher needs to ask the right person that question to receive relevant answers.
- Understand the overlap and any limitations of various fields' databases and be able to search those databases effectively. The researcher should be able to search using more than just keywords or subject terms. For example, the person should be able to limit a search to articles in a specific journal or search by *CAS* registry numbers if desired within some databases.
- Be aware of the fundamental interdisciplinarity of scientific research.
- Be aware of citation indexing tools and use some of their advanced features. With citation indexes, the researcher should be able to follow citation chains forward in time. With all other references, the researcher should be able to follow them backward in time.
- Be able to use current awareness services.
- Understand the importance of abstracts in scientific research.
- Have knowledge of government documents and "gray literature" and an ability to locate the full text of those documents.

- Be aware of nonbibliographic databases. For example, depending on the subject area, the researcher should be aware of databases in climatology, seismology, spectroscopy, or genome research. The researcher should be able to extract meaning from nontextual data sources, whether from a nonbibliographic database or not.
- Understand the importance of review articles and publications.

CONCLUSION

Scientists are interested in exploring the world and the universe around them. They read the scientific literature to learn what others have observed in the past, and they write articles and books to publish the research they have conducted. Scientists write journal articles and books as a way to document their research for posterity. Science students, faculty, and librarians use that literature to learn from past researchers. Much of the core literature can be found in journals, and it is imperative for students and librarians to know how to find those journal articles. To be scientifically literate, one needs to understand what information sources to use, where to find those sources, how to use them effectively, and why some sources are better than others. I hope this chapter pointed you in the right direction.

SCIENCE RESOURCES

Databases

ACM Digital Library. New York: Association for Computing Machinery. www.acm.org/dl.

ACM Guide to Computing Literature. New York: Association for Computing Machinery. portal.acm.org/guide.cfm.

ArXiv.org. www.arXiv.org.

Biological Abstracts. Philadelphia, PA: Thomson Scientific. thomsonscientific.com/support/products/ba.

Biological Sciences. Bethesda, MD: CSA. www.csa.com/factsheets/biolclust-set-c.php.

Chemical Abstract Service. Columbus, OH: Chemical Abstracts Service. www.cas.org.

CiteSeer.IST. State College, PA: Pennsylvania State University. citeseer.ist.psu.edu.

Computing Reviews. New York: Association for Computing Machinery. www.computingreviews.com.

CrossFire Beilstein. San Ramon, CA: Elsevier MDL. www.mdl.com/products/ knowledge/crossfire_beilstein.

CrossFire Gmelin. San Ramon, CA: Elsevier MDL. www.mdl.com/products/ knowledge/crossfire_gmelin.

GEOBASE. New York: Elsevier. www.elsevier.com/homepage/sah/spd/site/locate _geobase.html.

GeoRef. Alexandria, VA: American Geological Institute. www.agiweb.org/georef.

IEEE Computer Society Digital Library. Piscataway, NJ: IEEE Computer Society. www.computer.org/portal/site/csdl/index.jsp.

INSPEC. London: IEE. www.iee.org/Publish/INSPEC.

Journal Citation Reports. Philadelphia, PA: Thomson Scientific. scientific.thomson .com/products/jcr.

Landolt-Bornstein. New York: Springer. www.springer.com/sgw/cda/frontpage/ 0,,4-10113-2-95859-0,00.html.

Lecture Notes in Computer Science. New York: Springer. www.springerlink.com/ link.asp?id=105633.

Lecture Notes in Mathematics. New York: Springer. www.springerlink.com/ openurl.asp?genre=journal&issn=0075-8434.

MathSciNet. Providence, RI: American Mathematical Society. www.ams.org/ mathscinet.

MEDLINE. Bethesda, MD: National Library of Medicine. www.ncbi.nlm.nih .gov/entrez.

NASA Astrophysics Data System (ADS). Cambridge, MA: Harvard-Smithsonian Center for Astrophysics. adsabs.harvard.edu/abstract_service.html.

Science Citation Index Expanded. Part of the Web of Science. Philadelphia, PA: Thomson Scientific. scientific.thomson.com/products/wos.

Scopus. New York: Elsevier. www.info.scopus.com.

Zentralblatt MATH. Berlin: European Mathematical Information Service; Karlsruhe, Germany: FIZ Karlsruhe. www.emis.de/ZMATH.

Zoological Record. Philadelphia, PA: Thomson Scientific. thomsonscientific .com/support/products/zr.

Encyclopedias and Reference Tools

Chemical Abstracts Service Source Index. Columbus, OH: Chemical Abstracts Service. The most recent quinquennial edition covers the years 1907 to 2004.

CRC Handbook of Chemistry and Physics. New York: Chapman & Hall/CRC. www.chemnetbase.com.

Dictionary of Inorganic Compounds. New York: Chapman & Hall/CRC. www.chemnetbase.com.

Dictionary of Organic Compounds. New York: Chapman & Hall/CRC. www.chemnetbase.com.

Encyclopedia of Life Sciences. London; New York: Nature Publishing Group, 2002. els.wiley.com.

Grzimek's Animal Life Encyclopedia. Detroit: Thomson Gale, 2003–2004.

Handbook of Optical Materials. Boca Raton, FL: CRC Press, 2003.

McGraw-Hill Encyclopedia of Science & Technology. 9th ed. New York: Mc-Graw-Hill, 2002. www.accessscience.com.

Meyers, Robert A., ed. *Encyclopedia of Physical Science and Technology.* 3rd ed. San Diego: Academic Press, 2002. www.sciencedirect.com/science/reference works/0122274105.

Periodical Title Abbreviations. 16th ed. Detroit, MI: Gale Research Co., 2006.

Guides to the Literature

Anderson, Nancy D., and Lois M. Pausch, eds. *A Guide to Library Service in Mathematics: The Non-trivial Mathematics Librarian.* Greenwich, CT: JAI Press, 1993.

Bazler, Judith. *Chemistry Resources in the Electronic Age.* Westport, CT: Greenwood Press, 2003.

Boorkman, Jo Anne, Jeffrey T. Huber, Fred W. Roper, eds. *Introduction to Reference Sources in the Health Sciences.* 4th ed. New York: Neal-Schuman Publishers, 2004.

Davis, Elisabeth B., and Diane Schmidt. *Guide to Information Sources in the Botanical Sciences.* 2nd ed. Englewood, CO: Libraries Unlimited, 1996.

Douville, Judith A. *The Literature of Chemistry: Recommended Titles for Undergraduate Chemistry Library Collections.* Chicago: Association of College & Research Libraries, Division of the American Library Association, 2004.

Fowler, Kristine K., ed. *Using the Mathematics Literature.* New York: Marcel Dekker Inc., 2004.

Gould, Constance C., and Karla Pearce. *Information Needs in the Sciences: An Assessment.* Mountain View, CA: Research Libraries Group, 1991.

Guide to Reference Books. 11th ed. Chicago: American Library Association, 1996.

Hurt, Charlie Deuel. *Information Sources in Science and Technology.* 3rd ed. Englewood, CO: Libraries Unlimited, 1998.

Kellerman, Frank R. *Introduction to Health Sciences Librarianship: A Management Handbook.* Westport, CT: Greenwood Press, 1997.

Larsgaard, Mary Lynette. *Map Librarianship: An Introduction.* 3rd ed. Englewood, CO: Libraries Unlimited, 1998.

Maizell, Robert E. *How to Find Chemical Information: A Guide for Practicing Chemists, Educators, and Students.* 3rd ed. New York: Wiley, 1998.

The New Walford: Guide to Reference Resources. 9th ed. London: Facet Publishing, 2005. Volume 1 covers science and technology resources.

Ridley, Damon D. *Information Retrieval: SciFinder and SciFinder Scholar.* Chichester: John Wiley & Sons, 2002.

Schmidt, Diane. *Guide to Reference and Information Sources in the Zoological Sciences.* Westport, CT: Libraries Unlimited, 2003.

Schmidt, Diane, Elisabeth B. Davis, and Pamela F. Jacobs. *Using the Biological Literature: A Practical Guide.* 3rd ed. New York: Marcel Dekker, 2002.

Somerville, Arleen N., ed. *Chemical Librarianship: Challenges and Opportunities.* New York: Haworth Press, 1997.

Stern, David. *Guide to Information Sources in the Physical Sciences.* Englewood, CO: Libraries Unlimited, 2000.

Tucker, Martha A., and Nancy D. Anderson. *Guide to Information Sources in Mathematics and Statistics.* Westport, CT: Libraries Unlimited, 2004.

Wyatt, H. V., ed. *Information Sources in the Life Sciences.* 4th ed. London; New Providence, NJ: Bowker-Saur, 1997.

NOTES

1. Jean-Claude Guedon, "The Perspective of Scientists and Scholars," in *In Oldenburg's Long Shadow: Librarians, Research Scientists, Publishers, and the Control of Scientific Publishing* (Washington, DC: Association of Research Libraries, 2001), 15.

2. Michael Seringhaus, "Scientists, Consider Where You Publish," *Yale Daily News,* September 8, 2004, www.yaledailynews.com/article.asp?AID=26120 (accessed April 7, 2006).

3. Ann C. Weller, *Editorial Peer Review: Its Strengths and Weaknesses* (Medford, NJ: Information Today, 2001); and David Shatz, *Peer Review: A Critical Inquiry* (Oxford, UK: Rowman & Littlefield Publishers, 2004).

4. Chris Woolston, "The Scientific Paper Mill," *The Chronicle of Higher Education,* September 24, 2001, chronicle.com/jobs/2001/09/2001092401c.htm (accessed April 7, 2006).

5. One of the proponents for the open access movement is Peter Suber, a professor in the department of philosophy at Earlham College. He provides an overview of OA at www.earlham.edu/~peters/fos/overview.htm.

6. This provides more detail concerning their plan: www.oxfordjournals.org/our _journals/nar/announce_openaccess.html (accessed April 7, 2006).

7. "Feedback (Letter to the Editor)," *New Scientist* 175, no. 2350 (July 6, 2002): 108. An updated flowchart is available here: library.osu.edu/sites/geology/files/ComptesRendus .pdf (accessed April 15, 2006).

8. Einar H. Fredrikson, "The Dutch Publishing Scene: Elsevier and North Holland," in *A Century of Science Publishing: A Collection of Essays* (Washington, DC: IOS Press, 2001): 61–76.

9. Ad Hoc Committee on Economics of Publication, *Economics of Scientific Journals* (Bethesda, MD: Council of Biology Editors, 1982), 23.

10. Richard K. Johnson, "A Question of Access: SPARC, BioOne, and Society Driven Electronic Publishing," *D-Lib Magazine* 6, no. 5 (May 2000), www.dlib.org/dlib/may00/ johnson/05johnson.html (accessed January 3, 2006).

11. Robert H. Marks, "Learned Societies Adapt to New Publishing Realities," in *A Century of Science Publishing: A Collection of Essays* (Washington, DC: IOS Press, 2001), 92.

12. Robert H. Marks, "Learned Societies Adapt to New Publishing Realities," 94.

13. Blaise Cronin and Helen Barsky Atkins, *The Web of Knowledge: A Festschrift in Honor of Eugene Garfield* (Medford, NJ: Information Today, 2000).

14. Many articles are in a special section "50 Years of Citation Indexing," *Current Science* 89, no. 9 (November 10, 2005): 1502–54, www.ias.ac.in/currsci/nov102005/contents .htm (accessed March 16, 2006).

15. *A New Universe to Explore: Careers in Astronomy* (Washington, DC: American Astronomical Society), www.aas.org/education/careers.html (accessed April 7, 2006).

16. For these two fields, I consulted the *Occupational Outlook Handbook* (Washington, DC: U.S. Government Printing Office, 2006–2007), www.bls.gov/oco/ocos049.htm and www.bls.gov/oco/ocos074.htm (both accessed November 15, 2006).

17. The most recent is from 1977, see Robert A. Seal, *A Guide to the Literature of Astronomy* (Littleton, CO: Libraries Unlimited, 1977).

18. Brenda G. Corbin, "The Evolution and Role of the Astronomical Library and Librarian," in *Information Handling in Astronomy: Historical Vistas* (Dordrecht; Boston: Kluwer Academic Publishers, 2003), 139–55; and Uta Grothkopf, "Astronomy Libraries 2000: Context, Coordination, Cooperation," in *Information Handling in Astronomy* (Dordrecht; Boston: Kluwer Academic Publishers, 2000), 165–74.

19. Uta Grothkopf, ed., *Library and Information Services in Astronomy III (LISA III): Proceedings of a Conference Held in Puerto de la Cruz, Tenerife, Spain, April 21–24, 1998* (San Francisco, CA: Astronomical Society of the Pacific, 1998), www.stsci.edu/stsci/ meetings/lisa3 (accessed April 7, 2006); and Brenda G. Corbin, Elizabeth P. Bryson, and Marek Wolf, eds., *Library and Information Services in Astronomy IV (LISA IV): Proceedings of a Conference Held at Charles University, Prague, Czech Republic, July 2–5, 2002* (Washington, DC: U.S. Naval Observatory, 2003), www.eso.org/gen-fac/libraries/lisa4 (accessed April 7, 2006).

20. Constance C. Gould and Karla Pearce, "Biology," in *Information Needs in the Sciences* (Mountain View, CA: Research Libraries Group Inc., 1991), 24.

21. Constance C. Gould and Karla Pearce, "Chemistry," in *Information Needs in the Sciences*, 13.

22. Constance C. Gould and Karla Pearce, "Geology," in *Information Needs in the Sciences*, 36.

23. Claude Ellsworth Siebenthal, "Notes on Glaciation in the Sangre de Cristo Range, Colorado," *Journal of Geology* 15 (1907): 15–22.

24. Lura E. Joseph, "Geology Librarianship: Current Trends and Challenges," *Science and Technology Libraries* 21, nos. 1–2 (2002): 65–85.

25. Martha A. Tucker and Nancy D. Anderson, *Guide to Information Sources in Mathematics* (Westport, CT: Libraries Unlimited, 2004), 8.

26. Jill Newby, "An Emerging Picture of Mathematicians' Use of Electronic Resources: The Effect of Withdrawal of Older Print Volumes," *Science and Technology Libraries* 25, no. 4 (2005): 65–85.

27. Paul H. Ginsparg, "@xxx.lanl.gov: First Steps Toward Electronic Research Communication," *Los Alamos Science* 22 (1994): 157, library.lanl.gov/cgi-bin/getfile?00285556 .pdf (accessed January 17, 2006).

28. Kate Manual, "Generic and Discipline-Specific Information Literacy Competencies: The Case of the Sciences," *Science and Technology Libraries* 24, nos. 3–4 (2004): 279–308.

8

Engineering Research

Joseph R. Kraus

INTRODUCTION

Historically, and for a variety of reasons, engineers have not been heavy users of libraries.[1] Many engineers have been trained to focus on local extralibrary resources, such as personal collections of books, input from colleagues, or company technical reports. Engineers are more concerned with the creation of an engineered object than with documents.[2] This does not mean that engineers do not need library-based resources—they just use information in different ways when compared to researchers in other disciplines. For example, engineers use the journal literature, but not to the same extent as scientists. Libraries of all types have been providing more and more end-user searchable databases, and just like many patrons, engineers prefer to do their own research.[3] Since most engineers prefer to do their own information searching, librarians have been working to provide the best tools for those who want to find library-based resources on their own.

In this chapter, I discuss engineering information-based research methods and tools. Just as with scientists, engineers also conduct research in the laboratory. Some laboratory-based research methods are mentioned but are not fully explored. At the beginning of the chapter, I describe some of the standard research methods common to all parts of engineering, moving on to some of the unique research methods for some of the subgroups. Near the end of the chapter, I cover the major library-based research tools engineers use to find information for their education and jobs.

What does an engineer do? The *Occupational Outlook Handbook* provides a thorough description:

> Engineers apply the theories and principles of science and mathematics to research and develop economical solutions to technical problems. Their work is the link between perceived social needs and commercial applications. Engineers design products, machinery to build those products, plants in which those products are made, and the systems that ensure the quality of the products and the efficiency of the workforce and manufacturing process. Engineers design, plan, and supervise the construction of buildings, highways, and transit systems. They develop and implement improved ways to extract, process, and use raw materials, such as petroleum and natural gas. They develop new materials that both improve the performance of products and take advantage of advances in technology. They harness the power of the sun, the Earth, atoms, and electricity for use in supplying the Nation's power needs, and create millions of products using power. They analyze the impact of the products they develop or the systems they design on the environment and on people using them. Engineering knowledge is applied to improving many things, including the quality of healthcare, the safety of food products, and the operation of financial systems.[4]

What types of engineers are there? While some engineers might not classify themselves as belonging to a specific category, some commonly known engineering areas are aerospace and aeronautical, bioengineering, chemical, civil, computer, electrical and electronic, industrial, materials, mining, mechanical, nuclear, and systems engineering.

STANDARD RESEARCH METHODS
COMMON TO ALL ENGINEERS

In general, how do engineers use information, and what kinds of research questions do they ask? Constance Gould and Karla Pearce address this in a concise manner:

> Above all, engineers are problem solvers. They are also concerned with predictability—to design a device or system . . . so that when it is built it will function as predicted. The questions they ask are generally focused on un-

derstanding what is happening in a given system, whether mechanical or subatomic. This requires knowledge of general scientific principles, mainly drawn from physics, mathematics, and chemistry, coupled with experimental data. After general analysis of the problem, they will ask specific questions of the engineering literature, such as: What is the thermodynamic property of a certain metal under particular conditions? What is the effect of one compound on another? How should a particular type of tube be coated? How should one test for a leak? What is the standard . . . for testing the compressive strength of cement?[5]

Even though engineers use scientific principles to solve engineering problems, the way engineers use information is quite different from scientists. Several authors make the case for distinguishing engineers from scientists.[6] An encyclopedia entry by the same set of authors provides a historical overview of the literature on engineers' information-seeking behaviors.[7] Even though this encyclopedia article was written in 1993 before the advent of the Web, many of the research methods and the types of resources used by engineers have not changed much since then. For example, they noted the importance of information networks involving coworkers and colleagues;[8] the importance of that network holds true today.[9]

Engineers use information in different ways throughout their education, their career, and their position in a company. Undergraduate engineering students use different types of information than graduate students. As engineering students begin their undergraduate education, they are likely to use basic sources of information such as textbooks, monographs, and handbooks. Most notably, textbooks are very important to undergraduates because they are assigned problem sets in their textbooks to solve. Compared to undergraduates, graduate students use more abstracting sources, conference papers, journal articles, and technical reports.[10] Lastly, practicing engineers who are out in the workforce use a completely different set of resources because they now use a corporate library. Corporate libraries have traditional published business and engineering literature, but they also house internally published documents and technical reports not found in academic libraries.

Even though many people assume that engineers need only current information, many engineers use older literature. For example, an electrical or computer engineer might need to find an electrical schematic diagram concerning a component from the 1970s. A mechanical engineer might need a technical report concerning hypervelocity impact damage for a particular metal that was published in the 1960s. A civil engineer might need historical standards concerning a bridge construction project.

THE ACADEMIC ENVIRONMENT

Undergraduate Students

Many engineering students use traditional library resources such as books, journal articles, and reserve readings, but they do not use the library to the same extent as undergraduates in other disciplines. In a study comparing undergraduate students studying life versus nonlife, hard versus soft, and applied versus pure disciplines, Ethelene Whitmire found that engineering students did not use the library as often as students in other disciplines.[11] Part of the reason could be that engineering undergraduates rely heavily on their own textbooks. Undergraduates are assigned many problem sets from their textbooks and often use their own collections of books to find information to solve those problems.

Common Research Methods for Undergraduate Students

Quick access to information is very important to just about every engineer,[12] whether he or she is studying as an undergraduate or working at an engineering firm. The first point of reference for an engineering student is to look through the books one has on hand. From personally collected anecdotal evidence, if textbooks do not provide needed information, then students will use the following resources to complete their homework, loosely in this order:

1. Search the Internet.
2. Ask a friend who is enrolled in the same class.
3. Ask a friend who is enrolled in a similar class, or who took the class in a prior term.
4. Ask a friend outside of the class.
5. Ask the professor for clarification.

6. Go to the library to
   - use handbooks and/or reference materials,
   - get reserve readings,
   - find and print out journal articles,
   - work with a study group,
   - study in a quiet place, or
   - use technical reports, patents, or standards.

Faculty may assign problem sets or projects to groups of undergraduate students. The students are expected to work as a team to solve the problems. If this is the case, the students will work collaboratively on the project, and they will ask each other questions about how to solve the problems at hand. Depending on the space available in the library, students might find a group study area that is conducive to their research.

In general, Carol Tenopir and Donald King found that many engineering patrons ask for help from a librarian as a last resort, after all other resources have been exhausted.[13] Once a student does contact a reference librarian, what types of questions do engineering students ask?[14]

   - I need information on X topic.
   - Do we have the Y journal or book? How can I get item Z?
   - What does this abbreviation mean?
   - Where can I find the property, structure, or cost for a known material?
   - Where can I find a particular procedure or technique?

Since the baccalaureate degree is the terminal degree for most engineering students, many jump from being undergraduate students into a professional engineering position. This is quite different from the training that many scientists receive. For the most part, scientists are taught through the rigorous academic PhD system. Since most engineering students go right into the workforce (without any graduate school), they learn that advancement in the profession is tied to their work within an engineering firm.[15] In this sense, engineering researchers are similar to business researchers, since their careers are tied to the success of a company. To be successful in the business world, engineering students are concerned with financial success and professional preparation.[16]

Graduate Students

Many engineering graduate students have previously been in the work-force and may have picked up some research methods common to practi-tioners as discussed in a following section. If they did not obtain any en-gineering work experience between their undergraduate and graduate studies, their faculty adviser may begin the process of introducing re-search methods common to faculty or practitioners, depending on the field the graduate student is pursuing.

Faculty

Because faculty are in the academic realm, they tend to use more aca-demic journals and books in their research because academic library re-sources are available at their institution. Most engineering faculty also write journal articles since they are expected to publish the results of their research. If they had engineering firm experience before joining the fac-ulty, they may integrate some of their engineering practitioner research skills with academic research methods.

PRACTITIONERS

Once an engineer starts work with a company, he or she will learn to use information provided by the company. This local store of information will often include proprietary technical reports, memos, briefings, market re-ports, or other publications that are for in-house use only. Companies want to guard their research and development reports and trade secrets from leaking to competitors.

Research on practicing engineers reveals various rankings for how they use information.[17] Generally, engineers try to find information within their office, and then they will branch out geographically as needed. The fol-lowing is a representative list of how engineers seek information. They search through

- memory;
- personal files;

- personal books;
- departmental files, books, and databases;
- other records of previous work;
- other engineers;
- the company library; and
- other sources such as
  - clients,
  - manufacturers and suppliers,
  - manuals and brochures, and
  - conference publications and training course materials.

TYPICAL RESEARCH METHODS FOR SUBGROUPS OF ENGINEERS

While it is impossible to generalize to say that certain types of engineers use information a certain way, and another segment of engineers uses information a different way, it is possible to note some distinctions among the various subgroups of engineers.

In a recent article documenting the citation patterns of master's engineering students at Mississippi State University, Virginia Williams and Christine Fletcher found differences in the citation patterns between different engineering majors.[18] For example, they found that students in electrical and computer engineering cited a high percentage of conference papers, while those in chemical, agricultural, and biological engineering cited more journal articles in their research. An older study shows how engineers in research and development, design, operations, and management positions use various information sources, such as internal documents, external sources, publications, courses, and media. Russel Jones, William LeBold, and Becky Pernicka found, for example, that engineers in R & D and management were higher users of technical journal articles when compared to engineers in design and operations.[19]

John Kennedy, Thomas Pinelli, and Rebecca Barclay showed how different types of aerospace engineers use information.[20] Many other articles cover the information-use patterns of engineers in a variety of specific areas, such as computer;[21] construction;[22] design, process, and manufacturing;[23] innovation;[24] and software engineering.[25] Another study looked at engineers in the oil and gas industry.[26]

RESEARCH TOOLS

Engineers use a great number of research tools to gather the data and information they need. The following are presented roughly in order of the amount of time and energy needed to extract data from the source. Engineers use handbooks and encyclopedias because they can look up data very quickly. They also use library databases, but these resources take some time for engineers to learn how to use effectively. Engineers also join societies and professional organizations to meet with others to discuss engineering problems. Most of these societies publish journals, magazines, trade literature, and other reports in their specialties. Many engineers use gray literature such as technical reports, standards, patents, dissertations, and theses in their research. While few engineers use the guides to the literature, they can be handy resources for engineering librarians to consult.

Handbooks and Encyclopedias

As previously mentioned, engineers use handbooks because it is easy to retrieve the practical information contained within them. One of the best general sources is the *Engineering Handbook* by Richard Dorf. There is a wealth of subject-specific handbooks such as *The Computer Engineering Handbook*, the *Mechanical Engineers' Handbook*, or the *Standard Handbook for Aeronautical and Astronautical Engineers*. There are too many subject-specific handbooks to list here, but many of them are noted in the engineering resources section at the end of this chapter. Engineers also use general encyclopedias such as the *McGraw-Hill Encyclopedia of Science & Technology* or the *Encyclopedia of Physical Science and Technology*. They also use subject-specific encyclopedias such as the *Encyclopedia of Materials: Science and Technology* or the *Kirk-Othmer Encyclopedia of Chemical Technology*.

Databases

Engineering students and engineers use library databases to find articles published in journals, trade publications, conference publications, or magazines. *Compendex* is the best and most comprehensive engineering database since it covers all of the subdisciplines from aerospace through systems engineering. The database is the electronic version of the print *Engineering Index Annual*. It covers about 2,600 sources and has over six million abstracts of journal articles, technical reports, and conference papers. Many engineering patrons find *Compendex* easy to use, but some have difficulty finding source documents. One example concerns SPIE papers and the way they are indexed in the database. *Compendex* catalogs over 170,000 SPIE papers as articles in the serial *Proceedings of SPIE*.[27] When a patron clicks on a link to find the paper in a local library catalog, the system tries to find that serial title. *Compendex* considers those papers to be articles in a journal, but many libraries consider those papers to be chapters contained within books. Hence, the library may have the conference paper in a book cataloged with a different title, but the patron might not find it because of the way he or she was directed by the system.

Because *Compendex* can be somewhat daunting, a smaller database such as the *Applied Science and Technology Abstracts* can be used to identify core journal literature. The *Science Citation Index (SCI) Expanded* also covers the major engineering journals. The advantage to the *SCI* is its ability to track citations forward and backward in time. The *SCI* database is covered in greater detail in chapter 7. Another multidisciplinary engineering database is the *CSA Technology Research Database*. This database has three components: the *CSA Materials Research Database*, the *CSA High Technology Database with Aerospace*, and the *CSA Engineering Research Database*, which indexes many civil, computer, electrical, information systems, communications, mechanical, and transportation engineering sources.

In addition to searching *Compendex*, engineers should use databases that are specific to their fields. For example, aerospace engineers should search the *CSA High Technology Database with Aerospace* and *INSPEC*. *INSPEC* is a comprehensive database that covers a wide range of high-technology fields in physics, electronics, computing, information technology, and materials science, so it is a useful tool for patrons in many of the engineering subdisciplines. Biomedical engineers should look through *MEDLINE*. Chemical engineers should be familiar with the *Chemical Abstracts Service*. Civil engineers should be familiar with the *Civil Engineering Database* published by the American Society of Civil Engineers. The abstracts are freely available, but access to full-text articles is dependent upon a library subscription. Civil engineers should also be familiar with the *International Civil Engineering Database* and the *Transportation Research Information Service.*

Patrons in computer or electrical engineering should search specialized databases such as the *ACM Digital Library*, the *ACM Guide to Computing Literature*, *Computing Reviews*, *INSPEC*, the *IEEE Computer Society Digital Library*, and *IEEE Xplore*. When patrons search through *IEEE Xplore*, the default search option is set to search the entire database. Depending on the library subscription, engineers may not have full-text access to all of the *Xplore* database.

Some patrons may want to get information on a specific high-technology company or industry. For example, materials engineering students wanting information about the semiconductor industry should look through business databases such as *Business Source Premier* or *ABI/ Inform*. They should become familiar with company and industry sources discussed in chapter 5.

Societies and Professional Organizations

There are a huge number of engineering societies and professional organizations. Engineers like to work together to solve engineering problems and will attend meetings and conferences to learn from others in their discipline. The most important societies and organizations are listed in the "Engineering Resources" section at the end of this chapter. Most of those societies publish journals and magazines that members receive free or at reduced subscription rates.

Gray Literature

For the most part, gray literature consists of documents that are not meant for wide circulation; they are written for a small audience, and they often have a very narrow topical focus. Most are not indexed by the major indexing and abstracting sources. Many of them are categorized as technical reports, standards and specifications, patents, and dissertations and theses. Other examples include journal article preprints, translations of journal articles, supplementary data, some conference proceedings, and poster papers. The key characteristic of gray literature is that the information is not readily available as a traditional published book or a journal article.

Conference Literature

While many publications in the categories listed above are difficult to track down, not all items in those categories should be considered gray literature. For example, though many conference proceedings papers are published in a book or within a journal issue, many conference organizers provide the text of presented papers only to the attendees of a conference. These conference papers might not be sold as a book or published in a journal issue once the conference is done, or indexed in standard abstracting and indexing databases. About the only way patrons and librarians can learn of the conference is if an attendee donates a copy of the publication to the library.

Technical Reports

A technical report is a document that describes the progress or results of technical or scientific research. Such reports are often prepared specifically for the financial sponsors of a research project. They are often created just for internal distribution, but to make distribution easier, many technical reports are placed on the Internet or on a company intranet. They are rarely indexed by standard article databases.

Some technical reports are published on the Web, but they might only be posted there for a short period of time, or they might be posted in a hidden directory to which only certain people can gain access. The technical report could be hidden in a database that does not allow webcrawlers to index the content. In such cases, engineers may learn the lesson that "whom to ask" is just as important as "where to look" for information. An engineering librarian could direct the engineer to the correct publishing agency, author, or document supplier.

The U.S. government provides funding to many organizations and educational institutions to perform research in narrow areas, and technical reports are often the end results of that type of funding. The following government agencies provide greater indexing, abstracting, and sometimes the full text of these reports. Since technical reports often come from government sources, please see chapter 6 for more information concerning some of these indexing services.

- Defense Technical Information Center (stinet.dtic.mil)
- NASA Technical Reports Server (ntrs.nasa.gov)
- National Technical Information Service (NTIS, www.ntis.gov, also available from a variety of information vendors)
- U.S. Department of Energy, Office of Scientific and Technical Information (www.osti.gov)

Many citations to NTIS reports have leading letters and a series of about eight to eleven numbers and letters. Some examples are "PB2002104614," "N20050182124," and "ADA435888." If a patron asks for a report using one of these codes as a citation, then it may be an NTIS document; the patron should check the NTIS database or other technical report servers to verify the citation.

Many technical reports are created for private organizations in need of outside research. The engineering librarians at the University of Maryland created a "Virtual Technical Reports Center" (www.lib.umd.edu/ENGIN/ TechReports/Virtual-TechReports.html). This website points to hundreds of organizations that provide technical reports, preprints, reprints, dissertations, theses, and other types of research reports.

Standards and Specifications

A standard or a set of specifications is a document written by a group of experts and approved by an organization that provides rules, guidelines, or characteristics for technical activities or products. Standards are formulated by standards developing organizations (SDOs). An SDO could be a government agency, trade group, professional society or association, international or regional organization, or private company. The following websites provide information or abstracts concerning standards:

- Defense and Federal Specifications and Standards (also called "Military Standards," assist.daps.dla.mil/quicksearch)
- IHS Standards Store (www.global.ihs.com)

- National Standards Systems Network (www.nssn.com)
- TechStreet (www.techstreet.com)

Many citations to standards have leading letters indicating the standards-creating body. Some are ASTM (American Society for Testing and Materials), ISO (International Organization for Standardization), NEMA (National Electrical Manufacturers Association), NFPA (National Fire Protection Association), or SAE (Society of Automotive Engineers). Engineers either purchase standards or retrieve standards in a technical library. Many libraries do not catalog individual standards, so engineers should contact an engineering librarian for help in obtaining a standard.

Patents

Through the patenting system, most governments provide the creator of an invention with the sole right to make, use, and sell that invention for a set period of time. In the United States, that time period is twenty years from the date of application. There are many databases that index and abstract patents from the United States and abroad, but in the past, many patrons had difficulty getting their hands on the full text of a patent. The Internet has changed that in most cases, but engineers still need to know where to look for patents. For U.S. patents, many engineers download patents through the U.S. Patent and Trademark Office (USPTO) website (www.uspto.gov). This service is also described in chapter 6. Another website, free.patentfetcher.com, provides PDF versions of U.S. patents when the patent number is known.

Patents published outside the United States can be harder to find. For European patents, there is a good database called *esp@cenet* (www.espacenet.com), which provides full-text access to the patents of many European countries.

While many patents can be found using simple keyword searching, some engineers want to find *all* patents that incorporate a particular method or are in a particular subject area. If an engineer has a patentable idea and he or she wants to be sure that a patent has not already been granted on the idea, then the engineer should discuss the search with a librarian who is familiar with various patent classification systems. In the

United States, the researcher should visit one of the patent and trademark depository libraries (www.uspto.gov/go/ptdl).

Dissertations and Theses

Dissertations and theses are considered gray literature because there are only a small number of copies available for any given title. Most dissertations and theses are never published as a journal article or book. Once patrons know where to look, doctoral dissertations written at U.S. or Canadian universities are easy to find since they are indexed in the *Pro-Quest Dissertations and Theses* database. The ProQuest database does not index very many master's theses. Since most colleges and universities catalog their dissertations and theses, the patron could also use the *WorldCat* database from OCLC. If an author, title, or degree-granting institution is known, then it might be possible to request the dissertation or thesis through Interlibrary Loan. While many practicing engineers do not use dissertations and theses, master's students and PhD candidates find prior dissertations and theses useful to consult.

Guides to the Literature

There are a number of reference guides that cover engineering topics. Four books entitled *Information Sources in Engineering*, *Guide to Information Sources in Engineering*, *Information Sources in Science and Technology*, and *Information Sources in Grey Literature* are traditional guides to the literature marketed to librarians. The article "Engineering" within the book *Information Needs in the Sciences: An Assessment* is also geared to the same audience. There are other books that are nontraditional guides to the literature. The *MIT Guide to Science and Engineering Communication* is written for undergraduate science and engineering students. It explains to the student how to search the literature, document sources, organize and draft documents, write memos, develop proposals and progress reports, make presentations at conferences, and write CVs and resumes. Another book entitled *Communication Patterns of Engineers* should be consulted if one wants to learn more about how engineers perform research and use the literature. It explains engineers' communication framework, information seeking and use, reading patterns, the amount of engineering information output, the nature of engineering scholarly journals, and how engineers' communication patterns differ from scientific and medical communication.

RESEARCH SKILLS WITHIN THE ENGINEERING DISCIPLINE

Just as is the case for science researchers (or researchers in any other discipline for that matter), there are core research skills that engineers should learn. In addition to the core set of skills discussed in chapter 9, engineering researchers should also

- Know where to find government documents and gray literature (such as patents, technical reports, standards, and the like) in their field.
- Recognize the importance of "invisible colleges" in the research process. They should also be aware of the major professional engineering associations and organizations.
- Have a certain level of Internet fluency. They should understand that not everything can be found via Google, and not everything is on the Web. The engineering researcher may need to search within specific databases, such as NTIS or the USPTO to get the required document, or visit the library to photocopy an article from a journal.

CONCLUSION

Like all other library users, engineers need quality information. To access information, they may use the path of least resistance and rely on the information they can retrieve in their office or over the Internet. When they use the Internet, they may find useful journal articles or reports because the library subscribes to the sources. If they do not find the information available in their workspace, they will ask other students or colleagues working on the same project. If that does not suffice, they will expand their information-gathering umbrella to encompass other people in their organization.

It is usually at this point that the library will become critical. The researcher may have spent days or weeks looking for a certain piece or type of information, all to no avail. Since the engineering and technical literature is so wide and varied, engineering librarians can show engineers where quality information is located and the breadth of engineering literature. The librarian has the skills, the ability, and the mandate to show engineers how to navigate through the wide technical and engineering information landscape.

ENGINEERING RESOURCES

Databases

ABI/Inform Complete. Ann Arbor, MI: ProQuest Information and Learning.

ACM Digital Library. New York: Association for Computing Machinery. www.acm.org/dl.

ACM Guide to Computing Literature. New York: Association for Computing Machinery. portal.acm.org/guide.cfm.

Applied Science and Technology Abstracts. New York: H. W. Wilson Co.

Business Source Premier. Ipswich, MA: EBSCO.

Chemical Abstracts Service. Columbus, OH: Chemical Abstracts Service. www.cas.org.

CiteSeer.IST. State College: Pennsylvania State University. citeseer.ist.psu.edu.

Civil Engineering (CE) Database. Reston, VA: American Society of Civil Engineers. www.pubs.asce.org/cedbsrch.html.

Compendex. New York: Elsevier Inc. www.ei.org.

Computing Reviews. New York: Association for Computing Machinery. www.computingreviews.com.

CSA Engineering Research Database. Bethesda, MD: CSA. www.csa.com/factsheets/engineering-set-c.php.

CSA High Technology Database with Aerospace. Bethesda, MD: CSA. www.csa.com/factsheets/aerospace-set-c.php.

CSA Technology Research Database. Bethesda, MD: CSA. www.csa.com/factsheets/techresearch-set-c.php.

esp@cenet. Munich, Germany: European Patent Office. www.espacenet.com.

IEEE Computer Society Digital Library. Piscataway, NJ: IEEE Computer Society. www.computer.org/portal/site/csdl.

IEEE Xplore database. Piscataway, NJ: IEEE. ieeexplore.ieee.org.

INSPEC. London: IEE. www.iee.org/Publish/INSPEC.

International Civil Engineering Abstracts. Bradford, UK: Emerald Group Publishing. www.emeraldinsight.com/info/products_services/abstracts/ICEA.

MEDLINE. Bethesda, MD: National Library of Medicine. Available online through a variety of vendors. It is also available through PubMed. www.pubmed.gov.

Science Citation Index Expanded. Part of the Web of Science. Philadelphia, PA: Thomson Scientific. scientific.thomson.com/products/wos.

Transportation Research Information Service. trisonline.bts.gov/search.cfm.

Handbooks & Encyclopedias

ASM International Handbook Committee. *ASM Handbook.* 10th ed. Materials Park, OH: ASM International, 1990.

Bronzino, Joseph D., ed. *The Biomedical Engineering Handbook.* 2nd ed. Boca Raton, FL: CRC Press, 2000.

Buschow, K. H. Jürgen, et al., eds. *Encyclopedia of Materials: Science and Technology.* New York: Elsevier, 2001.

Chen, W. F., and J. Y. Richard Liew, eds. *The Civil Engineering Handbook.* 2nd ed. Boca Raton, FL: CRC Press, 2003.

Chen, Wai-Kai., ed. *The Electrical Engineering Handbook.* Amsterdam; Boston: Elsevier Academic Press, 2005.

Davies, Mark, ed. *The Standard Handbook for Aeronautical and Astronautical Engineers.* New York: McGraw-Hill, 2003.

Dorf, Richard C., ed. *The Electrical Engineering Handbook.* 2nd ed. Boca Raton, FL: CRC Press; New York: IEEE Press, 1997.

——. *The Engineering Handbook.* 2nd ed. Boca Raton, FL: CRC Press, 2005.

Kreith, Frank, and D. Yogi Goswami, eds. *The CRC Handbook of Mechanical Engineering.* 2nd ed. Boca Raton, FL: CRC Press, 2005.

Kroschwitz., Jacqueline I., ed. *Kirk-Othmer Encyclopedia of Chemical Technology.* 5th ed. Hoboken, NJ: Wiley-Interscience, 2004.

Marghitu, Dan B., ed. *Mechanical Engineer's Handbook.* San Diego: Academic Press, 2001.

McGraw-Hill Encyclopedia of Science & Technology. 9th ed. New York: McGraw-Hill, 2002. 9th ed. www.accessscience.com.

Meyers, Robert A., ed. *Encyclopedia of Physical Science and Technology.* 3rd ed. San Diego: Academic Press, 2002. www.sciencedirect.com/science/referenceworks/0122274105.

Moore, James, and George Zouridakis, eds. *Biomedical Technology and Devices Handbook.* Boca Raton, FL: CRC Press, 2004.

Murray, G. T., ed. *Handbook of Materials Selection for Engineering Applications.* New York: M. Dekker, 1997.

Kutz, Myer. *Mechanical Engineers' Handbook.* 3rd ed. Hoboken, NJ: John Wiley & Sons, 2006.

——. *Standard Handbook of Biomedical Engineering and Design*. New York: McGraw-Hill, 2003.

Oklobdzija, Vojin G., ed. *The Computer Engineering Handbook*. Boca Raton, FL: CRC Press, 2002.

Ricketts, Jonathan T., M. Kent Loftin, Frederick S. Merritt, eds. *Standard Handbook for Civil Engineers*. 5th ed. New York: McGraw-Hill, 2004.

Salvendy, Gavriel, ed. *Handbook of Industrial Engineering: Technology and Operations Management*. 3rd ed. New York: Wiley, 2001.

Schwarz, James A., Cristian I. Contescu, Karol Putyera, eds. *Dekker Encyclopedia of Nanoscience and Nanotechnology*. New York: Marcel Dekker, 2004.

Shackelford, James F., and William Alexander, eds. *CRC Materials Science and Engineering Handbook*. 3rd ed. Boca Raton, FL: CRC Press, 2001.

Ullmann's Encyclopedia of Industrial Chemistry. 6th ed. Weinheim: Wiley-VCH, 2003.

Webster, John G., ed. *Wiley Encyclopedia of Electrical and Electronics Engineering*. New York: John Wiley, 1999.

Yip, Sidney, ed. *Handbook of Materials Modeling*. Dordrecht: Springer, 2005.

Zandin, Kjell B., ed. *Maynard's Industrial Engineering Handbook*. 5th ed. New York: McGraw-Hill, 2001.

Societies and Organizations

American Ceramic Society (www.ceramics.org).

American Chemical Society (www.acs.org).

American Institute of Aeronautics and Astronautics (www.aiaa.org).

American Institute of Chemical Engineers (www.aiche.org).

American National Standards Institute (ANSI) (www.ansi.org).

American Society for Testing and Materials (ASTM) (www.astm.org).

American Society of Civil Engineers (www.asce.org).

American Society of Heating, Refrigerating, and Air-Conditioning Engineers (www.ashrae.org).

American Society of Mechanical Engineers (www.asme.org).

ASM International: The Materials Information Society (asminternational.org).

Association for Computing Machinery (www.acm.org).

Biomedical Engineering Society (www.bmes.org).

IEEE Computer Society (www.computer.org).

IEEE Engineering in Medicine and Biology Society (embs.gsbme.unsw.edu.au).

IEEE (Institute for Electrical and Electronics Engineers) (www.ieee.org).

Institute of Industrial Engineers (www.iienet.org).

Materials Research Society (www.mrs.org).

Minerals, Metals & Materials Society (www.tms.org).

Society for Mining, Metallurgy, and Exploration Inc. (www.smenet.org).

Society for the Advancement of Material and Process Engineering
(www.sampe.org).

Society of Automotive Engineers (www.sae.org).

Society of Manufacturing Engineers (www.sme.org).

Guides to the Literature

Auger, Charles P. *Information Sources in Grey Literature.* 4th ed. London; New Providence, NJ: Bowker-Saur, 1998.

Gould, Constance C., and Karla Pearce. "Engineering." In *Information Needs in the Sciences: An Assessment*, 54–62. Mountain View, CA: Research Libraries Group, 1991.

Hurt, Charlie Deuel. *Information Sources in Science and Technology.* 3rd ed. Englewood, CO: Libraries Unlimited, 1998.

Lord, Charles R. *Guide to Information Sources in Engineering.* Englewood, CO: Libraries Unlimited, 2000.

MacLeod, Roderick A., and Jim Corlett, eds. *Information Sources in Engineering.* München: K. G. Saur, 2005.

Paradis, James G., and Muriel L. Zimmerman. *The MIT Guide to Science and Engineering Communication.* 2nd ed. Cambridge, MA: MIT Press, 2002.

Tenopir, Carol, and Donald W. King. *Communication Patterns of Engineers.* Hoboken, NJ: John Wiley & Sons, IEEE Press, 2004.

NOTES

1. Maurita Peterson Holland, "Engineering," in *Scientific and Technical Libraries*, vol. 2, *Special Formats and Subject Areas* (New York: Academic Press, 1986), 122.

2. Nancy Jones Pruett, ed., "Scientific and Technical Literature and Its Use," in *Scientific and Technical Libraries*, vol. 1, *Functions and Management* (New York: Academic Press, 1986), 58.

3. Carol Tenopir and Donald W. King, *Communication Patterns of Engineers* (Hoboken, NJ: John Wiley & Sons, IEEE Press, 2004), 67.

4. *Occupational Outlook Handbook* (Washington, DC: U.S. Government Printing Office, 2006–2007), www.bls.gov/oco/ocos027.htm (accessed March 29, 2006).

5. Constance C. Gould and Karla Pearce, "Engineering," in *Information Needs in the Sciences: An Assessment* (Mountain View, CA: Research Libraries Group, 1991), 55.

6. John M. Kennedy, Thomas E. Pinelli, Rebecca O. Barclay, and Ann P. Bishop, "Distinguishing Engineers from Scientists—The Case for an Engineering Knowledge Community," in *Knowledge Diffusion in the U.S. Aerospace Industry: Managing Knowledge for Competitive Advantage* (Greenwich, CT: Ablex, 1997), part A: 177–213. A similar article was later published by Thomas E. Pinelli, "Distinguishing Engineers from Scientists—The Case for an Engineering Knowledge Community," *Science and Technology Libraries* 21, nos. 3–4 (2001): 131–63.

7. Thomas E. Pinelli, Ann P. Bishop, Rebecca O. Barclay, and John M. Kennedy, "The Information-Seeking Behavior of Engineers," in *Encyclopedia of Library and Information Science* (New York: Marcel Dekker Inc., 1993), 52:167–201.

8. Pinelli et al., "The Information-Seeking Behavior of Engineers," 194.

9. Morten Hertzum and Annelise Mark Pejtersen, "The Information-Seeking Practices of Engineers: Searching for Documents as Well as for People," *Information Processing and Management* 36, no. 5 (2000): 761–78.

10. Rebecca O. Barclay, Thomas E. Pinelli, John M. Kennedy, and Laura M. Hecht, "The Production and Use of Information by U.S. Aerospace Engineering and Science Students at the Undergraduate and Graduate Levels," in *Knowledge Diffusion in the U.S. Aerospace Industry: Managing Knowledge for Competitive Advantage* (Greenwich, CT: Ablex, 1997), part B: 425–65.

11. Ethelene Whitmire, "Disciplinary Differences and Undergraduates' Information-Seeking Behavior," *Journal of the American Society for Information Science and Technology* 53, no. 8 (2002): 631–38.

12. Several articles support this—Raya Fidel and Maurice Green, "The Many Faces of Accessibility: Engineers' Perception of Information Sources," *Information Processing & Management* 40, no. 3 (2004): 563–81. Another one is from Gillian Kerins, Ronan Madden, and Crystal Fulton, "Information Seeking and Students Studying for Professional Careers: The Cases of Engineering and Law Students in Ireland," *Information Research* 10, no. 1 (October 2004), informationr.net/ir/10-1/paper208.html (accessed January 17, 2006).

13. Carol Tenopir and Donald W. King, *Communication Patterns of Engineers*, 67.

14. Susan B. Ardis, "Internet Engineering Reference," *The Reference Librarian* 74 (2001): 75–89.

15. Nancy Jones Pruett, "Scientific and Technical Literature and Its Use," 58.

16. Nancy Jones Pruett, "Scientific and Technical Literature and Its Use," 57.

17. Several articles document the steps engineers take to track down information: Martin Ward, "A Survey of Engineers in Their Information World," *Journal of Librarianship and Information Science* 33, no. 4 (2001): 168–76; Tenopir and King, *Communication Patterns of Engineers*, 65; Hertzum and Pejtersen, "The Information-Seeking Practices of Engineers: Searching for Documents as Well as for People," 761–78.

18. Virginia Kay Williams and Christine Lea Fletcher, "Materials Used by Master's Students in Engineering and Implications for Collection Development: A Citation Analysis," *Issues in Science and Technology Librarianship* 45 (Winter 2006), www.istl.org/06-winter/refereed1.html (accessed March 29, 2006).

19. Russel C. Jones, William K. LeBold, and Becky J. Pernicka, "Keeping Up to Date and Solving Problems in Engineering," in *Proceedings, 1986 World Conference on Continuing Engineering Education: May 7–9, 1986, Lake Buena Vista, Florida* (New York: IEEE), 2:784–92.

20. John M. Kennedy, Thomas E. Pinelli, and Rebecca O. Barclay, "The Production and Use of Information by U.S. Aerospace Engineers and Scientists—From Research through Production to Technical Services," in *Knowledge Diffusion in the U.S. Aerospace Industry: Managing Knowledge for Competitive Advantage* (Greenwich, CT: Ablex, 1997), part A: 263–91.

21. Barbara D. Farah, "The Information Seeking Behavior of Academic Computer Engineers," in *Looking to the Year 2000: Information Professionals Chart the Course; Professional Papers from the 84th Annual Conference of the Special Libraries Association* (Washington DC: SLA, 1993), 65–101; Sandra G. Hirsh and Jamie Dinkelacker, "Seeking Information in Order to Produce Information: An Empirical Study at Hewlett Packard Labs," *Journal of the American Society for Information Science and Technology* 55, no. 9 (2004): 807–17.

22. David Veshosky, "Managing Innovation Information in Engineering and Construction Firms," *Journal of Management in Engineering* 14, no. 1 (January–February 1998): 58–66.

23. Lishi Kwasitsu, "Information-Seeking Behavior of Design, Process, and Manufacturing Engineers," *Library & Information Science Research* 25, no. 4 (2003): 459–76.

24. E. De Smet, "Information Behaviour in a Scientific-Technical Environment: A Survey with Innovation Engineers," *Scientometrics* 25, no. 1 (1992): 101–13.

25. Moshe Yitzhaki and Gloria Hammershlag, "Accessibility and Use of Information Sources among Computer Scientists and Software Engineers in Israel: Academy Versus Industry," *Journal of the American Society for Information Science and Technology* 55, no. 9 (2004): 832–42.

26. David Ellis and Merete Haugan, "Modelling the Information Seeking Patterns of Engineers and Research Scientists in an Industrial Environment," *Journal of Documentation* 53, no. 4 (1997): 384–403.

27. *Proceedings of SPIE—the International Society for Optical Engineering* (Bellingham, WA: SPIE).

9

Integrating Discipline-Based Library Instruction into the Curriculum

Carrie Forbes

Librarians have always seen themselves as keepers of knowledge, and they treasure the responsibility of showing others how to find information. Melvil Dewey wrote in 1876, "The time is when a library is a school, and the librarian is in the highest sense a teacher."[1] While librarians have always viewed their role as part educator and part gatekeeper, not much was written about library instruction during the early years of the profession. Interest in instruction really began to emerge in the 1960s. As stated by Francis Hopkins,

> Just as the decline of BI [bibliographic instruction] early in the century had been the product of social forces in the professional and academic environments, so was its revival in the 1960s. Two problems related to developments in education can be tackled only through systematic group instruction, and librarians, equipped now with better training and higher status, were ready for the challenge.[2]

As library instruction took flight during the 1960s and 1970s, a new specialization began to emerge. Library Orientation Exchange (LOEX), a nonprofit, self-supporting educational clearinghouse, was founded in 1971 after the first conference on library instruction was held at Eastern Michigan University.[3] Within the next two decades, new information technologies, the explosion of the World Wide Web, and online catalogs meant that library instruction filled a greater and greater need. While the increase in technologies created a great demand for user instruction, it also forced librarians to add complexity to bibliographic instruction. Users needed to develop crucial critical-thinking skills to be able to effectively evaluate all the information content. For teaching in a virtual world, librarians could use the same basic teaching principles they had always used, but these principles needed to be adapted to the new learning environment.

The expression "information literacy" (IL) came into use in 1974, but its use in the literature was not noticeable until the 1990s.[4] An increased emphasis on critical-thinking skills and lifelong learning needed for the Information Age led to a greater awareness of information literacy. IL was more than instructing users in the use of the library. Instruction needed to include not only teaching students how to navigate databases, but teaching them how to learn so that the principles they learned at the library could be applied to other assignments, other classes, and outside the classroom. Information literacy principles came to the forefront of the library world when in 2000 the Association of College and Research Libraries (ACRL) adopted the Information Literacy Competency Standards for Higher Education.[5] While these standards have been the subject of some criticism, they granted information literacy a higher place in the values of libraries and institutions of higher learning.

Now that we live in an age when the concepts of library instruction and information literacy are accepted or at least widely debated, the question has now become how to most effectively employ these concepts. Are one-shot sessions enough? Should we offer specialized workshops, credit classes, or online tutorials? As early as 1978, Lennart Pearson discussed the importance of teaching students library skills by building them into the overall curriculum. While the article was not written in a library journal, it did advocate the importance of librarians and library skills in the educational development of students and implored faculty to work with librarians on incorporating the necessary skills into appropriate classes.[6] These days, the idea of integrating information literacy outcomes into the larger higher-education curriculum is supported by the ACRL standards and accreditation. Librarians conducting instruction have seen many changes since the Middle States Commission on Higher Education made academic library instruction a requirement for accreditation. By adding library knowledge to the mix of skills that students needed to graduate, the accrediting organization relayed to all of academe the important role of libraries and librarians in the teaching and learning paradigm.[7]

Integrating information literacy into the larger curriculum has been attempted for the most part, not from the top down, but from the bottom up. Librarians have been sneaking, conspiring, cajoling, and collaborating for years to infuse library instruction concepts one class at a time. One widely used method of integration includes collaboration with English programs, particularly first-year English programs, or argument and research classes. First-year English classes are an effective means of advancing library instruction goals since they are usually required of all students in an entering class. They also provide a unique opportunity to set the foundational framework for later advanced studies in research skills development. First-year English programs are also often taught by teaching or graduate assistants, which provides the library with yet another opportunity to convey the value of information skills. As stated by Janet DeForest, Rachel Fleming May, and Brett Spencer in an article in 2004, "The EN 101 program modeled an example of librarian-instructor partnership that, hopefully, the teaching assistants will remember in completing their own research (they too are, of course, students first) and when they become professors."[8]

In addition to first-year English programs, library instruction is also often incorporated into basic first-year programs. While these programs do not offer the research component that English classes offer, they do allow librarians to introduce students to the library and the basic organization of book stacks. First-year programs are often called orientations and include tours or simple demonstrations on how to find book materials. First-year program orientations are intended to be exciting and interactive, engaging freshmen in scavenger hunts, quiz-bowl games, and parties. The ultimate goal is to acclimate students to the library so that they will be more at ease when they first come to the library to do *real* research. First-year programs have faced some criticism, however. They have been called overly simplistic, mundane, unnecessary, and a waste of time for librarians. In order to combat some of these negative impressions, librarians have looked for new ways to reach first-year students. Often this is through the use of technology like Web tutorials, online virtual tours of the library itself, podcasting, or Web research guides. Generation Y students, more in tune with the latest technology, respond well to these interactive lessons.[9] Librarians can create the modules or guides ahead of time and use them repeatedly, thereby saving staff time. These new technology-driven initiatives can also be adapted and reused to supplement more advanced levels of instruction.

In addition to instructing first-year students in the ways of an information literate culture, librarians can also facilitate workshops and seminars for faculty on research instruction. Incorporating information literacy programs into new faculty orientations also allows librarians to reach a fresh group of faculty members who may be more receptive to information literacy concepts. Teaching faculty to teach information literacy is particularly effective with faculty members who do not want to give up class time to come to the library. This method also allows classroom faculty to implement the concepts seamlessly into their course over the quarter or semester as they have time. The concept of allowing faculty members to teach information literacy concepts is not without its detractors, however. Allowing faculty members to teach information skills abdicates a primary responsibility of librarianship. After all, librarians are information experts and may be the best qualified to teach these concepts. Librarians also keep up to date on the latest databases and print resources and are thus able to incorporate these new resources into library sessions. It would be very difficult for classroom faculty to keep on top of the changing information world, even if they attended various workshops.[10]

Team teaching and collaboration are perhaps a more ideal way to incorporate library instruction into the curriculum. Librarians are able to spend more time with a class than they would simply during a one-time session. Librarians are also able to see their impact on a class and the long-term development of the skills. This kind of in-depth contact with a class provides librarians with the feedback that is so often missing from library instruction. Collaboration also allows classroom faculty to fully integrate research skills into their courses without feeling that they must be solely responsible for development and implementation. This teamwork approach also gives the classroom instructor a chance to keep his or her own information skills up to date.

While integration into English programs and first-year orientations provides an exceptional opportunity to reach a core group of students, it does not reach all students. Many colleges and universities now offer separate information literacy or research skills courses either as electives or as part of a general education program. These kinds of courses have become particularly popular now that accreditation standards are starting to emphasize the importance of information fluency as a graduation requirement. Information literacy courses that are part of the general education curriculum ensure that all students, regardless of major, receive a basic framework of information skills. While these courses may reach all students, they do not succeed in reaching students over the course of their academic careers. These courses also lack the context and relevancy that is present when library instruction is incorporated into a specific class.

Despite extended efforts and a plethora of methods, integration of information literacy concepts into the overall curriculum has not been widely accomplished. Current approaches to integration include a lack of context and relevancy, such as what happens with first-year programs, stand-alone courses, and general overviews. Students do not remember concepts unless they need to use them at that moment. Point-of-need instruction—instruction done at the reference desk and in course-integrated instruction—provides students with the context they need but fails in reaching all students and all majors. Using point-of-need instruction results in some students attending multiple library sessions, while other students may never set foot in the library. Furthermore, attempts at information literacy implementation have a library-centered orientation and do not effectively convey the importance of lifelong learning. After all, information skills are not just useful when you are forced to go to the library with your class but are needed all throughout life. What is causing these implementation problems? Why can't librarians succeed in spreading the good news of research skills? Part of the problem lies in the fact that librarians are not able to implement new courses or effectively suggest new curricula. As stated by Barbara D'Angelo and Barry Maid, "The ability of librarians to effect curricular change remains limited."[11]

If university students are to become lifelong learners, universities must incorporate information literacy into the curriculum on a larger and more effective scale. Current methods of pushing library instruction into the curriculum one class at a time have had only limited success. Discipline-based library instruction offers librarians the opportunity and collaboration they need to effectuate change within the curriculum. Library instruction at its best is not taught in a vacuum but instead thrives in the environment of context and relevancy that subject disciplines provide. Ann Grafstein writes that

> being information literate involves being literate about something. . . . In a
> robust, holistic IL program, these skills are presented and developed as the

curriculum of each course is taught. Librarians and classroom faculty share the responsibility for teaching them so that each teaches the skills that their credentials and background best qualify them to teach. Librarians are responsible for imparting the enabling skills that are prerequisite to information seeking and knowledge acquisition across the curriculum, while classroom faculty have the responsibility of teaching those skills that are required for subject-specific inquiry and research.[12]

Many librarians would argue that discipline-based library instruction is already being conducted and that it has not produced any better results than orientations or information literacy credit classes. Discipline-based library instruction amounts to more than just one-shot library instruction sessions for a given subject. A discipline-based approach to information literacy is not library centered but university centered. Both librarians and classroom faculty have specific and complementary roles. In this environment, librarians are recognized subject experts on discipline-specific resources, searching techniques, critical-thinking skills, and source evaluation. Classroom faculty, on the other hand, take responsibility for teaching students specific course content and how to evaluate the validity of subject-specific evidence.

But how should libraries begin to expand discipline-based instruction into the curriculum? New technologies provide a wonderful beginning for advancing discipline-based instruction. Technologies such as tutorials, Web guides, and more also provide an easy and nonconfrontational way to integrate information literacy concepts into the curriculum. Furthermore, many technologies that libraries are already using can be easily adapted for discipline-specific research. Many libraries already have online tutorials that teach the basics of searching and are usually used in first-year classes. By simply adapting these tutorials with discipline-specific examples and adding more advanced research concepts, librarians can create customized tutorials for use in upper-division classes. Web guides can also be made more specific and can even be created on a class-by-class basis. Voice over IP (VoIP) and podcasting technologies allow librarians to offer specialized instruction sessions online or to provide video downloads of the sessions. While many librarians are familiar with this newest technology, only a few have seen it as a way to advance library instruction through the disciplines. The key to making discipline-based library instruction work is to look for ways to modify and adapt existing technologies and then promote, promote, promote. As a university begins to see the technologies that the library has to offer, interest in information literacy concepts will increase. At the very least, library instruction will be incorporated into a number of subject classes virtually, and the impact of library instruction will increase both horizontally and vertically.

Another way to get started expanding discipline-based instruction into the curriculum is to consider offering supplementary courses to subject-specific classes that have a heavy research emphasis. A 1998 article by Colleen Bell and Juanita Benedicto refers to these types of classes as "companion courses." The University of Oregon piloted companion courses for journalism, management, psychology, and women's studies. These courses were offered as credit and were taught by subject specialist librarians. Students enrolled in targeted subject classes were also encouraged to enroll in the library companion course. While enrollment was low, the classes generally received positive feedback from faculty, librarians, and students.[13] While not all libraries are able to offer credit courses, the idea could be adapted on a smaller scale. Librarians might consider asking select courses to add a lab onto a course. This lab section could then be taught by a subject librarian. Lab credit might even be the better way to go, as students would be required to enroll in the lab if they enrolled in the subject course, thus taking care of the problem of low enrollment. If lab courses are not possible, librarians could consider offering frequent workshops to coincide with a specific class and assignments, a different version of course-integrated instruction. Library-related classes typically have the highest enrollment when they are mandated rather than optional, so these options should be considered beginning steps while librarians look for more structured university-wide opportunities to include information literacy.

A wonderful example of embedding information literacy principles into the curriculum on a larger scale can be seen at Weber State University. The expressed mission of the Stewart Library's instruction program "is to provide Weber State University (WSU) community with the skills and knowledge needed to effectively identify, find, evaluate and use information for academic success and to support lifelong learning."[14] WSU offers instruction on the access and evaluation of information across the disciplines. Of course many libraries offer similar instruction programs, but what makes Stewart Library and WSU unique is the comprehensive curriculum of credit-based classes, discipline-integrated instruction, and orientations. All instruction sessions incorporate learning outcomes specific to the level of the class, and the most important outcomes are frequently assessed. An outcomes framework on the Stewart Library website organizes these learning outcomes into tiers related to the level of instruction. For instance, first-year students have basic learning outcomes associated with library orientation tours and basic search strategies. Discipline-specific skills are then articulated in later years when the level of subject knowledge expectedly increases.[15] Weber State models an effective library instruction program that is easily attainable by many other institutions. The majority of library instruction programs in the United States already provide orientations, subject-specific sessions, and in some cases for-credit information literacy classes. All that is needed for most libraries and institutions is a comprehensive plan that aligns specific information literacy standards to tiered levels of instruction (instruction that already exists in many cases). This allows libraries to better plan their learning outcomes for specific classes and outlines the needs that are missing. Furthermore, having an organized set of outcomes and standards facilitates collaboration with classroom faculty in academic departments, as they can then see how their classes fit into the overall instruction goals of the library and university.

There have also been many recent examples of integrating information literacy across the curriculum through a more formal process. The Five Colleges of Ohio consortium received a grant from the Andrew W. Mellon Foundation in order to enhance and expand the teaching of information literacy across the curriculum. A key part of their approach involved collaborative teamwork between librarians and faculty members to instill the needed skills in students. They recognized not only the importance of basic introductory skills but of advanced discipline-specific skills as well. As stated in their proposal, "The fact that students need to master both basic information literacy competencies as well as library research skills at higher, discipline-specific levels suggests that a more structured curricular approach needs to be developed."[16] Some of the more advanced skills included learning about the important indexing and abstracting tools of the discipline, becoming familiar with additional indexing and abstracting tools for current literature and more elusive gray literature for a discipline, and discovering how researchers in a discipline convey new research results or theoretical advances. Because of the emphasis on collaboration with classroom faculty and on discipline-specific skills, the Five Colleges of Ohio grant is an excellent example of embedding information literacy principles across the curriculum through the disciplines. A subject-specific focus increases classroom faculty buy-in and makes information literacy a university goal as well as a library goal.

Another excellent example of embedding information literacy principles into the curriculum is provided by the California State University (CSU) Initiatives. In 1994, CSU libraries made information competency an important cornerstone of library instruction and suggested that CSU as a whole provide an outline of basic skill levels in the ability to use written information. They also asked that the framework provide a way to assess these acquired skills. A work group was formed that identified information competence as "the integration of library literacy, computer literacy, media literacy, technological literacy, ethics, critical thinking, and communication skills."[17] This definition was then used to form a set of information competency standards. These standards have then been used to incorporate IL concepts into discipline-specific areas through such projects as "Furthering the Information Competence of the 21st-Century Agribusiness Manager," "Information Literacy and Black Studies," "Promoting Information Competence in Nursing Students,"[18] and many more. Another CSU task force has also been asked to formulate plans for the assessment of these standards and to ensure that the standards are part of the learning outcomes of individual academic departments. It is through the incorporation of these information literacy elements in the departments that the ultimate success of the CSU initiative will be decided.

Whether through grants, university-wide initiatives, or structured library instruction programs, information literacy worked into the disciplines provides an ideal framework for implementation across campus. But all this is easier said than done, right? Not all libraries have the support of grants or are fortunate enough to be part of universities where information literacy principles are widely accepted. Say a library offers all the right sessions, creates an organized plan of learning outcomes, and succeeds in convincing a number of university staff outside the library that information competency is an important component to an academic curriculum, where does the library go from there? Earlier in the chapter, it was mentioned that librarians have had a hard time effecting curricular change. This is in fact why discipline-based models of information literacy are so important. Disciplines provide a context and framework for advancing the information literacy agenda. If a library has a grant proposal or a university-wide information literacy initiative, the task becomes a little easier. Either way, discipline-based library instruction needs a catalyst to help with widespread implementation. What if the library can't find a catalyst? Should it create its own?

Libraries should not necessarily have to create their own fire to spread the warmth of information literacy to the disciplines and across the whole curriculum. Instead, jump on the bandwagon of another university-wide initiative. In response to the need to provide library instruction that is both context driven and spread across the academic experience, collaboration with writing-across-the-curriculum (WAC) programs has now become in vogue. Collaboration with WAC programs can offer library instruction programs many benefits. Writing-across-the-curriculum programs usually have an academic home in the English department, something that library instruction programs lack. Having a departmental base provides clout, authority, and sustainability to initiatives. WAC emphasizes critical-thinking and problem-solving skills, which have long been the key goals of information literacy. These programs also often contain curricula that cross several years, thereby allowing librarians to teach students relevant skills over a good part of their academic studies. Furthermore, the discipline-specific nature sets writing-across-the-curriculum programs apart from former collaborators of information literacy instruction programs. As James K. Elmborg states in a 2003 article, "Whether WAC is a partner, a model, or simply an institutional friend, it can teach information literacy a great deal about being successful in working in the disciplines."[19]

Not only can writing-across-the-curriculum programs help advance information literacy principles, but taking tips from WAC programs will in the long run help librarians formulate better and more attainable goals for information literacy programs. Librarians are known for their practical nature, and this can be widely seen in information literacy programs. Library instruction has long emphasized learning library terminology, search techniques for various databases, Boolean operators, truncation, and tips for locating the much-needed full-text article. While all of these lessons are necessary for effective research, this overemphasis on practical tips is placing research as a process in the backseat. While librarians may understand that search skills are only the tip of the iceberg and that real research involves much trial and error and critical thinking, undergraduates come away from library class sessions feeling that once they have mastered a particular database, search engine, or print resource, they will have forever learned how to use the library and conduct research. This feeling often results in the familiar complaint from students, "I've already been to a library instruction session with my other class!" In contrast, through designated writing-intensive courses, writing-across-the-curriculum programs teach students the specific discourse of a discipline but emphasize heavily that students must find their own voice through writing. As researchers know, knowledge is created through disagreement, debate, and building upon prior information. Learn the rules and then make your own way. Likewise, library instruction needs to emphasize that librarians are available to explain the rules of a database and offer search guidelines, but there is no one path to finding the perfect research article. Many librarians fully believe that information literacy is a liberal art, just as much as writing or rhetoric, but a lack of foundational educational pedagogy has hurt information literacy and led to this overly practical nature. James Elmborg states that "in order to work with WAC and other instructional programs on campus, information literacy will need to begin to find the language to articulate key theoretical positions, and all librarians who work in information literacy need to be willing to articulate their own philosophies in the context of those positions."[20]

In order to be the most effective when working with writing-across-the-curriculum programs or other instructional programs on campus, librarians should heed several cautions. First, it is important to have a student-centered focus. The whole point of advancing information literacy concepts is to help improve the educational curriculum for all students and to help undergraduates become better prepared for the real world. It is not a competition, and librarians should not feel that they need to prove that information literacy is just as important as writing or other general education requirements. If librarians are perceived by other university officials to be using every possible opportunity to advance and promote the library, tensions will be strained. In order for information literacy to reach its full potential, it needs to become a university goal and not just a library goal. Librarians can be considered experts on information literacy, but they do not need to be the sole flag bearers.

Instruction librarians should also make use of the jargon of each discipline. Integrating information literacy into the disciplines means adapting terminology and making use of already existing modes of thought.

Librarians know that research skills are transferable from one discipline to another, but each discipline has its own way of conducting research. The hope of discipline-based library instruction is to teach students these differences, and it is also important to remember that same context when speaking with classroom faculty. Faculty members are much more likely to sign on to the concept of information literacy if they see the relevance for their own classes. Finding common ground with writing-across-the-curriculum programs and academic disciplines will only help information literacy grow as it should.

Along with looking for opportunities to collaborate with university-wide programs, assessment of overall library instruction programs needs to be conducted, but it can be a tricky business. In recent years, outcomes-based assessment has become one of the most popular methods. Both quantitative and qualitative methods can be used with outcomes-based assessment. The overall goal of assessment is to improve student learning and show that the library plays a large role in the educational development of students. Many libraries conduct pre- and posttests of individual instruction sessions to gauge the effectiveness of the content. Quizzes tied to online tutorials provide a way for instruction librarians to assess a large group of students and are often used in first-year instruction programs. Embedded assessment techniques, such as examining student work within senior-level capstone projects, provide a more effective means of evaluating discipline-based instruction. Discipline-based instruction also allows assessment to be conducted within a larger context—it's not just library skills that are being tested, but the overall research skills for a discipline. While all of these methods provide useful feedback, they are primarily library centered. They provide data on what and how much students remember regarding databases, Boolean operators, or searching skills, but these assessment attempts do not provide much data on how students integrate these concepts into their other classes or their overall major. In other words, many currently used assessment techniques provide a snapshot of what students know at one moment in time.

Several researchers have described unique assessment techniques to reach students beyond the moment. In 1991, Mary Ochs wrote about a technique in which surveys were sent to graduates of a library school program in an attempt to measure the skills they retained. Similar surveys were also sent to the employers to assess how well the students' education met the job requirements.[21] A similar method has been described by several researchers in which students were followed on the job after graduation to see how they used information literacy skills at work. Observation after graduation also helps to determine if students are being prepared with needed skills in the academic environment. While difficult, instruction librarians should employ a variety of assessment techniques (both quantitative and qualitative) so that they can be provided with a large picture of the impact of library instruction on the university. Integrating information literacy assessment into the disciplines, general education requirements, and other university programs will also help librarians to share the burden. Finally, librarians should also be cautious about taking assessment too seriously, as it is only one component of a successful program. As Elmborg relates, "When assessment goes bad, it can become a heavy-handed tool to certify competency (and, by implication, the incompetency) of teachers or students, often based on very simplistic or culturally biased definitions of competency."[22] To help librarians develop fair assessment methods and begin or extend discussions on their campuses, there are a number of standards and guidelines already in place.

The Information Literacy Competency Standards for Higher Education approved by ACRL in January 2000 provide a rubric for evaluating the information literate student. The competency standards include five standards and twenty-two performance standards, with specific outcomes listed for each performance standard. Ideally an information literate student should be able to demonstrate all of the competencies by graduation. Because the standards generally follow a progression from basic to advanced skills, many libraries have assigned specific standards to each academic level. For instance, first-year students will be taught how to define their topic and look for basic sources (Standard One), while senior seminar students will be taught about intellectual property, copyright, and plagiarism (Standard Five). Caution should be used, however, in applying the standards so strictly. Rather, the standards should be taken as guidelines that can be used as a framework for local discussions concerning information literacy goals and assessment. The best use of the standards perhaps lies in their incorporation into subject discipline research and writing classes. As stated in the standards, "Faculty and librarians should also work together to develop assessment instruments and strategies in the context of particular disciplines, as information literacy manifests itself in the specific understanding of the knowledge creation, scholarly activity, and publication processes found in those disciplines."[23] Another reason for applying the standards to specific disciplines instead of wholly across the board to academic levels is that "some disciplines may place greater emphasis on the mastery of competencies at certain points in the process, and therefore certain competencies would receive greater weight than others in any rubric for measurement."[24]

In order to help librarians effectively apply the standards to various disciplines, the Teaching Methods Committee of the ACRL Instruction Section has created a website on "Information Literacy in the Disciplines." The goal of the website is to provide librarians with relevant articles, books, and accrediting standards for specific subject areas. First, each subject area section provides a link or citation to relevant standards for the discipline accepted by accrediting agencies or professional associations. For instance, the psychology section provides a link to an APA (American Psychological Association) task-force report on Undergraduate Psychology Major Competencies. Second, each subject section on the website also provides a list of articles or reports on library instruction in that discipline, as well as discussions of subject-specific resources. Overall, this wonderful website yields a large amount of information for subject bibliographers or instruction librarians looking to keep up to date on a certain discipline.[25]

The California State University (CSU) Information Competence Initiative described earlier in this chapter has led the way in developing student learning outcomes for different disciplines based on the ACRL standards. A series of workshops were held in 2003 that allowed librarians and teaching faculty to share their experiences in developing appropriate outcomes. Workshops were organized for the biological sciences, history, educational psychology/counseling, and first-year experience/freshmen seminars. All of the represented disciplines were able to create specific relevant outcomes that demonstrated information competence for each ACRL standard. In many cases, specific classes were identified where relevant outcomes could realistically be achieved. When necessary, lower- or upper-division classes were created or modified to facilitate the implementation of new learning outcomes.[26] The application of the ACRL standards to the sciences has also been discussed in a 2004 article by Kate Manuel. In her article, she relates the difficulties of applying "generic" standards to specific discipline needs and outcomes, but she further states that with some work, a balance can be found. Faculty members in disciplines such as the sciences may at first find it difficult to embrace information literacy outcomes, but this lack of enthusiasm is primarily related to narrow definitions of information literacy and not to the concept itself. Manuel emphatically writes, "The sciences are certainly more interested in information-as-knowledge than in information-as-information."[27] To help achieve relevant and useful learning outcomes for various disciplines, librarians should make sure to define information literacy in ways that are pertinent to the discipline. Redefining IL concepts based on the discipline is not only helpful in creating partnerships with faculty as described earlier in the chapter, but it further helps infusion into learning outcomes, which is the ultimate goal.

As stated by Jeremy Shapiro and Shelly Hughes,

> Information and computer literacy, in the conventional sense, are functionally valuable technical skills. But information literacy should in fact be conceived more broadly as a new liberal art that extends from knowing how to use computers and access information to critical reflection on the nature of information itself, its technical infrastructure, and its social, cultural, and even philosophical context and impact.[28]

Because of this broad conception of information literacy as a liberal art, many have argued that information literacy should be a subject in its own right and that librarians should not have to give up territory to others who are less knowledgeable on the subject. For instance, Edward Owusu-Ansah argues that the library itself should be the solution for the problem of information literacy integration.[29] Librarians, however, should not feel that they alone hold the answer to helping students prepare themselves for the world of information. Rather, the university as a whole should accept responsibility for preparing and educating information literate citizens. Just as universities have begun to recognize the importance of writing for all students, so too are they beginning to recognize the importance of research skills to lifelong learning. The greatest hope for the future of library instruction and information literacy perhaps lies in a full integration into all disciplines along with the basic orientation classes that librarians have always provided.

INFORMATION LITERACY SKILLS ACROSS THE DISCIPLINES

All disciplines share common knowledge as well as core research skills. Providing students with these foundational research competencies will help to ensure that they are successful in doing research in their chosen discipline. An information literate student should be able to

- understand the scope of information needed;
- define a problem and identify appropriate keywords;
- differentiate different resource types (books, journals, reference materials, etc.) and select appropriate tools to find specified resources;
- locate material in the library or through online subscriptions and understand library classification systems;
- name the key parts of citations, distinguish book citations from journal citations, and create bibliographies in the correct citation style for a chosen discipline;
- explain and use basic library services such as Interlibrary Loan, as well as operate various library technologies like microfilm readers, copiers, and so on;
- devise search strategies, effectively use Boolean operators, and adapt these strategies for specific databases;
- understand the difference between keyword and subject searching in databases;
- specify and effectively use core research tools (indexes, databases, bibliographies, dictionaries, etc.) within a chosen discipline;
- understand the difference between scholarly (peer-reviewed) and popular sources and know major scholarly and professional journals for a chosen discipline;
- list major associations and the respective publications for a given discipline;
- identify prominent authors within a discipline and research additional writings or upcoming works by these authors;
- identify the major methods for communicating within the discipline, including relevant conferences, websites, blogs, and electronic e-mail lists;
- distinguish between online library subscription sources and the World Wide Web;

- reflect on initial readings and adopt additional search strategies and approaches, such as citation chasing, browsing, and so on;
- effectively evaluate resources and determine their appropriateness, strengths, and weaknesses for different assignments; and
- express an understanding of the ethical and legal issues surrounding information use (plagiarism, copyright).

NOTES

1. Melvil Dewey, "The Profession," *American Library Journal* 1 (September 1876): 5.

2. Francis L. Hopkins, "A Century of Bibliographic Instruction: The Historic Claim to Professional and Academic Legitimacy," *College and Research Libraries* 43 (May 1982): 195.

3. LOEX, "About LOEX," *LOEX Clearinghouse for Library Instruction*, 2004–2005, www.emich.edu/public/loex/about.html (accessed December 18, 2005).

4. Shirley J. Behrens, "A Conceptual Analysis and Historical Overview of Information Literacy," *College and Research Libraries* 55, no. 4 (July 1994): 309–22.

5. Association of College and Research Libraries, *Information Literacy Competency Standards for Higher Education* (American Library Association, 2000), www.ala.org/ala/acrl/acrlstandards/standards.pdf (accessed December 18, 2005).

6. Lennart Pearson, "What Has the Library Done for You Lately?" *Improving College and University Teaching* 26, no. 4 (Fall 1978): 219–21.

7. Mignon S. Adams, "The Role of Academic Libraries in Teaching and Learning," *College and Research Libraries News* 53 (July–August 1992): 442–45.

8. Janet DeForst, Rachel Fleming May, and Brett Spencer, "Getting Our Foot (Back) in the Door: Reestablishing a Freshman Instruction Program," *The Reference Librarian* 85 (2004): 160.

9. Julia K. Nims and Ann Andrew, eds., *First Impressions, Lasting Impact: Introducing the First Year Student to the Academic Library* (Ann Arbor, MI: Pierian Press, 2002).

10. Mary Beth Applin and Thelma Robertson, "Sharing the Responsibility of Teaching Information Literacy: Educating the Educators," *Mississippi Libraries* 66, no. 1 (Spring 2002): 3–5.

11. Barbara J. D'Angelo and Barry M. Maid, "Moving Beyond Definitions: Implementing Information Literacy across the Curriculum," *Journal of Academic Librarianship* 30, no. 3 (May 2004): 212.

12. Ann Grafstein, "A Discipline-Based Approach to Information Literacy," *Journal of Academic Librarianship* 28, no. 4 (July 2002): 202.

13. Colleen Bell and Juanita Benedicto, "The Companion Course: A Pilot Project to Teach Discipline-Specific Library Research Skills," *Reference Services Review* 26 (Fall–Winter 1998): 117–24.

14. Weber State University, Stewart Library, *Information Literacy Program: Mission and Statement of Purpose*, 2004, library.weber.edu/il/team/mission.cfm (accessed December 20, 2005).

15. Weber State University, Stewart Library, *Information Literacy across the Curriculum at Weber State University*, 2005, library.weber.edu/il/ilprogram/diagram.cfm (accessed January 6, 2006).

16. Five Colleges of Ohio, *Integrating Information Literacy into the Liberal Arts Curriculum* November 1999, www.denison.edu/collaborations/ohio5/grant/development/proposal.html (December 3, 2005).

17. CSU Information Competence Work Group, *Information Competence Initiative*, 2001, www.calstate.edu/LS/infocomp.shtml (accessed December 4, 2005).

18. Wendell Barbour, Christy Gavin, and Joan Canfield, "Integrating Information Literacy into the Academic Curriculum," *Educause Center for Applied Research Bulletin* 18 (August 2004): 5–6.

19. James K. Elmborg, "Information Literacy and Writing across the Curriculum: Sharing the Vision," *Reference Services Review* 31, no. 1 (2003): 69.

20. Elmborg, "Information Literacy and Writing across the Curriculum," 72.

21. Mary Ochs, *Assessing the Value of an Information Literacy Program* (Ithaca, NY: Cornell University, 1991), ERIC ED340385.

22. Elmborg, "Information Literacy and Writing across the Curriculum," 78.

23. Association of College and Research Libraries, *Information Literacy Competency Standards*, 8.

24. Association of College and Research Libraries, *Information Literacy Competency Standards*, 8.

25. ALA/ACRL Instruction Section, *Information Literacy in the Disciplines*, 2005, www.ala.org/ala/acrlbucket/is/projectsacrl/infolitdisciplines/index.htm (accessed January 6, 2006).

26. Iilene F. Rockman, "Integrating Information Literacy into the Learning Outcomes of Academic Disciplines: A Critical 21st-Century Issue," *College & Research Libraries News* 64, no. 9 (October 2003): 612–15.

27. Kate Manuel, "Generic and Discipline-Specific Information Literacy Competencies: The Case of the Sciences," *Science and Technology Libraries* 24, no. 3–4 (2004): 292.

28. Jeremy J. Shapiro and Shelly K. Hughes, "Information Literacy as a Liberal Art: Enlightenment Proposals for a New Curriculum," *Educom Review* 31, no. 2 (March–April 1996): 3.

29. Edward K. Owusu-Ansah, "Information Literacy and Higher Education: Placing the Academic Library in the Center of a Comprehensive Solution," *Journal of Academic Librarianship* 30, no. 1 (January 2004): 3–16.

10

Knowledge Out of Bounds: Reflections on Disciplinary and Interdisciplinary Research

Jennifer Bowers

Students become acculturated into disciplinary communities during the course of their academic careers. By selecting a major or concentrating on a specific area, they learn the parameters of a chosen discipline—its approach to inquiry, its predominant concepts, its unique vocabulary, and its ways of communicating. Doing research and understanding the research process in a discipline is integral to becoming part of the disciplinary community. Janet Donald outlines the important role that disciplines play in this transformation:

> Disciplines provide examples of systematic scholarly inquiry, and therefore serve as scaffolding for students in the process of exploring different ways of constructing meaning. In disciplines, faculty need to explain the main principles and tenets governing their field of study, describe how they establish and validate knowledge, and show the necessity for engaging in further research and discussion. Modeling inquiry in the discipline and explaining how theory is developed and tested is foundational to students' intellectual development.[1]

The process of acculturation continues for students who pursue advanced degrees. Graduate students adopt the beliefs, language, and practices of their disciplinary culture as they learn through research to become members of the community. And finally, as full-fledged disciplinary scholars, "individual faculty identify themselves with their departmental colleagues and cultures."[2] The discipline becomes the source of the individual's professional identity.

The chapters in this book illuminate the particular characteristics of the research process within general broad disciplinary groups—the humanities, social sciences, and sciences—and highlight the distinctive components of research within the individual disciplines of music, history, business, and engineering. To complement these discussions, the chapter on government documents emphasizes the particular challenges to researching specialized resources and shows how they can be used in a wide range of disciplinary inquiry. What emerges from this overview of the disciplines and their research practices are some common themes.

The disciplines are founded on a tradition of learning, yet they are not static entities. Continually evolving and changing, certain elements nevertheless remain constant—these are the characteristics that shape the discipline's identity. Thus, humanities research is concerned with human creations and their interpretation, social sciences pursue an understanding of humans within their social context, and the sciences investigate the natural and physical world in all its manifest properties. In conjunction with these different pursuits, each discipline has developed a body of knowledge with central concepts, theories, and language. Research pursues new questions in a continuing engagement with the disciplinary discourse and places those questions within the context of this ongoing conversation. As the chapters in this book show, understanding the research process in any discipline entails learning about the principal features of the discipline's knowledge base and how this foundational identity shapes the kinds of questions asked, the vocabulary used to articulate these questions, the particular methods of investigation, and the primary tools used for finding answers. Integral to this process is an understanding of how each discipline communicates and disseminates its ideas and the external ways it maintains and promotes its identity through professional associations and societies, conferences, and journals. Each chapter also addresses the role that technology has played and continues to play in influencing the research process within the disciplines. Not only have technological developments increased the variety of source formats and means of scholarly communication, but they have opened up traditional sources in new ways that affect the very nature of disciplinary inquiry. To understand research within the disciplines, then, it is critical to learn both the epistemological foundations and the cultural constructs of the discipline's identity, as well as the mechanics of the research process.

Librarians serve as partners in the research component of disciplinary acculturation by developing library collections to meet the needs of the community, by assisting students and scholars with research questions, and by teaching strategies and techniques for using general and specialized resources. To fulfill this collaborative role, librarians need to grasp both the epistemological foundations of disciplinary inquiry and the practical components of the research process. Disciplines are distinguished not only by their subject fields, but also by their particular information-seeking characteristics and professional apparatus. The preceding chapters point out the kinds of questions asked and the methods used in disciplinary research; they also present a selection of the specialized research tools and professional resources unique to each discipline, including principal databases, bibliographies, professional associations, and scholarly journals. In addition, the authors address the different kinds of research needs and practices characteristic of undergraduate students, graduate students, and faculty, as well as the special needs of practitioners.

Every discipline has its own distinctive voice. Fundamental to research across all the disciplines, however, as the chapter on library instruction and information literacy illustrates, is the need to teach students to think critically and creatively in order to identify, evaluate, and most importantly integrate and synthesize information. Research, as a process of engagement with varying ideas and disciplinary knowledge, enables students to develop intellectually as they acquire and refine these skills in the course of their academic careers. Proficiency with elemental research skills and techniques helps to set the foundation for disciplinary-specific research competencies. Together, both general and specialized research skills prepare students to assess and integrate information throughout their lives.

Disciplinary research is central to the intellectual development and identity of both students and faculty. In turn, the disciplines are the foundation upon which academia is physically and intellectually structured. University and college departments are organized by discipline, many classes and degrees are discipline based, and the knowledge community is characterized by disciplinary associations, conferences, journals, and resources. The library supports this disciplinary structure through its traditional classification schemes and discipline-oriented research tools and instruction. Disciplines are the "primary means for dividing up and organizing both *how we know* and *how knowers get socially grouped*."[3]

As much as disciplines define the state of knowledge, however, current scholarship is equally influenced by the intersections between disciplines. Scholars are engaged in crossing disciplinary borders, and interdisciplinarity is pervasive at every level. Indeed, to claim that scholarship is "increasingly interdisciplinary" has become somewhat of a cliché. Julie Thompson Klein, who has written extensively about interdisciplinary research, notes that during the latter part of the twentieth century, "heterogeneity, hybridity, complexity, and interdisciplinarity become characterizing traits of knowledge."[4] The boundaries between disciplines are increasingly less distinct and permanent as scholars investigate topics and pursue questions that transcend traditional disciplinary lines. In fact, several chapters in this volume discuss the ways in which research in their fields is becoming more interdisciplinary in nature. Although interdisciplinary scholarship varies in its intent and level of integration, Lisa R. Lattuca argues that a growing number of scholars, especially those in the humanities and social sciences, are not interested merely in borrowing concepts and methods from other disciplines but are intent on the more revolutionary goal of "deconstructing disciplinary knowledge and boundaries."[5] Whether interdisciplinary scholarship assumes a neighborly or radical stance toward the traditional disciplines, it nevertheless has become an acceptable and popular practice of knowledge production. And as a result, interdisciplinary inquiry has moved from "the academic periphery to a more central scholarly location."[6]

Interdisciplinary scholarship is not a new phenomenon. Thompson Klein ties interdisciplinarity to the general education movement of the early twentieth century. Her discussion of the historical relationship between interdisciplinarity and the humanities suggests that despite the fact that neither concept existed in the ancient world, the tenets of interdisciplinary research can be found in ancient Greek philosophy:

> Greek philosophers . . . developed a view of knowledge that promoted a
> broad synoptic outlook, harmonious unity of divisions, a holistic approach,

and the value of general knowledge. Humanists today trace precedents for interdisciplinarity to these ideas in the roots of Western philosophy and writings about education.[7]

Others argue that it doesn't make sense to discuss interdisciplinarity as a concept before the establishment of modern academic disciplines in the latter part of the nineteenth century.[8] The general education movement developed in conjunction with the growth and specialization of the disciplines during this period. In 1923, the Social Science Research Council was founded to encourage and support research across the social science disciplines. The 1930s saw the rise of area studies, which brought together different disciplinary perspectives to concentrate on specific geographic areas.[9] American studies, one of the oldest interdisciplinary fields, began in the 1920s and 1930s but expanded significantly after World War II. By the time the American Studies Association was founded in 1951, however, Thompson Klein notes that despite its goal of encompassing all of American culture, the field was dominated by literature and history subject areas, and practice was, in reality, multidisciplinary rather than one of interdisciplinary integration between the humanities and social sciences.[10]

The period following World War II fostered interdisciplinary research in the sciences, initially to meet military and political needs. In response to this climate, the National Science Foundation was created by Congress in 1950 to support basic and applied science endeavors.[11] Primarily problem based in nature, interdisciplinary research in the sciences continued throughout the twentieth century and is still the main type of scientific interdisciplinary work. Often involving teams of researchers from multiple disciplines, this kind of research "entails the collaboration of scientists with largely nonoverlapping training and core expertise to solve a problem that lies outside the grasp of the individual scientists."[12] Thomas R. Cech and Gerald M. Rubin suggest that the "movement toward interdisciplinarity is driven by the science itself,"[13] since complex problems, new fields, and technologies require the integration of ideas and methodologies from affiliated and previously unimagined partners.

The political and social movements of the 1960s and 1970s had a significant impact on the development of interdisciplinary studies. During this time, a greater awareness of political and social issues, such as poverty, racism, the environment, and feminism, led to curricular changes and the establishment of urban studies, environmental studies, ethnic studies, minority studies, and women's studies. These new fields combined different disciplinary approaches in order to address societal problems, often with an agenda of using scholarship to enact social change. To this effect, Thompson Klein remarks that despite differences between ethnic, minority, and women's studies, they exhibit "an implicitly shared epistemology that dismantles the boundary separating knowledge from action, discipline from politics."[14] In fact, this foundational epistemology complicates the interdisciplinary field's image as it moves more toward disciplinary status. In Eloise Buker's article, "Is Women's Studies a Disciplinary or an Interdisciplinary Field of Inquiry?" she suggests that the "politicized nature of its founding and its mission makes women's studies scholars ambivalent about becoming a discipline like the others."[15] Nevertheless, she argues that women's studies now can claim "a body of knowledge, set of technical terms, methodology, strategies of interpretations, and key questions that are acquired only through years of training,"[16] characteristics of disciplinary status along with tenure lines, graduate programs, journals, and a professional organization (the National Women's Studies Association). Critical to maintaining its identity in this transition, she asserts, is that women's studies "must sustain its intellectual roots in an open interdisciplinary epistemology."[17]

Concurrent with the social influences on interdisciplinary scholarship in the 1960s and 1970s was the rise and impact of theoretical movements that affected critical inquiry during the last part of the twentieth century and continue to exert their influence to varying degrees. Structuralism and semiotics "defied disciplinary boundaries in their search for underlying systems or forms that would unify theory in disparate areas."[18] Poststructuralist theory, following after, stimulated

> widening reflection on problems of language and representation, the role of gender and sexuality, a historically oriented cultural criticism, and categories of critical thought undertaken by deconstruction. New syntheses of Marxism, psychoanalysis, semiotics, and feminism also emerged as proponents tested their relationship to other practices.[19]

These theoretical movements challenged traditional disciplinary boundaries, especially in the humanities and social sciences, and seeded inquiry in such new areas as postcolonial studies, cultural studies, and gay and lesbian studies.[20] Postmodern theory, which initiated questions about the relationship between texts and their contexts, served to broaden the nature of disciplinary inquiry since it drew from multiple disciplines for its theoretical investigations. As a result, postmodern movements fostered a new generalism that was not unified but assumed instead a "cross-fertilizing synergism in the form of common methods, concepts, theories, and a metalanguage."[21] Indeed, much current scholarship across disciplines is characterized by these interdisciplinary epistemological and methodological approaches.

There are many definitions of what constitutes interdisciplinary research, yet no general consensus.[22] As suggested by the preceding discussion of interdisciplinary research, this kind of work can assume a wide range of guises, as varied as the scholars who practice it. In fact, lack of a standard definition is due in part to "the myriad positionalities of spectators and actors in interdisciplinary research,"[23] and to the fact that any definition, necessarily, will be subjective. First attempts at defining the term occurred in 1970. During this year, the Organisation for Economic Cooperation and Development (OECD) sponsored an international conference on interdisciplinarity, which categorized such endeavors into multidisciplinary, pluridisciplinary, interdisciplinary, and transdisciplinary levels of interaction.[24] Thompson Klein elaborates on her distinction between multi- and interdisciplinary research:

> Multidisciplinary approaches juxtapose disciplinary perspectives, adding breadth and available knowledge, information, and methods. They speak as separate voices in an encyclopedic alignment. The status quo is not interrogated, and disciplinary elements retain their original identity. In contrast, interdisciplinarity integrates separate disciplinary data, methods, tools, concepts, and theories in order to create a holistic view or common understanding of a complex issue, question, or problem.[25]

Matthew Miller and Veronica Boix Mansilla also define interdisciplinary work in terms of degrees of integration. For them, interdisciplinary research builds upon disciplinary perspectives to create something unique and not possible to derive from a single discipline. As such, "integration is not an end in itself but a means to attain a goal worth pursuing; disciplinary expertise is considered seriously; and disciplines are not simply juxtaposed but deeply intertwined."[26] John D. Aram interviewed twelve faculty directors of graduate liberal studies programs about the nature of interdisciplinary research, who when asked "What does 'interdisciplinary' mean to you?" revealed that some participants defined interdisciplinary in terms of the degree of knowledge integration, or the creation of

> "new knowledge" resulting from a confluence, fusion, or synthesis of disciplinary knowledge and others articulated a less integral relationship between knowledge sources, leading to a "new perspective" through the borrowing from one discipline to another or the interplay between disciplines.[27]

In contrast, Lattuca, who studied thirty-eight college and university faculty engaged in interdisciplinary scholarship, found it more productive to consider interdisciplinary research not by degrees of integration but rather as shaped by the kinds of questions researchers asked. From this study, she developed a fourfold, question-based typology of interdisciplinary teaching and research: informed disciplinarity, in which disciplinary questions require outreach to other disciplines; synthetic interdisciplinarity, in which the questions link disciplines; transdisciplinarity, in which the questions cross disciplines; and conceptual interdisciplinarity, characterized by questions that have no compelling disciplinary basis.[28] Whether interdisciplinary research is defined in terms of integration or motivating questions, the interaction between and among disciplines remains a central component. This abiding relationship underscores the importance of understanding the dynamic interdependence between disciplinary and interdisciplinary research.

Disciplines are constantly changing. Never static, they "serve as epistemological corrals of concepts, theories, and methods linked by specialized languages, but they are, above all, social groupings that make and break their own rules of scholarship."[29] To think of disciplines as social constructions in this way emphasizes how they are subject to social, political, cultural, and intellectual influences. The interplay of new ideas with foundational knowledge is what imparts to the disciplines their energy and vitality. Several chapters in this volume discuss how disciplines have changed over time, from their earliest intellectual roots through their foundation in the academy to their current established and transformative identities. Disciplines possess a certain elasticity; they expand into new territories and specializations and contract when subfields break off, sometimes to form their own disciplines.[30] As disciplines change in this way, so do their boundaries. Thompson Klein stresses that permeability is intrinsically part of a discipline's character. She suggests that permeability occurs primarily for the following reasons:

> the epistemological structure and cognitive orientation of a discipline; the borrowing of tools, methods, concepts, and theories; the pull of intellectual, social, and technological problems away from strictly disciplinary focus; the current complexity of disciplinary research; relations with neighboring disciplines; redefinitions of what is considered intrinsic and extrinsic to a discipline.[31]

Indeed, these points of permeation are the very places where, and the reasons why, disciplinary borders are crossed. Interdisciplinary work is sited at the nexus where disciplines interact and react with each other. Thriving at the borders, interdisciplinary research also frequently addresses gaps in knowledge, those topics or areas that fall outside disciplinary boundaries. Social and intellectual change encourages scholars to ask new questions and, from these different perspectives, to identify areas of exploration that have been forgotten or neglected. Such disciplinary exchange invigorates scholarship and furthers the aim of knowledge. As David J. Sill argues, "Boundary crossing . . . makes possible the redefinition of the boundaries themselves and provides the energy and means for synthesizing new orders of thought."[32]

Disciplinary and interdisciplinary research share a dynamic and interdependent relationship. In fact, it can be argued that disciplinary knowledge serves as the foundation for most interdisciplinary investigation. Scholars begin with their own disciplinary knowledge base that acts as a springboard for forays into other fields. As previously discussed, interdisciplinary scholars frequently borrow theories, concepts, and methodologies from external subject areas. In order to do this cross-borrowing, they need to become acculturated into the new discipline. Don Spanner learned in his study of the information-seeking behavior of interdisciplinary scholars that the early stages of interdisciplinary research were a particularly important time for faculty and students to acquire an introductory familiarity with disciplinary culture.[33] The challenge to becoming proficient with different vocabularies, methods, paradigms, and disciplinary cultures is a recurring theme among investigations of interdisciplinary research. Lisa Lau, a research fellow at the University of Durham, articulates some of the particular hurdles she faced in crossing between literature and geography:

> I found myself submerged in the language of cultural/human geography, which I barely comprehended, and more importantly was introduced to wholly new concepts, notions, and methodologies. Theory took on an entirely alternative meaning in my new environment, and I was challenged in my original premises, hypotheses and philosophical approaches. I found that there were definite areas of conflict, of theory and beliefs, especially at the most fundamental levels.[34]

Her experience emphasizes the necessity of learning the particularities of disciplinary knowledge, not just for students but also for scholars branching out into new areas of exploration. Knowledge of disciplines and their research tools can be critical to this process. As the example shows, terms and theories used in one discipline can possess a slightly nuanced or an entirely different meaning in another field. Although interdisciplinary scholars don't need to become experts in their newly adopted disciplines, they should obtain a proficient understanding of the working tools, methods, and theories they are borrowing in order to ground their work intellectually. Librarians can facilitate and support this process, just as they do for scholars conducting disciplinary research. A broad understanding of the different disciplinary tools and resources enables librarians to guide interdisciplinary scholars on their journeys across borders.

Faculty are trained in and continue to work from a disciplinary perspective. Lattuca's study confirmed that few interdisciplinary scholars abandon their discipline entirely. Instead, the participants expressed "the enduring impact of their disciplinary training; disciplinary concepts, theories, and ways of looking at the world."[35] Thompson Klein underscores this point by suggesting that interdisciplinary work "is *in* the disciplines as much as it is *outside* them."[36] Interdisciplinary scholars use their own and other disciplines as the touchstones for their integrative research:

Disciplines are needed to conduct interdisciplinary research. It doesn't discredit them or compete with them, rather interdisciplinarians ask questions in a different way about phenomena they see from various angles, and believe answers or solutions must come from common findings from these disciplines. In other words, interdisciplinarians believe that the search for knowledge to complex problems is transdisciplinary. Interdisciplinarity is a philosophy of integrative thinking.[37]

The integrative nature of interdisciplinary research fosters making connections in new and stimulating ways. Sill draws a direct correlation between interdisciplinary studies and higher-order thinking skills of integration, creativity, and evaluation. He emphasizes that integrative thought "consists of taking disconnected material or ideas and synthesizing them into something new, a task that is certainly a form of creativity."[38] Interdisciplinary research works at this integrative, synthetic level. Fernanda Morillo, María Bordons, and Isabel Gómez also attribute interdisciplinary research to creativity. Speaking specifically of work in the sciences, they suggest that "the importance of interdisciplinary research is widely recognized, since cross-disciplinary research is associated with creativity, progress, and innovation."[39] Its particular emphasis on problem solving and integrating disparate disciplinary forms of knowledge strengthens faculty and students' ability to thrive in a complex world. Whether scholars develop these skills in the process of disciplinary or interdisciplinary research, such proficiency contributes both to information literacy and the liberal education goal of providing an intellectual foundation for lifelong learning. Miller and Boix Mansilla's findings from the Interdisciplinary Studies Project affirm this idea:

In a world where most of the important dilemmas refuse to fit neatly into disciplinary boxes, fostering the capacity to synthesize knowledge from multiple perspectives, to capitalize on distributed expertise, and adapt to changing disciplinary and professional landscapes becomes an essential aim in our efforts to prepare young professionals for effective participation in contemporary life.[40]

Librarians can make a unique contribution to achieving these goals by continuing to encourage the integrative nature of the research process.

This book explores the instrumental role that disciplinary research plays in the production of knowledge from the particular perspective of subject reference librarians. The individual chapters discuss how research is conducted in metadisciplinary groups, as well as in specific fields, and provide librarians or scholars with the framework for research competency in new areas of investigation or responsibility. Disciplines still form both the primary intellectual and structural foundation for higher education. Although disciplines are dynamic, shaped as much by change as by tradition, they continue to influence the way in which knowledge is organized and communicated. Their mutable nature prompts scholars and librarians to be open to change as research assumes diverse directions and as subject areas interact with each other in innovative ways. To meet these challenges and opportunities, it is important to understand the underpinnings of disciplinary research, both to become acculturated into a specific academic community and also to transgress those boundaries by researching between and across disciplines.

NOTES

1. Janet Donald, *Learning to Think: Disciplinary Perspectives* (San Francisco, CA: Jossey-Bass, 2002), 292.

2. Lisa R. Lattuca, *Creating Interdisciplinarity: Interdisciplinary Research and Teaching among College and University Faculty* (Nashville, TN: Vanderbilt University Press, 2001), 36.

3. Matthew Miller and Veronica Boix Mansilla, "Thinking across Perspectives and Disciplines," Interdisciplinary Studies Project, Project Zero, Harvard Graduate School of Education, March 2004, www.pz.harvard.edu/interdisciplinary/pdf/ThinkingAcross.pdf., 4.

4. Julie Thompson Klein, *Crossing Boundaries: Knowledge, Disciplinarities, and Interdisciplinarities* (Charlottesville, VA: University Press of Virginia, 1996), 4.

5. Lattuca, *Creating Interdisciplinarity*, 3.

6. Lattuca, *Creating Interdisciplinarity*, 3.

7. Julie Thompson Klein, *Humanities, Culture, and Interdisciplinarity: The Changing American Academy* (Albany, NY: State University of New York Press, 2005), 13–14.

8. Lattuca, *Creating Interdisciplinarity*, 5.

9. Lattuca, *Creating Interdisciplinarity*, 8.

10. Thompson Klein, *Humanities*, 155.

11. Lattuca, *Creating Interdisciplinarity*, 8.

12. Thomas R. Cech and Gerald M. Rubin, "Nurturing Interdisciplinary Research," *Nature Structural and Molecular Biology* 11, no. 12 (December 2004): 1166.

13. Cech and Rubin, "Nurturing Interdisciplinary Research," 1166.

14. Thompson Klein, *Crossing Boundaries*, 118.

15. Eloise Buker, "Is Women's Studies a Disciplinary or an Interdisciplinary Field of Inquiry?" *NWSA Journal* 15, no. 1 (Spring 2003): 82–83.

16. Buker, "Is Women's Studies a Disciplinary or an Interdisciplinary Field of Inquiry?" 87.

17. Buker, "Is Women's Studies a Disciplinary or an Interdisciplinary Field of Inquiry?" 88.

18. Lattuca, *Creating Interdisciplinarity*, 9–10.

19. Thompson Klein, *Humanities*, 42.

20. Thompson Klein, *Humanities*, 43.

21. Thompson Klein, *Humanities*, 35.

22. For a good overview of the different definitions, see John D. Aram, "Concepts of Interdisciplinarity: Configurations of Knowledge and Action," *Human Relations* 57, no. 4 (2004): 379–85.

23. Lisa Lau and Margaret W. Pasquini, "Meeting Grounds: Perceiving and Defining Interdisciplinarity across the Arts, Social Sciences and Sciences," *Interdisciplinary Science Reviews* 29, no. 1 (2004): 49.

24. Thompson Klein, *Humanities*, 55.

25. Thompson Klein, *Humanities*, 55. For her views on transdisciplinary research, see Julie Thompson Klein, "Prospects for Transdisciplinarity," *Futures* 36 (2004): 515–26.

26. Miller and Boix Mansilla, "Thinking across Perspectives and Disciplines," 5.

27. Aram, "Concepts of Interdisciplinarity," 407.

28. Lattuca, *Creating Interdisciplinarity*, 81.

29. Lattuca, *Creating Interdisciplinarity*, 245.

30. Lattuca, *Creating Interdisciplinarity*, 73.

31. Thompson Klein, *Crossing Boundaries*, 38.

32. David J. Sill, "Integrative Thinking, Synthesis, and Creativity in Interdisciplinary Studies," *JGE: The Journal of Education* 45, no. 2 (1996): 142.

33. Don Spanner, "Border Crossings: Understanding the Cultural and Informational Dilemmas of Interdisciplinary Scholars," *The Journal of Academic Librarianship* 27, no. 5 (September 2001): 359. See also, Ethelene Whitmire, "Disciplinary Differences and Undergraduates' Information-Seeking Behavior," *Journal of the American Society for Information Science and Technology* 53, no. 8 (2002): 631–38; Carole L. Palmer and Laura J. Neumann, "The Information Work of Interdisciplinary Humanities Scholars: Exploration and Translation," *Library Quarterly* 72, no. 1 (2002): 85–117; and Carole L. Palmer, "Structures and Strategies of Interdisciplinary Science," *Journal of the American Society for Information Science* 50, no. 3 (1999): 242–53.

34. Lau and Pasquini, "Meeting Grounds," 52.

35. Lattuca, *Creating Interdisciplinarity*, 254.

36. Thompson Klein, *Crossing Boundaries*, 56.

37. John G. Bruhn, "Interdisciplinary Research: A Philosophy, Art Form, Artifact or Antidote?" *Integrative Physiological and Behavioral Science* 35, no. 1 (January–March 2000): 60.

38. Sill, "Integrative Thinking, Synthesis, and Creativity in Interdisciplinary Studies," 133.

39. Fernanda Morillo, María Bordons, and Isabel Gómez, "Interdisciplinarity in Science: A Tentative Typology of Disciplines and Research Areas," *Journal of the American Society for Information Science and Technology* 54, no. 13 (2003): 1237.

40. Miller and Boix Mansilla, "Thinking across Perspectives and Disciplines," 15. For a practical discussion about how to assess students' interdisciplinary work, see Veronica Boix Mansilla, "Assessing Student Work at Disciplinary Crossroads," *Change* 37, no. 1 (January–February 2005): 14–21. For a description of an exciting undergraduate interdisciplinary program, see Lucia Albino Gilbert, Paige E. Schilt, and Sheldon Ekland-Olson, "Engaging Students: Integrated Learning and Research across Disciplinary Boundaries," *Liberal Education* 91, no. 3 (Summer–Fall 2005): 44–49.

Index

About the Authors

Jennifer Bowers is the social sciences librarian at the University of Denver Penrose Library and teaches library instruction courses for the graduate and undergraduate programs in social work, psychology, anthropology, sociology, human communication, and mass communications. She is coauthor of *Literary Research and the British Romantic Era* and coeditor of the Scarecrow Press series Literary Research: Strategies and Sources. Jennifer received an MA in English literature from Portland State University and an MLS from the University of Washington. She is active in the ACRL Anthropology and Sociology Section (ANSS).

Christopher C. Brown is reference technologies coordinator and government documents librarian at the University of Denver Penrose Library. He teaches information access and retrieval, reference, and Internet reference in the library and information science program at the University of Denver. His book *United Nations Centre for Regional Development Publications: Bibliography and Index* covers publications of the Nagoya, Japan, research center through 2001. He often speaks to library groups regionally and nationally, and occasionally in Japan.

Carrie Forbes, instruction coordinator and reference librarian, joined the Penrose Library faculty at the University of Denver in June 2005. She manages a growing library instruction program and also collaborates extensively with the writing program to incorporate library research skills into the undergraduate writing curriculum. As a former distance education librarian, Carrie continues to have a strong interest in online learning and the application of new technology to instruction.

Esther Gil is the business and economics reference librarian at the University of Denver. She teaches graduate and undergraduate library instruction classes in marketing, management, international business, industry and company analysis, and finance. With the business marketing faculty, she has developed a program to teach business research strategies within the undergraduate group project structure. She obtained an MLS in 1992 from the University of Arizona and an MBA from New Mexico State University in 1990.

Peggy Keeran is the arts and humanities reference librarian at the University of Denver. She holds a BA in English and art history from Tulane University and an MA in art history and an MLIS from the University of California, Berkeley. She teaches library instruction for graduate and undergraduate programs in art and art history, literature, foreign languages, theater, and religious studies. She is coauthor of *Literary Research and the British Romantic Era* and coeditor of the Scarecrow Press series Literary Research: Strategies and Sources. She is active in ARLIS/NA.

Joseph R. Kraus is the science and engineering reference librarian at the University of Denver Penrose Library. He holds a BS in physics from Beloit College and an MLS from the University of Maryland. He teaches the science and engineering reference class in the library and information science program at the University of Denver. Joseph is active in the Special Libraries Association (SLA) and the Physics-Astronomy-Mathematics Division of SLA.

Michael Levine-Clark is the collections librarian at the University of Denver. He has an MS in library and information science from the University of Illinois, an MA in history from the University of Iowa, and a BA in history from Wesleyan University. His research interests include collections use and the history of the book trade. He enjoys hanging out with his daughter Isabel and his wife Marjorie.

Suzanne L. Moulton-Gertig, professor, is the head of the music library and teaches in both the music conservatory and academic divisions of the University of Denver's Lamont School of Music. She has served as editor of *Ars Musica Denver* and *The American Harp Journal*. She has published articles in musicology, harp, and library journals, as well as entries in *The New Grove Dictionary of Music and Musicians* (2001). She was an associate editor and contributing author to *Women and Music in America since 1900: An Encyclopedia* (2003). She serves as associate director of the Reznicek Society, which is dedicated to reviving the music of Emil N. von Reznicek and other forgotten late-nineteenth-century composers.

Nonny Schlotzhauer is social sciences librarian at The Pennsylvania State University, University Park. He has held positions at Juniata College, Miami University, and the University of Denver. He holds a BA in anthropology from Temple University and an MLS from the University of Pittsburgh. His interests include collection development, global issues, and the creative use of library space. He has written articles on the literature of conflict resolution, disaster psychology, and international assistance.